Wunnerful, Wunnerful!

The Autobiography of Lawrence Welk

Wunnerful,

By Lawrence Welk with Bernice McGeehan

Wunnerful!

Prentice-Hall, Inc., Englewood Cliffs, New Jersey

Design by Janet Anderson

Seventh printing........December, 1971

Wunnerful, Wunnerful! The Autobiography of Lawrence Welk
by Lawrence Welk with Bernice McGeehan
Copyright © 1971 by Lawrence Welk
Pictures from the personal collection of Lawrence Welk
Copyright under International and Pan American
Copyright Conventions
All rights reserved. No part of this book may be
reproduced in any form or by any means, except
for the inclusion of brief quotations in a review,
without permission in writing from the publisher.
ISBN 0–13–971515–0
Library of Congress Catalog Card Number: 70-155983
Printed in the United States of America T
Prentice-Hall International, Inc., London
Prentice-Hall of Australia, Pty. Ltd., Sydney
Prentice-Hall of Canada, Ltd., Toronto
Prentice-Hall of India Private Ltd., New Delhi
Prentice-Hall of Japan, Inc., Tokyo

*To my wonderful family,
who have been so patient and understanding
during the writing of this book;
to my wonderful musical family,
who have taken on added responsibilities and made me so proud of them;
and to my wonderful family of
fans and friends who have enriched my life . . .
and made it all possible*

Contents

PART ONE — THE FARM

1	Dummer-Esel	3
2	The Decision	12
3	My Four-Hundred-Dollar Accordion	20

PART TWO — THE ROAD

4	Proving Myself	39
5	The Peerless Entertainers	55
6	Fern	76
7	My Band Walks Out	92
8	Making Ends Meet	101
9	Honolulu Fruit Gum	118
10	Doubts	127
11	Champagne Music Makers	137
12	I Talk!	155

PART THREE — CHICAGO

13	The Trianon	169
14	Mother	180
15	Expensive Underwear and a Lady Drummer	182
16	Champagne Ladies and Prima Donnas	198
17	East and West	209
18	The Champagne of Bottled Beer	225

PART FOUR — TELEVISION

19	Reaching the Goal	239
20	The Lennons	263
21	Geritol, Sominex, and a Sleepless Night	273
22	My Musical Family	279
23	Tomorrow	288

Wunnerful, Wunnerful!

PART ONE

The Farm

1
DUMMER-ESEL

When I was about three years old, my mother used to say in her soft voice to one of my sisters, "Would you please go outside and find Lawrence for me?"

"And if we couldn't find you in the yard," says my sister Barbara, "then we'd always go and look in the summer kitchen—and there you'd be, trying to make a violin."

I don't remember trying to build a violin at the age of three, of course, but I do remember, a few years later, hiding up in the big shadowy hayloft, trying to make some kind of musical instrument out of a box and a few strands of horsehair. Even then I was dimly aware that I was different from the rest of the family in my single-minded devotion to music, and I was always worried one of them would find me up there. One day my brother Louie stole silently up the ladder and surprised me, and I was so startled I dropped my "violin" and broke it. Next day, however, I climbed right back up and glued the pieces back together and started in all over again. I just never gave up, I guess!

Sounds always fascinated me. My earliest clear memory is of crawling across the floor of our sod farmhouse toward my father, who was smiling and holding out his accordion. And I can still recall the wonder and delight I felt when he let me press my fingers down on the keys, which were round and shiny like pearl buttons, and squeeze out a few wavering notes!

I loved to hear my father play. We all did. At night he'd reach up and get the old accordion down from the top of the kitchen cabinet, and the minute he did we'd begin scrambling around for the best seats on the floor at his feet. He sat on the edge of his chair, with the accordion held slantwise between his knees and his head down so his dark, curly hair fell over his forehead. Then, after a moment's concentration, his right foot would begin to pound out the beat . . .

one two three *four*! (Years later I caught myself doing the same thing. As I would raise my arm to give my orchestra the downbeat, my right foot would begin to tap out the rhythm. I wasn't even conscious of it till someone pointed it out to me.) When Father played, he waited till he caught the beat, and then his head snapped up, his green eyes sparkled, and he whistled as he swung into a polka or an old-country waltz. He had a strong and perfect sense of rhythm and was in great demand in our part of the country for weddings and barn dances.

We really were a very musical family. In spite of the fact that we were so poor when I was a youngster that supper was often just a bowl of bread and milk, Father somehow managed to squeeze out enough pennies to buy us a small pump organ, and I just loved this instrument too. When I was about four he taught me how to play some simple "oompah" chords and I would lean against the bench (I was too small to sit on it) and pump furiously on the pedals while reaching up to play. Later he taught me a simple progressive melody to go along with the chords and life was never the same for me (or anyone else in the family) after that. I couldn't get that tune out of my head, and I practiced it for hours on end, nearly driving everybody crazy. In fact, if there is one phrase that lingers in my mind over the years, it is somebody groaning in agony, "Lawrence, *please! Stop that! I can't stand it one more minute!"* I'd stop, but after I figured they'd had enough rest I'd start in again, while they either gritted their teeth or went out for a long walk.

Music was my joy, my "home," the one place I felt happy and secure because I was absolutely convinced I was inferior to the rest of the family in every other way—the smallest, skinniest, homeliest member of the whole group, the *dummer-Esel* for sure. And I was not the only one who held that opinion! Not so long ago my sister Eva said, "Lawrence, none of us ever thought you'd amount to anything in this world. You were always off somewhere playing your accordion or else pounding away on that pump organ."

That was true. Every moment I could spare from farm

chores went into music. But we all had chores, even from our earliest years. My first tasks were to carry pails of water into the house for Mother and to help her with the sweeping. Later I was promoted to the barn, but that was one promotion I never really appreciated, because I always disliked farm work. For some reason I hated to milk cows more than anything else, and I'm sure the cows sensed it. More than once we ended up gazing mournfully at each other over an empty milk bucket. And I didn't much care for the other work either. I turned green the first time Father showed me how to kill a chicken, and I really did get sick the day he demonstrated how to butcher the hogs! He couldn't understand my attitude. He was an expert farmer himself and tried constantly to teach my brothers and me the fine points of running a farm. The other boys were apt pupils, but it was a lost cause with me, and Father sometimes got very exasperated. One day he called me over to help him work the bellows on his blacksmith forge, but as I approached he waved me aside. "Oh never mind, never mind," he said in disgust, "you wouldn't do it right anyway! I don't understand how you can mess up simple jobs!"

But he was proud of my musical abilities. Whenever company came he'd start shouting, "Lawrence... Lawrencell! Where are you? Come out now and play for our good friends here!" Finally I'd come slinking out from behind a chair where I'd been hiding (or in some cases I was dragged down bodily from the hayloft) and, white-faced and trembling, I'd begin to play. Once I got started playing, however, my shyness deserted me. Then the problem was to get me to stop!

In spite of the fact that our life was hard—very hard, with long work days that started at daybreak—I remember those years as very happy ones. Father was head of the house in true Germanic tradition, and not a one of us would have dared to cross him. Just one look from those sharp green eyes and we obeyed instantly! But he was always very fair and just with us, and my mother was the gentlest of women. She taught us, simply by the way she lived her life, that love

The Farm

is the strongest force in the world. "Mama just can't scold," my sister Agatha used to say, smiling, and that was true. I can never remember her raising her voice to any of us. If we did disobey, her eyes would fill with tears—and I would do almost anything to avoid seeing that.

I thought she was beautiful with wide blue eyes and curly brown hair. Her maiden name was Christina Schwahn, and both the Schwahn and Welk families came originally from Alsace-Lorraine. In 1878, after the Franco-Prussian wars, many Alsatian families went to Odessa, in the Ukrainian section of southern Russia, in order to escape religious persecution. My parents, who were children at the time, went along with that original band of settlers, and later on they were married there. While in Odessa they had one child, a son named Anton Welk, who lived to be only two years old. As time went on my father became increasingly dissatisfied with conditions in Odessa, and in 1892 he and my mother decided to emigrate to America. They had no money, no material possessions of any kind, except for the accordion and some leather-bound Catholic missals. My uncle M. A. Klein, who was married to Father's sister, had already settled in the Strasburg area of North Dakota, and he advanced my parents the money to make the trip. They traveled by steerage to New York, and then by train and horse cart to Strasburg, with Father carrying the accordion every foot of the way. It had been in the Welk family for generations. My grandfather once told him it had belonged originally to a blind ancestor of ours, a strolling player who had double-jointed fingers and thumbs. I have hands like that myself.

When my parents first arrived there, North Dakota had just been admitted to the Union, and the country around Strasburg, in the south-central part of the state, was still rather wild and harsh and sparsely settled. But to my parents this country offered the kind of wealth for which they had been searching all their lives—it offered freedom and a chance to achieve just as much as their own dreams and initiative inspired them to. Father immediately homesteaded a claim of land about three miles out of Strasburg and began to carve brick-shaped pieces of earth out of the land to build a sod house. It was a crude house, with walls three feet thick, but it served its purpose well, keeping the bitter cold out in the winter and providing a cool haven in the summer. My brother John was born in there in 1893, followed by Barbara, Ann Mary, and Louie. By that time the family fortunes had improved enough so that my father built another house, the one which still stands today. It, too, was a sod house with three-foot walls, but sheathed on the outside with white siding and painted and wallpapered on the inside. My sister Agatha was the first child born in the new house and then I was born in 1903, followed by Mike and our baby sister Eva.

Mother used to keep pots of red geraniums blooming on the deep windowsills downstairs. In later years she was able to hang lace curtains, and Father added an upper story to the house as a bedroom wing for us boys. It could only be reached by an outside stairway—which was nice in the summer, but a freezing trip to have to make at five o'clock on a cold winter morning. Sometimes when I stepped out onto that stairway the air was so cold it hurt to breathe, and I'd hold my hands over my face as I set out on a dead run for the barn. It always seemed a little cozier there with the horses moving around in the stalls and a few chickens squawking noisily. I'd feed them all as fast as possible and then run back to the kitchen for my own breakfast. The kitchen was always warm and always lighted, a bright spot in those cold, dark early mornings.

I admired my brothers extravagantly. John was a fine musician like Father and could farm very well, too. Mike was my special pal, being closest to me in age. And Louie was everybody's favorite. He was the tease of the family, the one who always got into trouble. Once at church he sat away from the rest of us with two other young boys his own age, and the three of them got into a fit of the giggles. The more they tried to suppress their laughter, the harder they laughed, in muffled snorts and spurts. Our priest, Father Max Speckmeier, favored them with a long, slow look of warning from the pulpit, and when that didn't work, he

The Farm

ordered the three culprits up to the front of the church where he had them kneel at the altar rail. There they stayed all during the rest of the service, in such an agony of embarrassment that the back of Louie's neck and ears turned first red and then purple. In those days the priest often preached for an hour or more, and Louie was numb on his knees long before the sermon was finally over. My parents were deeply mortified. To think that a child of theirs should be publicly reprimanded—and in church at that—was a source of terrible shame to them.

We all drove home in utter silence after Mass that day, Louie squirming miserably, knowing he was in for a real tongue-lashing from Father as soon as we got home. Instead, my father, who rarely laid a hand on any of us, walked into his bedroom and came out with his shaving strop. Louie took one look and with a yelp of terror streaked out of the house with my father right after him. "Louie!" roared Father. "Stop! You stop this minute!" But Louie, who decidedly did not want to be caught, kept right on running around the yard until finally he darted into the barn with my father right after him in hot pursuit. Inside the barn Louie climbed up into the hayloft and then dove into one of the feeding troughs, where, unhappily for him, he got firmly wedged. My father applied the strop with a good deal of vigor. We all stayed out in the yard listening with mingled terror and pleasure while my mother wrung her hands and turned pale. Louie came out of the barn bawling at the top of his lungs. My father put the strop away, and Louie never laughed in church after that.

When we were still very small, one of our special treats was to go into town with father and visit Uncle Klein's general store. It always seemed very exciting to me. The walls were jammed to the ceiling with all kinds of supplies—groceries, clothes, boots, bolts of dry goods: flannelette, calico, gingham, even some silk. There was a big barrel of pickles, and bins of sugar and flour, coffee and tea, and, always, a big round of cheese with a cheese knife stuck in the middle of it. Horse collars hung from the ceiling, and there was another big wooden barrel by the front door which was of special interest to me because it was filled with candy. The store was a kind of social center for the town, especially on Saturday night when all the farmers drove in to do their weekly shopping. During the winter months it was often much too cold for them to drive all the way home and then get back in time for Sunday Mass, and so they stayed in town. If they didn't have friends and relatives with whom they could spend the night, then they just bedded down around the pot-bellied stove in the middle of the store. Whole families brought their blankets and pillows and curled up close to the red glow of the little stove, while the North Dakota winds howled outside. In the morning after Mass, Uncle fed them all breakfast. He often told us that in all the years the Strasburgers stayed there, they never once took so much as a spool of thread or a piece of candy and they always left the store cleaner and neater than it was the night before.

But the real center of our town was our small white clapboard church, St. Peter and Paul's, and our choir. People came from neighboring states and even from Canada just to hear it, and it was truly wonderful. On Christmas Eve that small-town choir sang the Hallelujah Chorus better than I have ever heard it sung anywhere else, and this is not just sentimental memory on my part. The townspeople had gotten together at Father Max's suggestion and raised enough money to buy an organ and then import a choir director and organist from St. Francis Seminary in Milwaukee. His name was Max Fichtner and he had come originally from Leipzig, Germany. He molded those farmers and shopkeepers into one of the finest choirs in the world. A towering, almost legendary figure in our town, Max was a great influence on my life. A balding man with bright blue eyes and a sharp tongue, he could reduce some poor choir member to tears. "If you can't sing on key, go home! Go home!" he'd shout. Nevertheless the choir loved him. They all recognized that he demanded far more of himself than he did of them and they worked up to their top potential under his direction. He inspired me, too, and later on I was delighted when he condescended to play a few dances with me, although he groaned audibly and rolled his eyes to heaven every time I hit a sour note—which was fairly often!

Max and his music were part of the reason I loved to go to church, but even if there had been no music nothing could have kept any one of us from attending Mass every Sunday. We always went, even when the temperature dropped to thirty or forty degrees below zero and it took my father an hour or more just to shovel a path from the house to the barn in order to hitch up the horses to the sleigh. "Come now, we must not be late, children," my mother would say in her soft voice, and we would pile into the sleigh bundled to the ears in sweaters and coats and woolen scarves and mittens. Mother used to heat rocks in the kitchen stove for us to put at our feet and they helped somewhat, but even so the snow from the horses' hooves would fly up in our faces as we raced over the icy roads, and by the time we got to church we would all be stiff with cold. Nevertheless we went without fail. "It is God's day," said my father, "and we will honor Him." He and my mother set the pattern for our whole lives with their unfailing devotion.

When I was about five we had a school in our summer kitchen, but I didn't begin regular school until I was well past seven. I was always ailing with something or other as a youngster, and I wasn't strong enough to go until then. Our Strasburg school was run by Ursuline nuns who had been sent over from Germany to do missionary work in the wilds of North Dakota. We liked to think that they found a pretty civilized group of citizens when they arrived, but there must have been a few times when they longed to go home! In the winter it was too cold for us to make the round trip to school and so we all boarded with the Sisters, making their lives a true cross to bear, I am sure. I was generally well-behaved, partly because I was so shy I didn't talk much anyway, and partly because the punishment for disobedience was to have to sit on the girls' side of the room, right at the same desk next to some pretty little girl. In those days I would have killed myself cheerfully rather than do that, an attitude which, I must say, I got over in due time.

Max taught music at the school as well as in the choir, and you could have heard a pin drop on the day he strode through the door ready to give us the weekly lesson. Everyone sat motionless, hardly daring to breathe, and even Sister looked a little pale as she stood in the corner. Max marched up and down for a few minutes, stiff as a poker, hands clasped behind his back, head erect. Then suddenly he'd wheel around and say, "Now! We will sing the scales!" And we sang the scales, and no mistake about it!

The Sisters taught us to write in that fanciful flowing German script, and a good half of our lessons had to do with faith and morals. They tried valiantly to teach us in English at first, but since the entire community spoke only German, they eventually gave up, with the result that I never learned how to speak English until I was twenty-one years old.

In the pleasant summer weather we walked the three miles to school, swinging the tin lunch pails Mother packed, dawdling on the return trip, playing tag, picking crocuses, jumping over mud puddles in the road. Once I remember a neighbor stopping on the road as she drove her horse and buggy homeward. She extended a red and white striped paper sack toward me. "Have some candy, little Lawrence," she invited. I smiled and took the bag. "No no!" she cried, shocked, "not the whole bag! I only meant for you to take one piece!" My face went scarlet and I thrust the bag at her and ran all the rest of the way home in an agony of embarrassment over my mistake. She called after me. "Wait! Come back, come back and have one piece, at least!" But I kept right on running, and I remember thinking in a panic, "Well, *dummer-Esel,* you did it again. You never do anything right and now everybody will laugh at you again." I was worried sick for fear she would tell my parents, and sure enough she did. My mother reproved me gently and Father in somewhat stronger terms. Such are the faint memories of childhood which linger years later.

It never really occurred to me in those early years that I could ever be a musician. I expected to be a farmer like my father and brothers. Life seemed pleasant and orderly and the future well set—until one hot summer night in 1914. I had no idea when I went to bed that night that the whole course of my life would be changed before morning.

2

THE DECISION

SOMETIME DURING THE NIGHT I WOKE UP, CONSCIOUS that something was wrong but not sure for a moment what it was. I felt uneasy, troubled, and suddenly I was gripped by an intense pain in my right side, so severe that I doubled up and broke out into a cold clammy sweat. In spite of the fact that it was a warm summer night I pulled the quilt up around my ears and lay shivering. I tried not to disturb Mike, and he continued to sleep on peacefully throughout the night, but not I. The pains got sharper and deeper, and as the night wore on I became very nauseated.

Still the thing that bothered me most was not the pain but the fear that I might not be able to work the next day. We were in the middle of harvesting, and the threshing rigs, which traveled from farm to farm, had been at our place for several days. I had been driving loads of wheat from the threshing machine to the storage bins and I knew how important it was to get the job done as quickly as possible, so I decided to say nothing at all about how I felt, and I was sure I could get through the day somehow. But that night seemed endless. Try as I might I could not get comfortable. I tried to sleep. I said my rosary over and over and pushed my head into the pillow and turned this way and that. I finally discovered that if I lay on my right side with my knees pulled up to my chin I could get some relief, and I managed to doze off fitfully from time to time, but the nausea and burning pain kept me awake most of the night, and by morning, when I finally got up to get dressed I found I couldn't stand up straight. If Mike or Louie noticed my unusual color or quietness they said nothing, and we all went downstairs to the kitchen where Mother and the girls had our breakfast waiting.

I sat down at the table and looked at my dish of oatmeal, which seemed to be floating in circles. I was so dizzy I could hardly sit straight in my chair. Mother looked at me very closely for a moment with a kind of questioning look on her face (she later told me my unusual yellowish color had frightened her) but she said nothing, and somehow I managed to sit there till it was time to leave for the fields. But when I walked outside and headed for the barn, I felt as though I were wading through water, and the barn seemed endless miles away. I really do not recall much more of that morning. I realized finally that I couldn't reach the barn and I turned around and tried to get back to the house, but the last clear memory I have is my mother's anguished face as she ran toward me. After that I have spotty recollections of being lifted into the buckboard wagon and laid on top of a pile of patchwork quilts, and then being bounced around as if I were being jostled on a bed of hot nails. It was just the rutted road to Strasburg, and I'm sure my mother suffered far more than I did during that ride. I was unconscious during most of it.

We had no doctor in Strasburg, and the closest hospital was in Bismarck, seventy-five miles away. My cousin John Klein, who had the only car in town, volunteered to drive me there. I don't remember a thing about the trip because I was unconscious the whole time.

At the St. Alexis Hospital in Bismarck the doctors quickly diagnosed my case as a ruptured appendix and operated immediately. Peritonitis had already set in, however, and they told my parents that everything was in the hands of God. In those days, long before the discovery of penicillin and other miracle drugs, there was no treatment for peritonitis—or blood poisoning, as it was called then—and the only things the doctors could prescribe were rest, good care, and prayer. I got all three.

For weeks I hovered between partial consciousness and a deep coma-like sleep, with a tube in my side to drain off the poisons. And then one day I had a dream so vivid and real that even today I can recall every detail. I dreamed I was flying. I seemed to be wearing some kind of winglike apparatus on my arms and back, and I was flying in big, soaring circles, higher and higher in wide loops as a hawk would fly. It was a pleasant, wonderful sensation, and I had the feeling that if I would just try a little harder I could fly right over the top of the sky and everything would be all right. When I came to, I was out of bed and clawing at the wall while the nurses were struggling to pull me away. Weak as I was—so they told me later—I fought like a tiger and it was all they could do to drag me back into bed. All my brothers and sisters were crowded into the room and my mother was weeping uncontrollably. I wondered briefly why all my family was there, and why Mother was crying so, but I didn't seem to connect it with my own illness, and after that I lapsed into unconsciousness again. But I had passed the crisis. My vivid dream was the turning point, and I had been spared to live.

I had no real idea at the time of how sick I had been and what a miracle it was that I had recovered, but in later years I often thought about it. It seemed to me that God had given me a second chance at life and I prayed for guidance to use my life in ways that would please Him most. I was in the hospital for seven weeks before I was allowed to go home and I was delighted when John came back in his shiny new Ford to pick me up. Mother turned the back seat of the car into a bed with blankets and pillows and I slept heavily all the way home.

Back at the farm, Mother set up a cot downstairs where she could keep a close watch on me. It was right beside the pump organ, and I used to lie in bed looking at it and longing to play it, but I was still much too weak. The drainage tube stayed in place for several more weeks and I had to stay in bed all the time, but as my strength gradually returned I began to sit up and play tunes on the bedspread. At the end of two months I was able to get out of bed and play the pump organ itself. What a wonderful feeling! I also began to play my father's accordion more and more. I was in no shape to help around the farm, of course, so no one said anything as I sat out in the sun and wheezed along for hours at a time. I loved those long hours alone with the music, and something began to happen to me, deep inside, during those weeks. I had always accepted the fact that I would be a farmer, like my father and my brothers. All the Welk men were farmers, and it was taken for granted by everyone, including myself, that I would be one too. Now a thought so exciting, so overpowering that I could scarcely bear to think of it, began to inch its way forward into my mind. Maybe I wouldn't have to be a farmer! Maybe, just maybe, I could earn a living as a musician! I knew nothing of the life of a real musician, of course, but somehow I seemed to see myself standing in front of great crowds of people, playing my accordion. They were smiling and happy—it was an intoxicating vision—and the more I played, the more real that vision became.

I said nothing to anyone. I knew I would never be able to express how I felt anyway, and so I kept my dreams to myself for a while.

I was a full year convalescing from the peritonitis, which had sapped my strength entirely, and by the time September and time for school rolled around, I was as tall and gawky as a crane. The thought of going back to a class with children who were a full two years younger than I seemed shameful to me. "Please, Father," I begged, "don't make me go back to school. I don't want to sit with all those little kids." Surprisingly, he agreed with me. He reasoned, I suppose, that I had already learned enough arithmetic to run a farm; I could read and write, and there was no real reason for a farmer to have an extensive education, so he agreed that I could stay home.

I resumed my work around the farm and, for the time being, pushed my musical dreams to the back of my mind. But they were always there. Meanwhile I worked hard at the farm chores for the next five years, and I am thankful to God and my parents to this day for that privilege. True, I didn't like much of the work, and every time I shoveled out

another load of manure from the barn my inner resolve to become a musician was strengthened. But I developed such strong muscles and endurance that it has helped me all my life, and it also helped develop an almost effortless kind of self-discipline which has been of even greater help.

    I may not have liked the chores, but I did enjoy working the land. I loved the fresh breezes that blew in from the sweet fields of hay and clover; and I loved feeling the warmth of the hot sun on my back. I enjoyed hunting, too; all of us boys were crack shots with a rifle. John could catch a jackrabbit on the rise and we often shot game for our dinner. That part of farm life was a pleasure to me, and by the time I was fifteen I had regained my strength to the point where I was able to help with the threshing in such a way that I felt I made up partially for all those years when I was too sickly and frail to be much help to anybody. That year my job was to pitch wheat into the threshing machine. We were supposed to work with two men on each side of the machine, but one of the hired hands failed to show up so I ended up working alone, with two grown men working opposite me. I was determined to keep up with them, and after awhile they looked over and grinned, realizing that I was making a contest out of it, and they began to pitch extra hard too. I got myself into a rhythm, bending over all the time—fork, pitch; fork, pitch—and the three of us worked for fifteen hours without a break, except for lunch. Just talking about it today makes my back ache. We established a record which still stands to this day, so far as I know. We were paid by the bushel and we earned $15.01 apiece, at a time when the average farm hand earned only two or three dollars a day.

    This was a matter of deep satisfaction to me in one way, but in another it simply confirmed my feelings that I would never make a good farmer. Every bone in my body felt like it was broken and the muscles of my back and arms felt like they were on fire. I had muscle cramps all night long, and the next morning I couldn't move. For the first time in my life I stayed in bed. After awhile my mother came upstairs to see what was wrong. "Mama," I whispered, "I'm sick. I hurt all over."

She touched her hand to my forehead and smiled gently. "It's all right, Lawrencell," she said in her soft voice. "Today you take it easy."

I caught at her hand. "Mama, please help me. I just can't be a farmer! Please talk to Father. I have to find some way to get off the farm."

She looked at me, her wide blue eyes troubled. "But Lawrence, what would you do?"

"I can be a musician," I told her. "I know I can."

After a moment she said, "We'll see. We'll see. You rest now."

My father, of course, was assuming that all of us boys would stay on the farm. He planned to leave each of us a quarter share and he continually taught us the secrets of good farm management. Our farm was not as big as those of some of the other farmers in our community but Father always got a higher yield per acre than they did. That was because he plowed deeper, planted a better grade of seed, and gave his fields constant care. It was my first lesson in quality work, and it has been a guideline for me all my life. I have found quality to be far more important than quantity in any endeavor, and my father stressed this point to us over and over.

At about this time I began to play at barn dances, and the more I did, the more I dreaded the thought that I might have to live out my life as a farmer. Sometimes I wonder whether it was the fear of pushing a plow or the love of music that spurred me on the most. I suppose it was really the music. I still recall the day my brother John got married. It stands out in my mind as one of the happiest days of my life. I planned for it as soon as John announced his wedding day by immediately offering to stay home and do the chores. "Somebody has to do them," I announced virtuously, "so I will." If my family was surprised by this sudden show of generosity on my part, they refrained from commenting on it, and on the appointed day they set off for the church and the wedding celebration dressed in their best. The minute the buggy was out of sight, I ran for the cupboard—and John's accordion. I played and I played and I played. There was no one to hear me and plead, "Please! Lawrence, for goodness sake stop! Stop!" No one to see me if I got carried away and danced around the barn with an imaginary partner. I practically drowned myself in music that day, letting it wash over me. I played all day long until my arms ached, but it was a happy ache. The daylight started to wane before I realized it, and I ran around getting all the chores done before the family returned. I made it just in time. And I think now, as I look back, that on that day when I immersed myself in music, my mind was made up once and for all. I could not be a farmer. I must be a musician.

But in order to be a musician I had to have an accordion. I approached my father on the subject and he agreed with me completely. "Yes, Lawrence," he said, "certainly you should have one of your own. And just as soon as you earn the money for it, you may send away for one."

This was not exactly the answer I had been hoping to hear, but I went to work anyway. The only way we could earn any extra money was by trapping animals, and I immediately began to spend every spare minute after the daily chores were over setting up trap lines. Squirrels were a terrible nuisance at that time and the government was paying two cents bounty on each one. I'd cut the tails off and pack them into small Bull Durham tobacco bags to mail off to the government offices. I must have shipped dozens of those bags, but at two cents a tail it didn't add up very fast. I also trapped weasel and skunk, and the muskrats that lived in our lakes. Finally, I managed to save up fifteen dollars and sent away for my accordion.

I couldn't wait for it to arrive. Unfortunately, even in those days, as I soon discovered, a fifteen-dollar accordion was not much of a bargain. It fell apart after I had played it only a few weeks. I was heartbroken but determined to have another, so I went back to the trap lines and my rifle, and after what seemed an eternity, I had saved twenty dollars. I suppose I should have realized that a twenty-dollar accordion couldn't be much better than a fifteen-dollar one, but I didn't, and I sent hopefully away for the second one. Exactly the same thing happened. It, too, fell apart, and I finally learned my lesson. I had worked for months, and saved up thirty-five dollars in order to buy those two accordions, and neither one of them had been any good. It was a dramatic and painful lesson in the value of the kind of quality and craftsmanship my father had always practiced, and I never forgot it.

One day Father came home from town to tell us that a traveling musician named Tom Gutenberg was coming to Strasburg to play a series of accordion concerts and dances. "They say he's a fine musician, Lawrence," he told me at supper. "Maybe you'd like to hear him." I went into town the first night Mr. Gutenberg appeared, and from that moment on my life was changed. He had the first piano-type accordion I had ever seen, and I was overcome with admiration for its beauty and the clarity and brilliance of its tone. I'm afraid I was overcome with the sin of covetousness too. Oh, how I wanted one just like it! I went into town every night Tom Gutenberg played, and even though I loved to dance I sat glued to my chair watching every move he made. Once he left his accordion onstage while he went behind the curtain for a moment, and I moved up to the platform as though I were hypnotized and ran my hands over the keys, almost expiring with delight at the touch. Suddenly I heard a sharp voice behind me. "Take your hands off that, young man! It's not yours!" I turned quickly to face Mrs. Gutenberg. "I . . . I'm sorry," I tried to apologize lamely. "I just wanted to touch it." I doubt if I could have explained to her or anyone else how much I wanted to have one just like it.

For days after that I could think of nothing else. I wanted that accordion! I felt I had to have one just like it. But it cost four hundred dollars! I had to think of some way to earn it and for days I struggled with different ideas.

Finally I thought of a plan. But it meant I would have to

ask Father for help, and I was not at all sure that he would agree. Several times I had tried to express to him the overpowering joy I felt whenever I played music and my innate distaste for farm life, but I had never been able to explain my feelings very well. So I thought my scheme over from several angles before I worked up enough nerve to speak to him about it.

Finally I took the plunge. It was just after our evening meal and, for the moment at least, there were no special chores to be done. "Father," I said, "could I . . . that is . . . may I speak to you?"

"Of course, Lawrence."

I swallowed hard and my throat got so dry I couldn't talk at all. "Well?" he said, puzzled.

I looked at him and then looked at the ground and then suddenly I blurted out, "Father, if you'll give me four hundred dollars to buy an accordion like Tom Gutenberg's I'll work for you for four years on the farm and give you every cent I make playing for weddings and festivals and barn dances . . . and name days . . . and . . . everything." I stopped, appalled that I had said it so badly.

He looked at me for a long moment with those clear green eyes and didn't say anything at all. His expression didn't change. And then finally he said quietly, "I'll think it over."

3

MY FOUR–HUNDRED–DOLLAR ACCORDION

For the next few days I was on pins and needles waiting for father's decision, but he said nothing. Sometimes I would look up from my work to find him regarding me with a thoughtful, almost perplexed look on his face, but still he said nothing. Not until almost a full week later did he finally end the suspense. We had just finished unhitching the horses after a long day's work in the fields, and I was hanging the heavy harness over the wooden pegs in the side of the wall when I became aware that he was standing in the doorway of the barn, watching me again. "Lawrence," he said almost abruptly, "come over here. I want to talk to you."

He sounded so severe my heart sank. I was sure he was going to say no. Nervously I dusted off my hands against my overalls and went over to him. "Yes, Father?"

He began to walk slowly toward the house, with me right beside him. "I've been thinking over your offer . . . about the accordion," he began. Suddenly he stopped and looked right at me with those penetrating eyes. "You say you'll work four years on the farm?" I nodded eagerly. "And turn over all the money you make to the household?"

"Yes I will, Father. Every penny of it!"

He looked at me for a long, long moment, while I waited, hardly daring to breathe, and then at last he said gruffly, "All right. Go ahead. Order your accordion."

Heaven never smiled more benignly on a repentant sinner! I was overcome with joy, and even though I was almost seventeen years old and big for my age, I felt like turning somersaults. To this day I don't know exactly what motivated my father's decision. True, he had struck a very good bargain with me. On the other hand, he put himself voluntarily in debt to the tune of four hundred dollars, at a time when most farmers earned less than that in a full year's work, and this represented a staggering amount of confidence and trust in just one of his eight children. Perhaps he understood me and my dreams a great deal better than I thought. Then, too, I have always been sure my mother talked to him on my behalf. At any rate, he did agree, and I was beside myself with joy at the prospect of owning a special hand-crafted piano accordion.

We sent away for it immediately. Since it had to be built to specifications with Swedish steel reeds, I knew that it would take several weeks before it could be delivered, and so for the first six weeks or so I managed to restrain my impatience. After that, however, I was in a fever of anticipation, and every day I hitched up the horse and buggy and drove into town to see if it had arrived yet. My routine never varied. After a quick check of the train loading platform outside, I stuck my head into the dim interior of the depot where Mr. Meier, the stationmaster, was at work sorting packages, stamping tickets, or clattering away at the teletype machine. He would look up when he saw me, smile, and say, "No . . . no . . . didn't come today, Lawrence. Maybe tomorrow." And sometimes at my look of despair he'd add kindly, "Now don't worry. It will come one of these days."

After a few weeks of this, however, he got so he stopped talking entirely, just shoved his green eyeshade up when I peered in the doorway and shook his head slowly and mournfully from side to side.

I ached with frustration. On the ride into town I was always in a glow of hopeful expectation. Maybe the accordion would be there when I arrived! But the ride home was something else again. It was in the spring, and spring in North Dakota is the loveliest time of the year. The fields on either side of the road to Strasburg were beginning to sprout with wheat, covering the flat lands as far as the eye could see with a sort of golden haze. Blue-green crocuses and silverberry flowers grew in the clumps of buffalo grass along the roadway, and all the trees were bursting into full green. There was a heavy fragrance in the air which I have never noticed in any other part of the country, and the ride into town was always an almost unbearable mixture of hope and beauty and expectation. But the ride home was dreary. I let the horse plod along slowly through fields which didn't look nearly so fresh and beautiful as they had just an hour before, and sometimes, in spite of myself, my eyes would fill with tears. Up ahead lay the farm, and all the chores I hated—and another day without the accordion.

I began to entertain all kinds of doubts and suspicions. Maybe the money had gotten lost in the mail. Maybe the company had never received the order. Maybe it had gone broke and I would never receive the accordion. Then where would I ever earn four hundred dollars to pay my father back? Louie and Mike teased me quite a bit. It was a long wait.

One day, almost three months after I had sent in my order, I drove into town for my usual daily vigil. From far off in the distance I could see a figure standing out on the station platform, and as I drew closer I could see it was Mr. Meier. He was waving his arms and shouting something that sounded like "It's here. It's come," and finally, cupping his hands around his mouth, he yelled unmistakably, "Lawrence! Your accordion is HERE!"

I drove wildly up to the platform, jumped down from the buggy, threw the reins loosely around the hitching post, and rushed over to Mr. Meier. Sure enough, there was a huge packing crate, stamped "Fragile," tied securely with double twine, and addressed in large black letters to "Mr. Lawrence Welk, Strasburg, North Dakota." I was so excited I was very close to tears. I ran my hand over the packing crate, swallowing hard, and then I turned and grabbed Mr. Meier by the hand. "*Danke schön,* Mr. Meier, thank you," I said emotionally, over and over. "*Danke schön, danke schön!*" I never meant anything more in my life. He laughed good-naturedly, "Well now, that's all right, Lawrence," he said. "I'm just glad it finally got here." In truth I think he was; I don't think he could have stood many more of those daily mournful visits of mine.

"Now c'mon," he said, "I'll help you load it into your buggy." Together the two of us carefully eased it next to me on the front seat, wedging it in firmly so that it wouldn't bounce on the trip home. I turned and shook his hand once again and then I took off at a fast trot while he stood on the edge of the platform, smiling broadly as I drove away, relieved no doubt that the long ordeal of waiting was over for both of us.

Back home my shouts of excitement brought the whole family running into the yard, and Louie and Mike helped me unload the crate and carry it into the living room where we set it up on top of the table and carefully opened it. And there it was. I don't think I shall ever again experience the thrill I felt when I finally saw it.

It came encased in its own red plush-lined black case, and it was a beauty—black and silver and sparkling with rhinestones, with my name spelled out in block letters of rhinestones, winking brilliantly. The rest of the family was full of admiration, but I was overcome.

"Oh, it's beautiful," breathed Eva reverently. "Just beautiful."

Even my father was impressed. "That's a fine accordion," he said, examining it carefully. "Good workmanship." I lifted it out very gently and strapped it on. Suddenly I was as close to heaven as I had ever gotten. How I loved it! Today I sometimes wonder at the enchantment which accordion music held for me in those years. I still enjoy it, but then it delighted and fulfilled me as nothing else could, and I could never seem to get my fill of it. My family could, though, and that night they certainly did! I played all through supper and all evening and far into the night until even my mother looked faintly distressed, and finally Ann Mary said in exasperation, "Lawrence, *please*! I'd like to go to bed! Can't you stop now?" I retreated into the kitchen where my brothers were playing cards, and I sat in the corner playing until they threatened to throw me out bodily; and then I went outside where I strolled up and down playing under the stars. Finally I climbed the outside stairway to our bedroom and sat on the edge of my bed, still playing.

When Louie and Mike came up to bed they couldn't believe it. "Are you still playing that thing?" asked Louie incredulously. He climbed into bed and pulled the covers over his head and tried not to listen, but after a while he moaned, "C'mon, Lawrence, cut it out! Please! I can't stand it!" But I kept it up until my father roared from downstairs, "Lawrence! Stop playing and go to bed! We have to get some sleep around here."

Obediently I put the accordion down beside my bed where I could still reach out and touch it occasionally, but I got up again at four o'clock the next morning and slipped out to the barn where I began to play for the surprised chickens and horses. I played for more than an hour, while the dawn gradually cut through the morning darkness and turned the sky violet, and then gold, and then a clear shining blue. That was a moment I'll never forget. It made up for all the years of trapping muskrats and cutting off squirrel tails and dreaming in the cold and shivery darkness of my room. I felt as if I could conquer the world. And I set out immediately to try.

For such a small community, Strasburg had an unusual number of parties and celebrations. There were weddings and birthday parties and baptismal celebrations and name day festivities (celebrations in honor of various saints on the Catholic Liturgical Calendar). Most of these called for a party with lots of food, drink, and dancing, and it wasn't long before I began to play for a good number of them.

The wedding parties were by far the most profitable—especially the kind that went on for three days. By the third day the serious drinkers had taken over and the money flowed as freely as the *schnaps.*

Strasburg in those years was still a mixture of Old World and New World customs, and wedding parties usually followed the same routine. Since the community was almost entirely Catholic, the wedding mass was usually held at St. Peter and Paul's Church at ten o'clock in the morning, and then the wedding party and all the guests would return to the bride's home for the festivities. My part was to stand near the door and "play" the bride and groom into the house after they returned from the church. I remember this as a time of smiles: the bride flushed and smiling shyly, the groom beaming, Father Max smiling paternally, all the guests laughing and calling out good-natured jokes, and I—hair parted in the middle, slicked down neatly, and dressed in my best—beaming too. After the wedding party was safely inside, I rushed around to the wedding table and began playing dinner music. All the time the food was being served I hovered in the background, playing sentimental waltzes and wedding music, punctuating the toasts with a flourish on the accordion, and accompanying our local butcher, Pete Baumgarten, and his wife, who often sang at these parties.

Those wedding feasts certainly offered food to be remembered! Platters of fried chicken, roast beef, ham, sauerbraten, wurst (a German sausage), all kinds of home-canned fruits and vegetables and big bowls of sauerkraut, home-baked bread and rolls and German chocolate cakes and butter cookies and always a special confection called "Hochzeitkuchen" or "Kuka," a flat cookie-like cake which was heavily sprinkled with sugar and cinnamon and served traditionally in pie-shaped wedges at all German weddings. All of this was washed down with glass after glass of *schnaps* or cup after cup of hot coffee. It always seemed a wonder to me that the guests could even get up and walk, let alone dance, after such a feast. But dance they did, and that was the part I loved best. Sometimes wedding dances were held in the parlor of the family home, and sometimes in Bichler's Pool Hall in Strasburg, which served as everything from the town auditorium to a ballroom; but in most cases they were held in the hayloft of the barn, which was always ten times the size of even the largest farmhouse, and could handle as many as a hundred couples or more. The haylofts were always sturdily built with cross-beam construction and ship-lath floors so they could support the heavy weight of the hay which was stored there during the winter. And a good thing it was too, or they never could have supported the weight of all those dancers. These people didn't glide sedately around in a smooth waltz or fox trot. They *danced,* with a good deal of heel stomping and foot clicking. After an hour or so of these whirling shouting dances, the atmosphere got so thick it made your eyes water.

The excitement mounted as the dancers called out requests. "Lawrence, play 'Zu Strasbourg'! A polka! A German waltz! A *schottische*! A one-step!" I played them all, enjoying it so much I always had a smile on my face. I played as loudly as possible, since that was a main requirement for country dances. One day as I played with great abandon and many flourishes, one of the older couples waltzed by, and the man, red-faced and breathing hard, grabbed me by the arm. "You play pretty good there, Lawrence," he told me. "And so does your brother John." I beamed. But then as he waltzed off he shouted back, "But neither one of you boys plays as well as your father! You just don't have the rhythm!"

I was paid by the guests at these parties, the usual donation being a dime or a quarter for a set of three dances. Once in a while someone would drop a nickel on the plate. I'd go ahead and play anyway, but I might say those dances were on the short side. As the afternoon wore on, especially if it was a hot day, a general decorous shedding of clothes began. The men took off their heavy suit coats and piled them on the benches at the sides of the loft, and then they loosened their ties and rolled up their sleeves. But they never stopped dancing, even when they were drenched with perspiration and their shirts were plastered to their backs. The afternoon sun came streaming through the hayloft windows, gleaming on an occasional wisp of straw, catching a cobweb here and there, bathing the whole whirling mass of people in a warm glow. And I played and I played and I played, just as long as anyone wanted me to.

Whole families came along to those parties, and children were sometimes lost among the piles of coats and sweaters on the benches, sound asleep as their parents spun and stomped around them. They seemed never to tire; if they did get tired of a German waltz, which is a very fast dance, they would slip easily into walking around the floor, arm in arm, still in tempo with the music. After a brief breathing spell like this they would swing back into the dance.

It was not unusual for the festivities to go on well after midnight the first night. The next day the same thing started all over again. By the end of the second day many of the older folks bid the bride and groom goodbye and set off for home. But the rest of the guests, sometimes with a quick trip home to attend to necessary farm chores, kept on going.

It was the third day when the going was roughest for me. By that time, after so many hours of continuous playing, my left wrist was often raw and bleeding from the pressure of the leather strap. Generally I just tied a clean white handkerchief around it and kept on playing; if it bled through I just put on a fresh cloth. I never did get used to this, and even today the skin on my left wrist is thicker than that on my right. My mother was always upset when she noticed the bleeding. "Lawrence, you must not hurt yourself like that," she said, troubled. "Don't play so long." I told her it didn't bother me, and it didn't. I loved to play so much I would cheerfully have bled every night playing the accordion, rather than do any of the farm chores, which became more and more distasteful to me as time went along.

Music pulled at me continually. Everything about it fascinated me. Some nights I saddled up my pony and rode several miles to a dance—I loved to dance almost as much as I loved to play—and by the time I galloped home across the dark and silent prairies it was dawn and time to start the day's chores. I'd feed and harness the horses and clean out the stables automatically, but my mind was still on the music, still on the dancing, still dreaming of the tunes from the night before.

Occasionally my father would give me some spending money from what I brought home to him. "Here," he'd say, gruffly, "take this. You've earned it." I was always delighted to get it, and I gave it to my mother to save for me. I saved up enough to buy my first pair of long pants that way, and it was a red letter day for me when I first wore them. I was then seventeen years old, and up to that time I had worn either overalls or the short pants which boys much younger than I were accustomed to wear. I felt I finally had arrived and that I had made the right decision in planning to become a musician. My father, however, didn't feel the same way at all, and he frequently said so. "Accordion playing is all right for fun, Lawrence. But it's not a life's work. You're a farmer. We all are. You'd better start thinking more about the farm."

But I could not. Music obsessed me, and I reasoned that if I made enough money and proved to my father that I could earn a living at it, he might change his attitude. So I talked to everybody who was planning any kind of name day or birthday celebration and got myself hired for everything I could. One day I landed a job playing for a community dance at Ipswich. I thought it would be a great triumph which would impress my father mightily, but it turned out to be a disaster.

Ipswich was nearly a hundred miles from Strasburg, and my parents had allowed me to go only because my brother John and his wife, Theresa, lived there and had promised to keep an eye on me. I was in a fever of excitement. The day of the dance I carried a lunch my mother packed for me and took my first train trip, awed by the red plush seats and the ornately carved and gilded overhead luggage racks. That night I met the local drummer, who was to play with me at the dance, and my heart was pounding as we started in. Everything went well right from the beginning; the dancers seemed to be having a wonderful time, and when midnight came they passed the hat and hired us to play for another hour. Wonderful! I was beaming from ear to ear, tapping my foot on the floor as my father always did, happy that the people were having such a good time and I was making so much money! And at one o'clock the same thing happened all over again. The dancers passed the hat and hired us to play for another hour. It seemed too good to be true, and a little after two o'clock I nearly floated home to John's house, still so flushed with dreams of glory I couldn't sleep.

The next day was Sunday, and John and Theresa and I went to Mass. After a few moments I began to get very uncomfortable. The priest launched into a fiery sermon about "the Devil who had come to town the night before, and lured the people into sin, dancing and prancing even unto the Sabbath Day!" Suddenly all my joy of the evening before turned into ashes. I went scarlet with mortification and couldn't get out of the church fast enough as soon as the mass was ended. I felt terrible about unintentionally committing such a grievous sin. After awhile I began to worry even more for fear my father would find out about the whole thing and forbid me to play entirely.

"John," I begged, "please don't tell Father. He might stop me from playing. I didn't mean to do anything wrong. Please don't tell him!" John let me squirm for quite a while before he finally promised. Word of my misdeed never reached my parents, or if it did, they said nothing about it. For many years I thought perhaps I had exaggerated the whole incident in my mind, but in 1970 I was playing in a golf game in Aberdeen, South Dakota, and a group of three ladies, Mrs. William Thielen, Mrs. Ed Lass, and Mrs. Gertrude Egan, came over to talk to me. It turned out that they had been at the Ipswich dance that night. "I'm certainly glad to see you turned out all right," one of them twinkled. "The priest really gave it to you the next day!"

The engagement that stands out most vividly in my mind was the Assumption Day Festival in Hague, North Dakota, in 1923, because it was the first time I ever promoted a dance all on my own. The Hague celebration was always a big one. The farmers in that area had a special devotion to the Virgin Mary, in whose honor the Festival was held, and the town was always crowded with people eager for a day of fun. I knew that if I could get part of that crowd to attend a dance I would do very well, and so I made all kinds of plans. A few weeks before August 15, the day of the celebration, I talked to Pius Volk and Carl Fisher, two friends of mine in Hague who knew the owner of the local Opera House (any vacant building large enough to house a fair-sized group of people was automatically called the Opera House), and they made arrangements for me to rent the hall for the occasion. It cost me three dollars; already I was in the hole.

Once the hall was rented, I set to work advertising the event. I talked to everyone I knew, spreading the word about the dance, and I painted some signs myself in my best German script and tacked them up all over Strasburg and the surrounding countryside. My father was sufficiently impressed with this show of initiative to lend me the family car for the occasion, and very early in the morning on August 15 I got up, ready to make my debut as a local impresario. I loaded the car with my accordion, some more signs, tacks and a hammer, a roll of ribbon, a paper of pins, and a pair of scissors . . . (in place of tickets we used to snip off pieces of ribbon and pin them on the coats of ticket buyers). Then I drove carefully over the back country roads to Hague.

It was still early when I arrived, but already the town was beginning to fill up. Cars, buggies, and buckboard wagons soon jammed the main street, which was gaily decorated with flags and garlands of flowers in blue and white, the colors of the Virgin. The day officially began with a beautiful High Mass, and afterward the crowd began promenading up and down the street, talking and laughing together, while I ran back to the Opera House ready to sell my tickets. Not a soul showed up to buy any, and by one o'clock I realized with a twinge of panic that if I were going to make any money at all I would have to go out on the street and sell my own tickets.

I hated to do it. I was embarrassed about talking to strangers anyway, and it somehow seemed shameful to me to have to go out and advertise my own playing and my own dance. But I was determined to make a success of this project, so I took my spool of ribbon and my scissors and pins and went to work.

It turned out to be easier than I thought. For one thing, most of these people spoke German; and for another, I knew several of them from having played so many dances in the area. My first few sales went rather quickly and I was elated. Then I ran into a group of older farmers who didn't seem interested at all.

"It's only a dollar," I said, "and ladies free, of course." That was standard practice in those days.

"A dollar a ticket! Aaaagh! Way too much," said one of the men gruffly.

There were five men in the group and I didn't want to lose this sale. "Well . . . " I stalled a little, "then how about the five of you for four dollars?"

"Four! Two would be more like it! We don't like to dance that much." The other men laughed.

"Then I'll sell you five tickets for three dollars."

"Two," said the man instantly.

I did some rapid calculation. I had already sold enough tickets to pay for the hall and the cost of the gasoline for the car. One of my prime objectives was to fill the hall that night, so I would have sold the tickets for two dollars, but I made one last attempt. "Then how about the five of you for two-and-a-half?"

"Sold!" cried the man laughing, and the deal was made. I was so exhilarated by this exchange. I had forgotten about being shy while we talked. All the rest of that afternoon I sold tickets on that basis. If I got a flat turn down, I made a counter offer, and I was almost always able to work out some kind of "group" arrangement; little by little my roll of ribbon got smaller as I snipped off tickets.

It was much easier to sell tickets to fellows my own age. I could always promise them an introduction to some girl they particularly admired. Even though I was still rather tongue-tied around the girls, I was always very much at ease dancing with them and I knew them all—especially the pretty ones. The promise of an introduction usually would help sell tickets. "Come in about eight-thirty, " I told the boys, "and you can meet the girls before the dance starts."

One group of young farmers, however, seemed strangely reluctant to buy any tickets, and finally one of them confessed the reason why. "Heck, I'd like to come," he said, "but we was never to a dance before! We don't know how."

"Oh, is that all," I said. "Well, come in about eight o'clock and I'll show you. It's easy."

After a little embarrassed discussion among themselves they agreed. They all bought tickets—at a slightly reduced rate.

For the rest of the afternoon I kept at it and by seven-thirty my pockets were stuffed with money. Then I ran back to the Opera House. My stomach was churning with hunger. I had been so busy all day long that I had forgotten to eat, so I stopped and gulped down a quick cup of coffee and a hamburger. Back at the Opera House I turned on all the lights, shoved chairs and benches against the walls, and threw the doors and windows open, ready for my first self-promoted dance.

My dancing students were the first to show up, red-faced but determined, and I lined them all up and then stood in front of them ready to demonstrate the one-two-three waltz step. (That may be the first time I ever counted uh-one and uh-two!) They followed along as best they could but they were pretty bad, and one of them was the worst I've ever seen. He seemed to have no sense of balance or rhythm, and when he tried to waltz he looked just like a newborn calf, staggering around, knees together, feet wide apart, legs sprawling in every direction, as he tried desperately to keep his balance. It was all I could do to keep a straight face and I despaired of even teaching him how to walk in time to the music, but he kept at it and by the time the lesson was over he had managed a kind of resemblance to a waltz step, but it was nothing to worry Fred Astaire.

The other boys started to arrive, putting an end to the lesson, and finally the girls came in, all talking to each other and apparently paying no attention whatever to the boys. They sat together in bunches looking like flowers in their light summer dresses, and I began to drag embarrassed, anxious swains up to meet them. "Oh how do you do," they'd say, flirting demurely, while the boys shuffled awkwardly and tried to make a little conversation. I stayed long enough to make sure that each boy met the girl he liked and then rushed off to make some more introductions as more girls and boys kept arriving. By nine o'clock almost everyone I had sold a ticket to had arrived and the rising hum of conversation and general air of excitement made it clear that it was time to start the dance. The hall was packed. If folks hadn't bought a ticket during the day, there was no way for them to get in now.

It was just getting dark outside—that clear deep blue of a summer Dakota night—when I climbed up on a chair in the corner and began to play. The nervous exhaustion and long hard work of the day were forgotten as I swung into my first number. As always, the music filled me with that familiar sense of joy, and a new surge of strength and energy. I smiled at the crowd as they spun around in a fast waltz. I felt happy, very very happy.

I established something of a reputation that night. The word got around that Lawrence Welk must be a pretty good accordionist—"There was such a crowd at the Hague dance that half the people couldn't get in"—and I began to realize that we often make our own success. It helped make up for some of the embarrassment I had suffered during the day trying to sell my own tickets, and it taught me a valuable lesson. I learned that day that dreams are not enough. They have to be backed up with lots of hard work.

That night I made more money than ever before and I was anxious to get home and show it to Father. I dumped the big sack of silver and paper money onto the kitchen table and watched as he counted it all silently in the light of the kerosene lamp. When he finished it came to more than $150. He sat back in his chair, and looked at me with . . . what? Pride? Anxiety? Resignation? I didn't know. He said nothing.

Finally, I ventured, "That's pretty good money, Father."

"Yes. Tonight was good. But you only make that much every now and then."

"But if I worked in bigger cities I could make that kind of money every night," I said confidently.

My father began scooping the money into his money box, and he didn't answer me for a moment. Then he said, "A traveling musician . . . no . . . that's not the life for you, Lawrence. It's not a good life. You'd run into all kinds of conditions you know nothing about." He looked at me very directly. "I don't want you to lose your faith and fall into a life of sin."

"But I wouldn't! I can be a musician and still lead a good life. You know that, Father!"

He shook his head. "You don't know the temptations. You don't know the life at all. Besides, you could never earn a living at it. Tonight you made a lot of money.. There would be plenty of nights when you wouldn't earn anything at all. No." He got up from the table. "Stay on the farm. You can always make a living here. If you leave home and try the music business you'll be back here begging for a meal in six months' time!"

I would never have contradicted my father but I knew I would starve before I would ever do that. And so we said no more about it. But the question of my leaving the farm and pursuing a musical career hung between us all during the rest of my time on the farm.

I was filled with a feverish impatience as my four years of bondage drew to a close. My father still persisted in his attempts to dissuade me, sometimes by outright lectures and sometimes by indirection. Often after he and my mother returned from one of their hand-in-hand evening strolls around the farm, he'd say, "What do you think you'll plant in your share of the farm, Lawrence? That's good land . . . good land. The best in the world."

I had no way to answer him. I didn't want to plant anything in my share. I wanted only to make music. And so I said nothing.

As my twenty-first birthday approached I was filled with excitement. I sent away for a new suit. Mike twitted me about my new finery when it arrived, but he smiled when he said it. I packed and repacked my small valise a dozen times—a change of underclothing, two shirts, some hand-knit socks, a sweater, my missal, my rosary, my prayer book. I shined and reshined my shoes and I marked the days off on the calendar. I could not wait to leave.

On March 11, 1924, I woke up very early in the morning. I was twenty-one years old. I got dressed in my unfamiliar new finery, inspected the contents of my valise one more time, and counted my small hoard of money. I had enough for my train fare plus three one-dollar bills, which I pinned in my inside coat pocket, and a little loose change. I smoothed the patchwork quilt, which my mother had made, over my bed for the last time, and then looked around the room where I had spent so many hours with my brothers. I felt no unhappiness, only a great eagerness to begin my great adventure.

After breakfast I said my farewells, to Eva, to Mike, and to Louie, who thumped me on the arm in his familiar gesture of kinship. We said goodbye quickly and then I turned to my father.

"So you're going," he said with that level look of his. "Well, you'll be back. You'll be back just as soon as you get hungry. He'll be back in six weeks," he added, turning to the rest of the family, "looking for a good meal!" They all laughed and I did too, but I knew I would never return for help. I would never come back till I had proved myself. My father and I had made a bargain, and we had each kept to the letter and spirit of the agreement. He had kept his word and I was free to go. Now it was up to me to prove that my dreams were more than dreams. I shook my father's hand, and it was a moment of deep emotion for me because I felt we were shaking hands on both an ending and a beginning, something on which we had differed sharply and something that meant a great deal to both of us. I loved my father very much at that moment, but I was unable to tell him so, any more than he was able to tell me. I turned to my mother, and she took both my hands in hers and looked at me for a long long time. Then she took her hands away and patted my arm awkwardly. "Lawrencell," she whispered, her blue eyes brimming with tears. I nodded and turned away very quickly and, with my valise in one hand and my accordion case in the other, I jumped into the buggy and I began the three-mile trip to Strasburg. Once again it was springtime and I was on the same road I had traversed every day four years previously, waiting for my accordion. Now the fields stretched straight ahead of me, beckoning me toward my future. I was filled with a mixture of emotions—excitement, hope, joy, and a small tinge of sadness. Occasionally I would turn around and look back toward the farmhouse. All the rest of the family had returned to their chores, but my mother stood out where she could see me as I drove down the road; and whenever I turned around she would withdraw her hands from beneath her white apron and wave both arms in the air. I waved back, until finally I came to a turn in the road . . . and I could see her no more.

PART TWO

The Road

4

PROVING MYSELF

NOBODY WAS EVER AS DUMB AS I! FOR THE NEXT FEW weeks I continually ran into things which surprised, delighted, or shocked me, and I learned something new every day. I learned almost immediately that my father was right when he predicted that I wouldn't earn a lot of money every night. In fact, I was hard put to earn anything at all at first. I had gone to Aberdeen, South Dakota, the day I left the farm, partly because we had friends living there, and partly because I had only enough money to buy a ticket that far. I stayed with Mr. and Mrs. Jacob Faith and their two sons, John and Frank, who played the violin and piano, and they helped me get engagements around town. Most of them were at St. Mary's Hall on the north side of town, the German-speaking side, and I began to play for weddings and dances there, much as I had in Strasburg. But I barely made enough to pay for my room and board. In desperation I joined a children's band. I was two feet taller and ten years older than anybody else in the group, but I didn't care. I was earning money and gaining experience, and I just beamed and smiled right along with the other members of the Jazzy Junior Five.

After a few weeks I had saved enough to go to Bismarck, the capital of North Dakota and the most exciting city I had ever seen, with impressive state buildings on Capitol Hill and crowds of lawmakers and businessmen as well as shopkeepers and clerks thronging the streets. I rented a room in a boarding house for thirty cents a night, and landed a job right away in a music store, selling pianos on commission. It wasn't much of a job, but then I wasn't much of a salesman either. I never sold a single piano all the time I was there! But I did learn more about the music business, and a few other things as well. It was in Bismarck that I first learned there was such a thing as divorce, and I was shocked. My friends at the music store thought this was hilarious. "You mean to tell me you never heard of divorce?" demanded one of them. "Where is that place where you grew up anyway? Didn't they teach you anything?" My naïveté was a continual source of hilarity to them. Half the time I didn't even know what they were laughing at, so I just smiled and tried to laugh right along with them. I was struggling all the time to learn English better, too—and between trying to sell pianos, to find extra work at night or on weekends, and to keep up with this sophisticated new world, there were times when I had a sinking feeling that my father was right, I should have stayed home on the farm.

I kept on trying to find extra work playing my accordion, but I didn't do very well, partly because I was acutely conscious of my heavy accent. Frequently I couldn't think of the right words in English to express what I was trying to say, and I would grope around for a substitute word while my listener waited patiently—and sometimes not so patiently. That old feeling of being the *dummer-Esel* threatened to overwhelm me again, and I finally decided I'd be better off closer to home, so I returned to Aberdeen. There I had an immediate stroke of good luck. I ran into a friend of mine Frank Schalk, who had two outstanding attributes. He could play drums and he had a car. After we compared notes for a while he said, "Listen, I can't find many bookings either. What do you say we form a duo and travel around together . . . see what we can dig up that way? Would you like to do that?"

Would I! In two minutes flat Frank and I became a team, and we started scouring the countryside looking for engagements. One day we drove into the town of Oldham, South Dakota, and saw a poster advertising Mike Gibbs and his orchestra playing at a dance that night. Frank and I showed up early, partly to hear the band and partly in the hope we could get ourselves hired.

The hall was jammed. I stood at the foot of the bandstand tapping my foot in rhythm with the orchestra, wishing desperately that I were playing in it, too. Finally when Mr. Gibbs looked my way I blurted, "Uh . . . I play the accordion. Could I play with your orchestra for a little bit?" He looked at me for a moment and then grinned and nodded. I dashed outside to the car, grabbed my accordion, and rushed back into the hall where I sprang up on the platform and began to play with every flourish and run I had ever learned, and, as I had been taught in my Strasburg days, with all the stops out. The crowd seemed to enjoy it. I played a few solos to thunderous applause, and I was so delighted with my reception that I half expected Mr. Gibbs to offer me a job. But as I was putting my accordion back in its case at intermission, I overheard the trumpet player say to one of the other musicians, "Boy! If I had to play with an accordion player like that, I'd rather quit the business!"

I felt sick. I finished putting my accordion away and snapping the case shut, but everything suddenly seemed unreal. I couldn't quite believe what I had just heard, but when the trumpet player came out into the hallway from his dressing room and saw me standing there, he looked so embarrassed I know he had meant every word he said.

His words had far more effect on me than anything my father had ever said, far more than the constant turn downs and long stretches of unemployment of the preceding few months. For the first time in my life I lost confidence in my ability to play.

I told Frank to go on ahead. "I just feel like walking," I told him. "I'll see you later." And I walked back to our hotel that night, carrying an accordion case which suddenly seemed very heavy, wondering dully if I had made a mistake. Maybe the dreams which I had carried in my head all these years were just foolish dreams which could never be realized. I sat on the edge of the bed for a long time, too depressed even to get undressed and go to sleep. I kept thinking over and over, "You can't read music. You can't speak good English. And if that trumpet player is right, you can't even play the accordion! Maybe you *should* go back to the farm. Maybe that's all you're good for."

But then I would think, "No. I can't be that bad!" And after a while I thought, "All right. Maybe I'm not very good. But I'll get better." By morning I had decided to "stay in the music business"—a world-shaking decision for a young man who was barely in it—and I had also decided to learn to read music better and to play the correct chords. My chance to do both came along sooner than I had anticipated. In the fall of 1924, Lincoln Boulds, an orchestra leader from Chicago, was touring through that part of the country, and when he came to Watertown, South Dakota, Frank and I went to hear him. After the dance I talked to him for a while, and to my delight he offered me a job. I agreed, on the condition that he hire Frank also, and the two of us set off with high hopes, pleased to be associated with such a big band. A few weeks later we both discovered why it had been so easy to get a job with Mr. Boulds.

He had a terrible memory; he always forgot payday. Sometimes when we asked for our salary he seemed genuinely surprised to discover that he had forgotten to pay us; at other times he would tell us that he simply didn't have the money, and that was very often the case. Either way, we didn't get paid. He was a good musician, and I did learn more about reading music while I toured with him, but I didn't eat any too regularly and I certainly didn't earn any money. I learned something very valuable from Mr. Boulds, though. I learned how not to run an orchestra. He'd schedule engagements too far apart, or crisscrossing each other in such a way that we found ourselves backtracking one day over the same territory we had covered the day before. He invariably managed to run out of gas or oil a mile short of town, and then he'd have to borrow money from one of us to get to our destination. This comedy routine got to be so familiar we knew it by heart.

The car would wheeze to a stop and Mr. Boulds would look surprised. "Well . . . now what? You don't suppose we're out of gas, do you?"

The rest of us would look at each other and say nothing.

Lincoln would get out and look in the gas tank. "Well," he'd say worriedly, "it looks like we are. Which one of you

Proving Myself

wants to go into town and get a gallon or so? It's only a couple of miles down the road."

Finally one of us, not wanting to be stuck on a lonely country road for the rest of the day, would volunteer to go, and then to no one's surprise Lincoln would say, "Oh, by the way, just go ahead and pay for it, will you? I'll reimburse you when I pay your salary." Naturally he never paid us, and naturally no one stayed with him for very long—no one but me, that is, and at one point even I got fed up and quit and went to Chicago. Lincoln immediately hired another accordionist, a man who played far more nimbly than I. I had heard him one day in the basement of a dingy hotel in Estherville, Ohio, and I had been awed by the way his fingers flew over the keys. Technically he was a marvel of a performer but he always played with such a gloomy look on his face he took all the joy out of it and I always had the feeling he'd like to stuff his own ears with cotton. Perhaps the audiences felt that way too, because three days after I arrived in Chicago, Lincoln called me to come back.

"But you already have a new accordionist," I said. "And he's wonderful. What do you want me back for?"

"Well," said Mr. Boulds, "you may not play as well as that other fellow, but the folks like you better. They've been asking for you. Now listen, Lawrence, I'll pay you sixty-five dollars a week instead of thirty-five. Come on back!"

The combination of the compliment and the tremendous increase in salary knocked my better judgment right out of my head and I agreed to return. He might as well have offered me a thousand dollars a week, since he wouldn't have paid that either, as I soon found to my chagrin. I wonder, even today, why I stayed with him. Partly, I'm sure because I couldn't really believe he was dishonest; I thought that he would pay me whenever he got the money, and I suppose he would have, but he never seemed able to get that much together.

We were forever arriving in town two or three hours after we said we would, to find the dance hall closed, all the potential customers gone home, and a furious dance-hall manager pacing up and down. In vain Lincoln would explain, "My car broke down. We got here just as fast as we could!"

"Well that don't help me none!" replied the manager. "I'll never book you in here again."

I think the highest—or lowest—point of my tour with Lincoln occurred one Christmas Eve. As usual, we were limping along a snow-choked highway, and as usual, Lincoln had figured too close a time spread and we were three hours behind schedule. By the time we arrived in this small Iowa town it was eleven o'clock Christmas Eve. The dance hall had long since closed. Not even the usual red-faced manager was there to greet us. There was no hotel, no place to go. There we were, the Lincoln Boulds Chicago Band, stuck in a drafty touring car in the middle of a small and dark and almost deserted little town. Nobody said anything until Lincoln had a stroke of genius. "Well," he said, "I'll just ask the local policeman if he can help us out a little."

"If Lincoln fixes us up a room in jail I'll kill him!" muttered one of the boys. But the town policeman turned out to be an angel in disguise. He took us to the largest home in town. The owners had gone to Florida for the winter, and, those being the days when people trusted each other, the officer offered us the use of the house as a simple gesture of Christian generosity. "Bring the key back in the morning," he told us. We gratefully fell into bed (four to a bed, with everything piled on top of us in order to keep warm) and drifted off to sleep with the chimes from the local church tolling the birth of Christmas Day.

Perhaps the Christmas spirit imbued Mr. Boulds with generosity, because the next morning, to everyone's astonishment, he said, "Come on, fellows. It's Christmas Day. Let's forget last night and have a big celebration. I'll treat you to breakfast.

We were a little suspicious, but we were also hungry, so after returning the key to the police chief we marched into the local restaurant and for once I ordered a big breakfast instead of the usual nickel hamburger and coffee. We all did. We ordered ham and eggs and sausage and pancakes and

Proving Myself

fried potatoes, toast and jam and cup after cup of coffee. And then we sat back and waited for Lincoln to go into his usual act of fumbling around for the money. But to our surprise he whipped out a checkbook and signed for our huge breakfast, including a hefty tip for the waitress as well! We were surprised and delighted. Maybe things would work out after all. We'd work out a better schedule and begin to play for dances that would attract big crowds and everybody would be paid and all our problems would be solved. It was a happy group that Christmas Day, but a week later we found that things really had not changed at all. The check bounced.

I had had enough. Mr. Boulds owed me over six hundred dollars, and I felt that even though he was trying to act in good faith, I couldn't stand such a regular nonpaying job any longer and although he begged me not to, I left.

I went to Lake Okaboji in Iowa, a summer resort, for a short vacation. It was locally famous, that summer of 1925, because it had seven dance pavilions built at intervals of a mile or half a mile around the edge of the lake. I convinced myself that I was going primarily to hear all the different bands, and to find out which one was the best and why. But there was also a very lovely blonde Danish girl named Billie Sorenson vacationing there with her family that summer, and I think her company was at least as attractive to me as the music. Billie and I attended all the dances, walking hand in hand along the wooded paths. All the orchestras charged the same price—ten cents for a set of three dances—and the crowds moved from hall to hall, trying out each band. By eleven o'clock at night you could always tell which group had been playing the best. Their ballroom would be packed to the door, while the rest of the orchestras played forlornly to empty houses. It was a vivid demonstration of the free-enterprise system in action, and an example of the basic American ideas of competition and excellence. This experience gave me some lifelong ideas about the importance of always pleasing your audience. I spent hours attending the dances when I had enough dimes, or just standing outside under the pine trees and listening when I didn't. It was a worthwhile vacation.

After a while I decided I had better get back to Aberdeen, so I said goodbye to my lovely companion and started out. It was a maddening trip in some ways, because my old jalopy, for which I had paid sixty-five dollars, broke down regularly every ten miles unless I filled it with oil. I had to figure my route very carefully so I would always break down in or near some town. In other ways, though, the trip was wonderful. I think now of how kind people were in those days, how helpful. Often, when I didn't have enough money for a night's lodging, I simply knocked on the door of some small neat house and asked the owners if I could set up my folding cot in their back yard. I was rarely refused, and as often as not the family invited me inside to spend the night, and gave me breakfast in the morning before I left. Other nights, when such hospitality was not available, I just set up my cot in a cornfield somewhere and rolled up in a blanket. I never minded that; in fact I rather enjoyed it.

I almost always managed to eat well because usually I could play for my supper in some restaurant along the way, and sometimes I made very good tips that way, too. It was on this particular trip that I figured out one more way to earn money. I contacted every theater I could and tried to book myself as a single act. If the manager turned me down, which he usually did, I was ready with a helpful suggestion. "Why don't you charge a nickel extra for my performance, and I'll just take that as my pay?" Sometimes this worked, but if it didn't I was ready with yet another idea. "Well then, suppose you charge a nickel extra and we'll split it down the middle? We'll each take two-and-a-half cents." Almost always this did the trick. Those two-and-a-half cents royalties helped pay my way back to Aberdeen.

By that time I had made some decisions. I decided to form my own orchestra, and I sent for Frank to join me. He had had enough of Lincoln Boulds's erratic paydays and he came willingly; with the two of us as the nucleus, I set about building up a small band, first getting a booking of some kind, and then hiring the necessary number of musicians. We did fairly well, too, except that my car kept breaking down with frustrating regularity, and I spent almost every penny I made on oil. Obviously I needed a new car. The question was how to get it? If I had to make much of a down payment, then I wouldn't get to eat very often. I wrestled with the problem for a few days and finally went into the local Chevrolet dealer to see what I could work out.

As soon as I walked in I saw exactly what I wanted—a touring car glistening with chrome, equipped with running boards, an expandable luggage rack, and wire spoke wheels, and big enough to carry six musicians and all their instruments. I loved it on sight and was determined to have it.

"How much?" I asked the dealer.

"Standard price. Seven hundred dollars."

That was about seven hundred dollars more than I had. I walked around the car, stalling for time, trying to figure out some plan, kicking the tires, running my hand over the shiny trim. It was such a beautiful car. The owner watched me and finally said, "You don't have to pay it all at once you know. You can just make a down payment and pay the rest on the installment plan."

"Yes," I said, "I know." Suddenly inspiration struck. "Say . . . I think I might have an idea that could help us both!"

"You do? What's that?"

"Well if you could take my old car as the down payment, instead of cash, then I'd be able to give you an awful lot of free advertising."

He looked at me appraisingly. "And how would you do that?"

"Because my orchestra and I play at all of these small towns around Aberdeen . . . places where they don't have any car dealers at all. Everybody sees what kind of car we drive, and we could tell them exactly where you're located, what model cars you have here. It would be great publicity for you!"

The dealer considered my offer doubtfully. I plunged on. "And I won't wait to pay it off in monthly payments either.

I'll pay it off just as fast as I can, with the very first money I earn. I'll pay it right away!"

He grinned, and then almost in spite of himself he burst into laughter. "Well all right, son, you're quite a salesman. I think I'll take a chance on you. It's yours. Go ahead. Take the car."

I was so delighted I very nearly floated out of the place, and I was in my glory driving my new car down the street. But before long my sense of elation gave way to one of pure panic. All on my own I had managed to mortgage myself to the tune of seven hundred dollars. Suddenly I began to understand more fully why my father had taken a full week to decide about ordering a four-hundred-dollar accordion.

I redoubled my efforts to earn money. I worked day and night. Frank thought I was crazy. "What are you trying to do' Kill yourself?" he demanded, as I combed the countryside playing every fair, carnival, festival, theater, and restaurant or barn dance I could find. If I could play in a restaurant for a meal, then I ate well; otherwise I subsisted mostly on milk and nickel hamburgers, and I saved every penny I could. I was determined to pay off that car as soon as possible. It became almost an obsession with me.

In June of that year I had an idea which I hoped would earn me enough money to make a substantial payment on the car and ease some of the nagging worry. The Fourth of July was coming up, and in those days the Fourth was the biggest holiday of the year. There were always speeches and parades and band concerts and fireworks and civic celebrations. All businesses were closed and Independence Day was celebrated with a warmth and fervor that seem regrettably to have vanished today. When I was a small child, our whole family had always gone into Strasburg for the day, dressed in the best clothes we had, laden with a huge picnic lunch, ready to celebrate. My father gave each of us smaller children a dime apiece to spend—more than we ever got at any other time of the year—and I was always in agony of delight trying to decide just how to spend all that money. Mike and I would spend hours trying to make a choice between buying candy or lemonade or fireworks or maybe saving a penny or two.

I remember also the parades we had. Everybody gathered in town during the early part of the day, and in the afternoon the parade would start forming at one end of the main street. The little Strasburg band would come down the street playing a march for all it was worth, and everybody crowded to the edge of the sidewalk to watch it go by. The band always marched at the head of the parade and the town fire engine brought up the rear, with all the local dignitaries riding in floats or cards in between. And always, at the head of the parade, was the American flag, fluttering in the breeze, making small crackling noises as it passed by the rows of silent people—the men with their hats over their hearts, the women standing very straight and quiet, the children saluting. It was a hushed, almost reverent moment, a time of great emotion for all of us. I have often thought that those immigrant farmers, most of whom could not even speak English, were probably the most American Americans I have ever known. They appreciated the wonders of this country, more perhaps than those who had been born into it. They had all experienced deprivation and tyranny in the old country and they never got over the freedom and opportunity they found here. Deeply grateful for it, they taught all of us children to value it as they did.

We all loved those Fourth of July celebrations, with the red, white, and blue bunting stretched across all the storefronts, the spectacular fireworks at the end of the day, and the dance, which was one of the highlights of the Strasburg celebration. It was always a very profitable affair for the band that played it, and I decided to try and arrange a similar dance at Scatterwood Lake, a picnic area near Aberdeen which boasted one of the largest dance pavilions in the state. If I could fill that pavilion with dancing couples, then I could make a big payment on the car.

I contacted the owner of the pavilion and made my offer: I wanted sixty percent of the gross receipts of the dance. To my surprise he agreed without any further discussion. I should have realized then that there was something more to the deal than just a picnic and a dance, but, as is usual with me, I learn by doing. The pavilion arranged for and the percentage agreed upon, I set about getting together the best musicians I could find. The going rate for musicians in those days was five or ten dollars a performance. I offered twenty-five dollars for the day's work, and I came up with the best performers in Aberdeen. We got together for several rehearsals beforehand and I was full of optimism. "This is a great group, Lawrence," Frank said enthusiastically. "The best you've ever had."

The big day dawned warm and muggy . . . an ideal day for a picnic, I thought. I arrived early, with my own roll of tickets, to make sure everything was arranged for. I sprinkled cornmeal on the hardwood floor so that it would be smooth dancing, and checked all the benches to make sure they were clean and free of splinters which could tear stockings or dresses. The Scatterwood Pavilion, like most dance pavilions of the day, was built with latticed arches and grillwork, and wired with lights which sparkled at night. Benches encircled the inside for spectators to sit and watch the dancing, and the dance floor itself was roped off in the center.

As a rule, each dancer paid a nickel for a set of three short dances, and then the floor was cleared while everyone bought another round of tickets. And one of the things that has since vanished, along with the buggy whip, is the long rope which the dance attendants used to help clear the floor. Four men, working in teams of two, would stretch the ropes through the crowd in the center of the floor, and then begin herding the dancers toward the side exit-gates, where they walked out, bought more tickets, and walked right in again, through adjoining entry gates. People were so used to this procedure that the ropes were not really necessary, but it was part of the scene of the day.

My fine musicians began arriving in plenty of time for the two o'clock matinee, and we were all excited and pleased, because the park was jammed. Every table was taken and latecomers spread their picnic cloths under the shade of the cottonwood trees. Big granite pots of coffee boiled on the open-air cook stoves, and when the picnic hampers were opened, the aroma of fried chicken and hot dogs and lemonade and corn on the cob mingled with the smell of the coffee and wood smoke. Almost every family had a big watermelon for dessert, and some of them carved their initials in it and stuck it in the water to keep cold, while others used tubs of ice. Children ran around playing tag and screaming with delight when they set off firecrackers behind some unsuspecting adult, and the clank of horseshoes floated over all the other noises in the park. It was a typically happy, satisfying family-picnic kind of Fourth of July, and I could hardly wait to get the dance started.

A little before two o'clock we tootled a few practice numbers and were rewarded with a burst of applause from the nearest picnickers. By now most of the ladies had packed away the remains of their lunches and set the baskets aside for supper later on, and so we got set for a rush of dancers to enter the pavilion. Instead, everybody in our vicinity got up and began walking off in the opposite direction, away from us. From all over the park we could see crowds of picnickers calling to each other, walking around the horseshoe pits and open-air stoves, and disappearing into a grove of trees at the far end of the park. A few of the older ladies did come up and sit on the benches in the pavilion . . . even then I guess, the mothers liked me . . . but when I raised my baton for the opening number we had exactly three couples skimming around the huge floor. I could feel my stomach tighten at this ominous sight . . . and I felt even sicker when one of the dancers confirmed the suspicion which had been growing in my mind as I watched all those picnickers vanish from sight. "Boy," he called enthusiastically, as he and his partner swooped around the empty floor, "all this space is great . . . just great! I hope that ball game lasts all afternoon."

"Wait a minute," I said. "What ball game?"

"Oh, you know," he called as he waltzed off, "it's the county championship game. Everybody's there," he added unnecessarily.

My heart sank. In that part of the country local ball games were taken as seriously as the World Series is today, and I knew that no one would leave the game till it was over, by which time they probably would be ready to go home. I was angry at myself for not looking more fully into the situation and angrier at the owner for not telling me. Every time I looked at those three couples sailing around the floor I got sick all over again. Even if they danced all afternoon it wouldn't make much difference. I didn't know what to do. When the sky turned suddenly gray and lowering and a few thunder clouds rumbled in the west, I didn't pay much attention. I continued to smile brightly on the outside, but inside I was wondering how I would ever get out of this mess and how I would pay my musicians.

It started to rain, and I didn't pay much attention to that either. It often rained in the summer in the Midwest—brief thunder showers that are over even before they start—but after a while I realized that this was going to be one of those long heavy penetrating rains, the kind that just doesn't stop. For the first time I saw a ray of hope glimmering in those dark clouds. Some of the ladies began to make a mad dash back through the rain-soaked trees and bushes to put the food hampers back in their cars and to put on extra coats. When they saw the inviting shelter of the pavilion and heard the music, they crowded into the spectator sections, with their children alongside, climbing on the railing or clambering over the benches. As the rain continued without letup the men began to straggle back, too, and more and more of them came up into the pavilion. My men began to play with even greater enthusiasm, and soon the floor began to fill up with hundreds and hundreds of couples.

"Oh shoot," mourned the first dancers, "now it won't be nearly as much fun!" But my spirits were soaring. The rain continued to pour down. The skies got even blacker and there were flashes of lightning and continual rumbles of thunder, but inside the pavilion it was warm and dry and full of music and dancing and laughter. I began to feel very hopeful about the afternoon, and when I saw the two baseball teams, each in full regalia and each soaked to the

Proving Myself

skin, dash into the pavilion, I couldn't help but feel a thrill. If even the baseball teams had to come in out of the rain, then the game had been definitely canceled.

Maybe the rain and the postponement of the game had something to do with it—maybe it was just the fervor and excitement with which we played—but the crowd kept us playing for hours. The dancers thronged the floor and the tickets rolled off the reel as fast as the ticket sellers could make change. The men with the ropes had their work cut out for them when they tried to herd people off the floor. The owner of the pavilion walked by rubbing his hands. "Made a pretty good deal for yourself, young fella," he called out. I was too pleased to say anything; through a stroke of fate, and certainly no thanks to him, I had.

The folks seemed to be having such a good time that they didn't want to stop, even when dinner time neared. Wives slipped out to the car and brought back a chicken leg or a ham sandwich for their children and husbands, and, just as in the barn dances of my youth, they would often tuck a child to sleep under a pile of coats on the benches while they took a whirl around the floor. Some of them even brought their babies up in baskets and left them on the bandstand. "Just keep an eye on him, will you, Lawrence?" they'd ask, before spinning off. I played the accordion, conducted the band, and baby-sat, all at the same time.

The tiny lights outlining the arches of the pavilion sparkled against the mist of the rain as the skies darkened, and still the dancers showed no inclination to leave. My orchestra members were enjoying it, too; any musician will tell you he likes to play for a group which enjoys hearing his music. After a while we took turns stepping down from the bandstand and having a dance or two ourselves. By this time I was sure I had more than enough to pay my men and have plenty left over for myself, too, so I picked the prettiest girl on the floor and asked her for a dance. We spun around in a fast waltz while the lights on the pavilion arches sparkled and the music flowed all around us and I was sure I had picked the most wonderful way in the world to earn a living.

It was very late at night before the dance ended. The skies

had cleared completely, and stars twinkled brightly as some of the picnickers shot off one last burst of fireworks before heading for home. The owner of the pavilion and I went into his office to count out the receipts. I was trembling as he began dumping out canvas sacks of money on top of the wooden table. Nickels, dimes and quarters rolled all over the counter top, and we both made a lunge for them. Then we began counting silently, separating the nickels and dimes into piles of a dollar each, and the quarters and halves into two-dollar stacks. As the stacks grew, my excitement turned into wonder. I had never seen that much money in my life before! And to this day I cannot remember exactly how much it was. I just know I made more than enough to pay for the car in full, pay my musicians their twenty-five dollars and a healthy bonus . . . and have enough left over to go back home in style to Strasburg.

It had been a year and a half since I left. I had a new car fully paid for, I obviously was not hungry, and I had my pockets stuffed with money. I have been proud of a good many things in my day, but I think I was prouder when I first returned home to my parents with that brand-new car than at any other time in my life. I had tried so hard to prove, especially to my father, that I could earn a living as a musician. Now, in my mind at least, I felt I had.

The family listened to my glowing tales of success—I left out all the parts about working for Mr. Boulds as an unpaid musician—and my mother sat beaming at me. My father seemed gratified to learn that the car was fully paid for. Finally he said rather grudgingly, "Well, you did all right, Lawrence. Let's hope you can keep it up." My mother listened quietly and eagerly to all of my stories, and once she leaned forward and brushed the hair back from my forehead. "It's good to see you so happy, Lawrencell," she said. It was as much as she ever said to me but, as always, I felt that she understood me. In one way it seemed good to fall back into the German tongue, but in another way it was difficult. I had been trying to speak only English, with varying degrees of success, and now sometimes when I couldn't think of the proper German word, it both amused and surprised my parents, and perhaps saddened them a little, too. If any further proof were needed that I had definitely left the farm, it lay in the fact that I did not speak their language as well as I had.

5

THE PEERLESS ENTERTAINERS

FOR THE NEXT FEW WEEKS I BASKED IN THE ADMIRATION OF MY family and friends. Every day I drove slowly up and down the main street of Strasburg in my new car, smiling and beaming and waving grandly right and left. If I had any humility then, it certainly didn't show! I even drove over to show off my new car to Mr. Meier at the depot. He was impressed. "My goodness, Lawrence," he said running his hand over the shiny chrome, "you certainly must be very successful. That's a fine car." Max Fichtner, however, was not nearly so impressed. He looked at me dourly. "How could anybody who plays as bad as you do make so much money?" he demanded. But then he laughed and agreed to join me in a concert at the pool hall where Mr. Gutenberg had played nearly six years earlier. Everybody in town came to hear us and my father was very proud; he looked on with smiles as my mother and I waltzed around the floor. The Prodigal Son had returned and everyone was happy.

I enjoyed those few weeks at home and, looking at my family and friends through new eyes, I saw what good people they were and how deeply fortunate I had been in being allowed to grow up in a home and in an area where the emphasis was still on the simple virtues and where the love of God was still the dominant theme that underlay every other consideration. I did not feel that I had fallen away from the teachings of my youth, but those weeks at home made me realize with renewed clarity and how true those teachings were.

In September I went back to Aberdeen and landed a booking almost immediately, playing a week's engagement at a fair in Selby, South Dakota. It was quite successful; the fair pulled big crowds from all over the state and most of the people stayed on for our dance at night. We had one nightly visitor who intrigued those of us on the bandstand very much, because he stood out from the rest of the crowd like a peacock in a flock of hens. He was tall and thin with a long, slender, humorous "actor's" kind of face, and he wore a flashy striped suit and a big diamond ring which glittered and glowed on his left hand. He didn't dance, but just sat leaning against the wall smiling pleasantly at all the dancers and nodding occasionally to us up on the stage. Once in a while I would notice him looking at me closely and then conferring with the small group of friends who accompanied him every night, but he made no move to come up and talk until the last night of our engagement. Then he threaded his way through the crowd that was emptying out of the ballroom and approached me as I was stacking the sheet music away.

"Good evening, sir," he said, as I straightened up to meet him. "May I introduce myself? My name is George T. Kelly!" Extending his hand with just the suggestion of a bow, he wrung my hand heartily.

"Good evening," I replied.

"I've enjoyed your little novelty orchestra so much," he told me, beaming, "and may I say that you are the finest young accordionist it has ever been my pleasure to hear. Yes indeed, the very finest!" Right away I liked him.

"I have a little show of my own," Mr. Kelly went on, gesturing toward his group of friends, who now stood waiting for him at the door. "We've been playing at the carnival down the street for the past week. And . . ." he looked at me appraisingly, "I have a business proposition I'd like to discuss with you. That is, if you're not too heavily booked for the next few weeks."

Of course I had no bookings at all lined up, but after a year and a half on the road I had learned not to look too anxious, so I said I thought there might be a possibility of working something out.

"Well that's fine," said Mr. Kelly heartily. "Suppose we meet for coffee then, tomorrow morning, at the Selby restaurant, and we'll discuss the venture in more detail. Would that be agreeable to you, sir?"

I said it would, and after another firm handshake Mr. Kelly rejoined his friends. As he went out the door he flicked his cap in a jaunty little salute. I had never met anyone quite like him before. The next day I arrived a little ahead of time for our appointment and while I waited I began to wonder if he would even show up. But right on the dot I saw him come swinging down the street, striped coattails flapping in the autumn breeze, cap on the side of his head, smiling at everyone he met, bowing a little to the men, tipping his cap to the ladies. "Good morning, sir," he cried when he caught sight of me waiting outside the restaurant, "good morning to you. And how are you today?"

"Just fine," I replied, a little overwhelmed by his breezy personality. Mr. Kelly pushed open the door of the restaurant. "After you," he said, waving me in ahead of him, and then he led the way to a small table covered with red and white patterned oilcloth. "Now then, young sir, what would you like with your coffee? Some pie perhaps? A couple of doughnuts?"

I ordered some pie and coffee. The waitress who served us was obviously fascinated with Mr. Kelly and his expansive gestures which made his diamond ring glitter and glow in the morning sun. "Very good coffee, ma'am," Mr. Kelly told her after his first sip. "Simply delicious." She beamed and then turned away, and as she did Kelly began spooning sugar into his coffee. "Now then, young Mr. Welk," he said, "I have a show called The Peerless Entertainers. We tour all through this part of the country every winter playing the inland towns—those off the railroad tracks, you know," I nodded, "and it occurred to me that you could come along with us. You could perform in some of our dramatic sketches and then play for a dance after the performance." He stopped for a moment and then added casually, "Of course this would be a steady job. Regular pay all winter long."

Privately I was elated at the thought of a steady job, but I tried hard to look as though I was just considering his offer. "Well," I said cautiously, "maybe I could do it. How much does it pay?"

Mr. Kelly stirred his coffee thoughtfully and then looked at me across the table with keen blue eyes. "Thirty-five dollars a week," he said after a long pause.

This was less than I hoped for.

"Mmm," I said. "I usually get fifty."

"Fifty!" cried Mr. Kelly, as though he had been speared. "Now come on, man, this is a steady job I'm offering you! A regular paycheck every week."

I didn't know what to say, so I took a big bite of pie and thought quickly to myself that I had better try to settle for forty dollars, when suddenly Mr. Kelly leaned across the table and said, almost abruptly, "Well, young man, I'll tell you what I'll do. I think you're a fine accordionist, and you'll add a great deal to the show. We'll pay my wife fifteen dollars a week to handle the tickets and the props and the bookkeeping, so after I pay her and the other two actors, you and I will split the profits right down the middle. Fifty–fifty." He sat back in his chair. "There. How does that sound to you?"

I nearly choked on the pie. When I finally got it down I reached across the table and wrung his hand with delight. "Mr. Kelly," I said, "that sounds just wonderful!"

He grinned, and Kelly and Welk were in business. I often thought, in the happy days that followed, that it was the smartest move I ever made in my life. George T. Kelly taught me more about show business and how to get along with people than anyone I had ever met. He had a natural easy Irish friendliness that endeared him to everybody, and an almost courtly way of doing business. I learned a lot listening to him as he got on the telephone and set up future bookings for us. He would make it a point to find out who was the leading citizen or businessman in each of the small towns he played and then he would call in advance of our arrival.

"Good morning, sir," he would say, Irish charm oozing from every syllable. "Good morning! My name is George T. Kelly. I represent a little troupe of performing artists known as The Peerless Entertainers. We present a show consisting of songs and sketches, and then we have a dance after the show, featuring Lawrence Welk, America's Foremost Accordionist. Now I find, consulting my schedule, that we'll be in your vicinity in the next two weeks, and it occurs to me that perhaps we could work in a performance for you. When would be the best time for you to arrange our appearance in your Opera House?" The leading citizen almost always succumbed to the blandishments of Mr. Kelly, particularly if he had played there before, because The Peerless Entertainers did put on a good show. In no time at all Kelly would have arranged to rent a hall for two or three dollars for the night. If the leading citizen seemed hesitant, George T. would throw in his strongest bait. "Why don't you have the Ladies Aid or the women of the town put up a little light lunch—serve sandwiches and cake or coffee—" he would say, "and then you may keep all the profits for the benefit of the city?" This usually cinched the deal, and in one fell swoop George had arranged a booking for us with all the refreshments taken care of, and a certain amount of free publicity guaranteed by his exciting "long-distance" telephone call. We also mailed posters and handbills out in advance of our arrival.

The Peerless Entertainers consisted of George T., his wife, Alma, and their daughter, another married couple, Harry and Frieda Woodmansee, and myself. We did everything! There were times when I thought the show was almost incidental to all the other work we performed, and I strongly suspected that George had hired me as much for my muscles as for my prowess on the accordion. When The Peerless Entertainers pulled into one of those small towns we all sprang into immediate action, with George, Harry, and I handing out more posters and handbills, talking to all the merchants in town, chatting with people on the street about our show. Meanwhile Frieda and Mrs. Kelly were dusting and sweeping out the theater; if necessary, Harry or I would scrub the place down when we returned. Then we lugged in heavy planks and pop bottle cases which we borrowed from the local general store or lumber yard, and set up makeshift benches for seating.

At the end of the first act we changed from performers into candy butchers. George and I came out and sold candy; since there was always a prize in one of the boxes, sales were usually brisk. After that, America's Foremost Accordionist and its Leading Thespian shoved all the benches back against the wall to make room for dancing and then we swept the floor, which was littered with wrappers and boxes, while the audience milled around getting out of our way. And after *that* we changed back into performers again and played for a dance for the rest of the evening.

Our scenery was the simplest and we carried a minimum of props, just enough to suggest an illusion of what we were trying to convey. The scenery flats set the mood for the audience and also served as our dressing rooms, offering enough space behind them so that we could make costume changes. We carried no special lights or printed programs, and we generally played in bare rooms lighted as often as not by a single bulb hanging down from the end of a cord in the middle of the ceiling. But when the hall was filled with excited families and small children who hadn't seen a show in months or even years, and The Peerless Entertainers came out in costumes and makeup and began to perform, it was theater and it was exciting.

Kelly was a born actor, a great performer. I used to wonder why he had never tried for success in Hollywood or on Broadway; it seemed such a natural goal for him . . . and it was a long time before I discovered the reason why. On those inland tours, he was a smashing success. He did a character called Ole the Swede, and since we toured through a part of the country heavily populated by Swedes and Norwegians, they all loved him. If George was playing to a Norwegian audience, he'd come out in his "Ole" costume—loud checked pants, lumberman's boots, flannel shirt, knitted cap with a tassel on the end of it—and, with a wink at the audience, he'd say in his outrageous accent, "You all know what a Svede is, don't you? . . . Yah, sure, that's a Norwegian with his brains knocked out!" The Norwegians would roar with laughter. Next night he might be playing to the Swedes and he'd reverse the line and the Swedes laughed just as hard. They all recognized themselves in George's impersonations and laughed at their own quirks.

I played a Spaniard. I looked just about as Spanish as any other fair-skinned German, so Kelly had me dress up in short black satin pants, a white shirt with big balloon sleeves, and a red satin fringed bolero. As long as I kept my mouth shut, nobody seemed any the wiser. I also "acted" in some of the plays, although my parts were usually limited to mumbling, "Yes, ma'am," or "No, sir," in the murder-mystery comedy sketches we did. Kelly often said I was the best corpse he ever hired.

The curtain was my responsibility. Every night I had the job of threading a strong wire through a heading at the top of it and then attaching it to two nails which I drove into the walls at either side of our "stage." It was always a tedious job to take the wire out every night and wind it loosely into a coil, and then fold up the curtain, and when I discovered a new kind of flexible wire, I thought I had found a way to simplify the job greatly. "Look, George," I said, "the way this wire bends I can just leave it in the curtain and fold up the whole thing, wire and all, every night. It will save a lot of time." George was a little dubious but he let me go ahead with my new project, which worked very well for a few nights. But one night about two weeks later George retired behind the curtain to change costumes and I stayed out in front to play a few numbers for the audience. Suddenly they exploded into laughter with wild shrieks of feminine hilarity punctuating the uproar. I turned around to discover that the wire had snapped and the curtain had fallen, disclosing Kelly standing there in his long underwear with his back to the audience, and revealing a good deal more of Kelly than he intended to. That was one of the greatest laughs he ever got in his professional career, but Kelly didn't think it was so funny. He grabbed the curtain, held it around his middle, and ordered me in no uncertain terms to go back to rethreading the curtain every night with a good strong wire.

One season George hired an actesss named Vera Abek to tour with us and she brought along her five-year-old daughter Jeannie. Jeannie and I were inseparable, and I fell in love for the first time in my life. She followed me around like a little puppy, holding onto my hand, asking a thousand questions, holding up her arms and demanding imperiously, "Up, Lawrence, up." I'd hoist her on my shoulders, where she rode around contentedly, sometimes helping me arrange the curtain that way. She was my best audience, clapping furiously whenever I finished a number. George T. wasn't quite so fond of her as I was. She got so she knew all his routines by heart. "Now he's going to fall down!" she'd exclaim, just before George did so, and she often laughed loudly just before he got to his punch line. George was exasperated. "Get that kid out of the front row," he exploded to Vera one night. "She's ruining my act!'

"Now, George," said Mrs. Kelly placidly, "the audience thinks she's cute. They like it." George stopped fuming, and then he grinned; the next night Jeannie was back in the front row as usual.

"Why do you talk so funny, Lawrence?" she asked me innocently one day. I tried to explain to her, but my accent was still so bad that even my explanation proved difficult. "Well, never mind," she told me after listening for a while, her big eyes wide and solemn. "I *like* the way you talk." But I hated it, and though I tried constantly to improve, I made mistakes all the time and my accent remained terrible. I remember one time when we ran out of pins and I went off at a run to the local general store to get some more. I rushed and told the clerk I needed some pins.

"Some what?" he asked, looking puzzled.

"Some pins, pins . . . you know . . . pins," I said again.

"Oh, sure," he said, his face clearing. "Sure. Follow me."

And he led me to the back of the store and handed me a pair of pants!

Mrs. Kelly worked with me patiently, explaining meanings of words and the correct pronunciation, but even though I talked freely with the Kellys and the other members of the troupe, it was still very hard for me to initiate any conversation with someone I didn't know. I was always in dread I would say the wrong thing, and frequently I did. I remember telling one young lady that she "appalled" me; I was trying to tell her she appealed to me but it didn't come out right. But the lack of language never seemed to matter on the dance floor. Conversation didn't seem necessary at all when I put the accordion down and swung some young lady around the floor, which I began doing more and more often.

George T. was as good as his word regarding our fifty–fifty arrangement. After each evening's performance we'd come back to his hotel room and dump all the money on the bed, just as I had dumped the money on the kitchen table for my father two years before. Nickels, quarters, dimes, half dollars, and paper money rolled all over the top of the white cotton bedspread which usually decorated those hotel beds. Mrs. Kelly methodically stacked it into separate piles, and then we'd count it out. On the one night a week when Kelly paid Mrs. Kelly and the other actors we'd split what was left, and on every other night we split the take right down the middle.

The first week with him I made eighty-six dollars and some weeks I made well over a hundred. I felt at the time I had made a wonderful financial arrangement with George T. Kelly, but it wasn't till years later I realized how rewarding our partnership really had been.

I admired him so much I began to imitate him in small ways—and big ones too. I bought clothes like his—flashy outfits with striped vests—and I learned how to tuck my right hand casually into the watch pocket of the vest as he always did, which made me feel very sophisticated. I really felt I had arrived the day I bought a diamond ring like his. It was a large double stone set into gold, and I thought it was beautiful. (I still do, and I still wear it.)

I learned so much from him, and not just about show business either. He was a shrewd judge of character and he knew more about how to get along with people than anyone I have ever met. One day the two of us were having the usual cup of coffee and piece of pie in a small restaurant. My pie was stale, and when I took one bite I exclaimed, "What kind of pie is this! It's terrible." The waitress said nothing but looked at me rather sourly, and George T. said nothing either, just regarded me with that quizzical little smile over the top of his coffee cup. But I noticed that he left a larger than usual tip on the table, and he complimented the cashier extravagantly on the quality of the coffee as we left. I was still grumbling about wasting my dime on a bad piece of pie as we left, but I thought no more about it during the rest of that busy day. It wasn't until we were on the road that night, driving along to our next destination, that Kelly brought it up again.

Tired out, I had propped a cushion under my head ready to go to sleep, when Kelly touched me gently on the arm. "Lawrence," he said, "just a minute. I want to talk to you."

He seemed very serious. "What is it?"

"Do you remember that piece of pie you had today . . . you remember complaining about it?"

"Yes," I said, a little surprised. "What about it?"

Kelly pursed his lips and then said something I've never forgotten. "Lawrence, wherever you go you leave an impression. Now it's up to you whether you leave a good one or a bad one. Today for example. You complained about that pie so loudly that everyone noticed it. When they think of you, they'll remember that. If you recall, I complimented them on their coffee . . . because it was good. When they think of me they'll remember that. It's just as easy to find something good as something bad." He drove silently for a moment and then said, "You think about that, Lawrence. Think about it."

"But the pie *was* bad," I argued stubbornly.

George T. glanced at me with that pleasantly amused expression he wore much of the time. *"I* know that pie was bad," he said, "but I also know that if you had spoken pleasantly to that waitress and asked her for another piece of pie she would have been glad to bring it to you. It's the *way* you do things, Lawrence. The kindness. Most people are basically nice, and the more consideration you show them, the more they'll show you. And that's a lot more important than one piece of bad pie."

He grinned at me and went back to his driving. After a while I settled down with my pillow and drifted off to sleep, but I realized the truth of what he said and I have never forgotten it. I made a conscious effort after that to look for something pleasant and to overlook anything bad, and I found, rather to my astonishment, that Kelly's words made a lot of sense.

We continued our tour. I think now about those hundreds of little towns we played, and they run through my mind almost like a litany—West Port, Driscoll, Beulah, Dawson, Madina, Streeter; all small, always cold, usually blanketed in snow or ice, but always friendly and anxious to see George T. and his Peerless Entertainers. In many ways I suppose it was a hard life, but to me it was sheer bliss. I was earning a very good salary doing the thing I loved best in the world. I could ask for nothing more.

Except maybe to go south. I loved the Dixieland jazz I had heard on the radio and records, and I was anxious to get to New Orleans and hear the artists who played there. I began to work on George to schedule our tours throughout the South so that we could wind up in New Orleans.

"Oh no, Lawrence," he said. "I know this territory like the back of my hand. I know what these good folks want and I'm earning a very good living at it. I don't think we should take the chance."

But as we continued to play our small-town circuit and our reputation grew, the crowds got larger and he began to weaken a little. I kept at him. "George, if you would schedule a tour working down through the southern states we could wind up with a real bang in New Orleans . . . and see the Mardi Gras!" I painted as glowing a picture as I could in my halting English, and somehow I managed to convince George to make the trip.

We packed up our green curtain, and our costumes, and Ole the Swede and Lawrence the Spaniard, and headed south. I was sure we would make a fortune. But George was right—as usual.

The farther south we went the worse we fared. The Southerners had no idea what George's accent was supposed to be, and the Swedish jokes that had seemed so hilarious to Scandinavian audiences made no sense whatever to these people who were nearly all of a different background. They sat in puzzled silence while George struggled through his routines, and I was certainly no help when I came on with my authentic accent. Even the dances afterward failed, because in some of the southern towns where we played the prevailing religion forbade dancing. I was very chagrined and I really felt bad the night we played to the smallest audience of all. I have since played to audiences in the thousands—I think our all-time high was 68,000 people at Soldiers Field in Chicago, where we played for the Music Festival sponsored by the Chicago *Tribune*—but on this particular night in a little town near Enid, Oklahoma, we had an audience of one lone little old lady.

As curtain time neared we peeked out from behind the famous green curtain, and there she sat, stone-faced, arms folded, waiting implacably for the show to begin. We waited for a few more customers to show up, but no one did; finally, about thirty minutes after our customary opening time, George sent me out to speak to her. "Tell her we just can't do a show for only one person," he said. I didn't want to do it. "Now look," he said, grinning a little, "you got us into this situation. You get us out!"

Finally I went out, smiling nervously, and tried as best I could to explain the situation to her. My accent sounded worse than ever, even to me, but she understood me well enough and she flatly refused to leave. "But lady," I said unhappily, "we can't put on a show and a dance for just one person!"

"Oh, yes you can," she said. "I came to see the show and I'm going to see the show!"

"We'll give you your money back," I offered. "We'll just be real happy to do that."

She gave me a look. "Ain't no money involved," she told me with some relish. "I have a lifetime pass here, young man. You see, I own this building."

That stopped me completely, so George finally came out and took over. "I'm sorry, madam," he said firmly. "I'm afraid we'll just have to cancel our performance. We make it a rule that there must be more people in the audience than in the cast. As you can see, that's not the case tonight."

The Peerless Entertainers closed down for the season.

George and Alma went home to Poplar, Montana, and I went to Texas, where I had been asked to lead a six-piece band for the summer. Right away this farm boy found himself in deep trouble! I thought I had picked up a fair degree of sophistication during my year with George, but West Texas was something else again, and I spent almost that entire summer in a state of shock. For one thing, my new band and I didn't see eye to eye on a number of things. I hadn't been with the group very long before I realized something funny was going on. A few of the fellows kept disappearing from the bandstand all during the evening, and when they returned they looked progressively glassy-eyed. I couldn't imagine what they were doing, until my new drummer, Johnny Higgins, took me aside and patiently explained that they were out in the back smoking marijuana. Even after he explained it to me I didn't know what it was.

Between the marijuana smokers who kept ducking outside for a smoke and the drinkers who just sat on the bandstand until they fell sound asleep—the sniffers and the snoozers I called them—I often wound up the evening playing all by myself. I really didn't mind too much. I strolled around the dance floor playing requests much of the time anyway, and it wasn't at all unusual for one of those big-hearted Texans to tip me with a twenty-dollar bill. I always made more in tips than I did from my regular salary all the time I played in West Texas.

In 1926 West Texas was still wide-open, rip-roaring frontier territory, crowded with people swarming into oil towns like Odessa and McCamey and Midland, looking for a quick fortune. A good many of them found it, too, and overnight oil millionaires were common. I remember one friend of mine who struck it rich and immediately began buying expensive sports cars as a hobby. One day when we were out for a drive he got a flat tire; instead of having it repaired he drove right into the nearest garage and ordered four brand new tires. "But you only have one flat," I cried, aghast. "Why are you buying four more?"

"Well, I don't want to take a chance on the other three going flat," he explained as though it were the most reasonable thing to do. I thought he was crazy.

There was a great deal of excitement all the time, partly stemming from the prospect of making a million overnight, and partly from the lack of formal law and order. Most of the men wore guns and liked to handle things in their own way. I found this out immediately at our first engagement. The saxophonist, Howard Kieser, smiled at a pretty girl as we left the bandstand at intermission, and her boyfriend got so enraged he grabbed a knife and slashed Howard right across the abdomen from hipbone to hipbone. Horrified, I grabbed Howard and rushed him off to the local doctor who placidly sewed him back together again. I wanted to have the assailant arrested. "Forget it," the doctor advised as he stitched and sewed. "Down here you just don't smile at another man's gal! This guy got just what was coming to him." Fortunately, Howard's wound was superficial and he recovered quickly, but after that he was very, very careful about whom he smiled at. Needless to say, so was I.

Those dances were different from any I had ever played before or since. As a rule there weren't any regular ballrooms in the territory, although occasionally we found one over a drugstore or a restaurant; for the most part dances were held in the local hotels, which usually had rooms big enough for dining and dancing.

Friday night the lobby of one of those hastily built wooden hotels would begin to fill up with burly Texans outfitted in their best attire—including their best guns—and accompanied by their beautiful wives. After they had all checked in—many of them had driven one or two hundred miles to attend the dance, so they generally spent the weekend at the hotel—the hip flasks would begin to appear and the men would settle down to do some serious drinking. Nobody ever started dancing till very late in the evening, mainly because so many Texans had been raised in areas where dancing was frowned upon, and consequently they had never learned how to dance. It took quite a few drinks before they worked up enough nerve to go out on the floor and attempt a waltz or a polka, and the accompanying jeers and catcalls from the men still on the sidelines were almost always enough to start a few spirited fist fights before the evening was over.

If the catcalls didn't start a fight, there was one other local custom which was practically guaranteed to. In this part of the country it was an established and accepted social habit for two or more married couples to arrive together. Then, as a matter of good-natured courtesy or as a kind of good sportsmanship, one man would spend the entire evening being very gallant and attentive to the other man's wife. You never spent the evening with your own spouse. Sometimes this worked very well, but sometimes—especially if the other man's wife was pretty—and those Texas girls were among the prettiest I have ever seen anywhere—all kinds of fireworks would erupt. One of the men might try to steal a kiss, at which point the good sportsmanship would fly right out the window and the trouble really started. If the men didn't settle things with a knock-down-drag-out fight in the middle of the room, then they would whip out their guns and start shooting, while everyone else screamed and shouted or threw themselves flat on the floor.

The first time I saw this happen I stood rooted to the spot, just frozen with terror, while my accordion wheezed to a stop and my entire band automatically hurled themselves on the floor. I was terrified listening to the bullets whine and ricochet all around the room, but I soon discovered that those fights were over almost as quickly as they started. Half the time the desk clerk didn't even bother to stick his head in the door to see what was going on. After the wounded had been carried away from the scene of the battle and the ladies had straightened their dresses and patted their hair back into shape, the dance went on just as though nothing had happened. In time I got very nonchalant about the whole thing myself. When folks would ask me what time the dance started, I said, "Well, the dance starts at ten and the fight starts about midnight." I could afford to be so nonchalant because I had rearranged our band setup so the piano slanted across one corner of the room in such a way that it made a natural protective barricade for us. Whenever Johnny spotted trouble in the offing he gave us a special drum roll as a signal and we all made a quick dive behind the piano. I developed split-second reactions that summer.

West Texas was really a land of contrasts; tucked in among all those rather lawless towns were several straight-laced religious communities where no dancing, drinking, or card playing were allowed. The people came to our performances just to listen to our music. It was in one of those small and neat towns that I met a beautiful young girl named Rosalind Adams. She and I became very fond of each other, and we might have become even fonder if she hadn't asked me one night what my religion was.

I smiled at her. She was really so pretty. "Well, I think I'll let you guess. What religion do you think I am?"

She considered. "Oh, I don't know," she said. "And anyway, it doesn't matter at all! It just doesn't make one bit of difference to me *what* religion you are . . . just so long as you're not a Catholic!"

Well, that ended this particular little romance. After a while the boys and I packed up and headed for our next engagement.

One time we were hired to play in the town of Wink, Texas. When we arrived we discovered there wasn't any town, only miles and miles of cactus-strewn desert. The only house in sight was the outhouse which the promoters had erected in anticipation of the big crowds they expected. At first it seemed almost insane for the six of us to be sitting outside in the middle of the desert playing waltzes and polkas while scorpions and rattlesnakes slithered by and the wind blew hot sand in our faces. But it turned out that those promoters had the right idea. They weren't interested in music so much as in selling land, and they had hoped our little band would have sufficient drawing power to attract some buyers. We did, and enough people bought city lots that day to get the town going. It's the only time in my career that I helped give birth to a whole town, and I have felt very close to Wink ever since. Land in the outlying districts was going for fifteen cents an acre that day, and I could have kicked myself later on for not buying any, because Wink eventually turned out to be a highly successful oil town with a population which grew to 15,000 people.

After those hectic days in Texas it was a relief to get back to George and The Peerless Entertainers again. At least we wouldn't have to duck behind the piano every time we heard a car backfire! Johnny and Howard came with me and joined the troupe, and we took off almost immediately. One of our first stops that year was Strasburg, where we played in the basement of the church. The place was packed; there were even people sitting huddled together in the windows. They were generous with their cheers and applause, and nobody laughed when I came out in my Spanish costume. "Say, you put on a really good show," Johnny Klein told me in surprise afterward. "That Kelly is a great comedian." My parents came too and enjoyed it. It was a happy night.

Our schedule was very heavy that year and we crisscrossed through hundreds of little inland towns—Steele, Washburn, Wilton, Stanton, Tuttle, Wing, Tappen. In November it turned unusually cold and occasionally we were stranded by a sudden blizzard, but we nearly always managed to reach our Opera House, and so did our audiences, no matter how miserable the weather. More than once we played in rooms so cold that the spectators wore heavy overcoats and boots and sat with woolen blankets or buffalo robes over their laps. Their applause sounded strangely muffled when they clapped with their mittens or gloves on. My Spanish outfit that year was a heavy red velvet matador suit with a lined cape, and I was grateful for it. I would have frozen to death in those short satin pants.

As the tour progressed, George and I began to make plans for a tent show in the summertime. George had been raised in carnivals and circuses and knew a great deal about it, and I was enthusiastic because I thought it would cut down our expenses and enlarge our audiences. We discussed it as we drove from one date to another, and by early spring we had our summer schedule all worked out.

One day, when we were playing a small North Dakota town just across the border from Canada, I looked at the calendar and realized it was March 11, 1927. "Hey, George," I said jubilantly, "today's my birthday. Let's celebrate."

George laughed. "I'll have Alma bake you a cake."

"No, listen," I said, "we're just a few miles from the border. C'mon. I'll treat you to a beer. They don't have Prohibition in Canada."

George hesitated for just a fraction of a second. Then he said, "I didn't think you drank, Lawrence."

"I don't. You know that. Oh, well . . . never mind. It was just an idea."

But George's eyes began to sparkle. "No, let's do it," he decided. "After all, it is your birthday and we should celebrate. One beer won't hurt."

We crossed the border and walked into a small, steamy restaurant where we settled into a booth with high wooden backs and a table covered with a soiled white cloth. "Two beers," I told the owner, and he served us each a glass apiece.

George smiled. "Happy Birthday, Lawrence," he said, "and many many more. You're a fine young man."

We clinked glasses and drank our beer slowly, talking idly of the days we had spent together and making plans for our summer tour. "Well," I said finally, "I guess we better go. We've got a show to do tonight."

"Oh, let's have another beer, Lawrence," said George quickly. "We've got time for another."

I was surprised. "No, I don't think we do. Come on, George."

But he insisted on ordering another round, and when I wouldn't drink mine he downed that also. I realized that he was beginning to get tight and I wanted to get him back to the show before he had another. It was a tough struggle. His whole personality began to change and his normally happy, easy-going disposition was replaced by a sharp and querulous manner. He insisted on having more drinks before I finally got him to leave, and then he bought a bottle of whiskey to take with him. My reaction was more one of surprise than anything else, but I was not really upset; I was just rather startled at this unsuspected side of George's character. I offered to help him down the street, but he flung off my arm indignantly. "I don't need any help," he said loftily. "No help at all." He staggered down the street stiff-legged but straight as a ramrod, and we crossed the border without incident and headed back to our hotel to get ready for the evening's performance.

When Mrs. Kelly saw us, she went white. "Where have you been?" she whispered.

I was embarrassed. "Well, it's my birthday and we went over to celebrate," I explained. "We just had some beer, Mrs. Kelly."

She seemed distraught. "Oh dear, you shouldn't have done that," was all she said, but I thought she was making too much of the incident.

"He's really all right," I told her. "Don't worry. I'll take care of everything."

And I did. I got the curtain up as usual and the show organized and set the scene for the first number, with Johnny helping me. When George showed up just before the program, he seemed as jovial as ever. But as he began his act I realized that he was not himself. He made several mistakes and his usually flawless timing was off considerably. But we finished the show somehow, and the rest of us went ahead and played for the dance afterward, without George at the drums.

I thought no more about it that night, but the next day George was still tight. We were scheduled to leave town that afternoon and make another appearance that night, and we didn't know whether or not he would be able to perform at all. Mrs. Kelly said nothing and we all worked in silence, carrying things into the cars, getting the scenery and props stowed away, talking only when necessary. George, on the other hand, talked volubly or not at all. I was at a loss to understand him. But I still thought that in a day or so his behavior would right itself. It did not.

He seemed lost in some world of his own, and nothing we said seemed to get through to him. Johnny tried, I tried, we all tried to get him to stop drinking, but none of us were successful. George not only continued to drink, he insisted on appearing at every performance, even though most of the time he stood uncertainly in the middle of the stage, unable to remember what to do or say next. We were all worried that he would hurt himself, and one of us stayed close to him at all times to keep him from falling off the edge of the stage. We tried hard to help by cueing him in his lines or making up extra dialogue as we went along, but the show just fell apart, and several times we had to cut everything short while I took over on the accordion. Word of our sorry performances began to reach towns ahead of us, and our audiences grew smaller and smaller; in a few cases our bookings were canceled outright. Before long our tour ground almost entirely to a halt. And still George kept right on drinking. It was an agonizing time for all of us, and I was torn between pity for him and anger that he was allowing this to happen. I couldn't understand how a man I loved and admired as much as I did George could change so drastically in a matter of days.

One night as I was packing away the props, wondering what would become of us, Mrs. Kelly, who was working alongside me, touched me gently on the arm and said, "Lawrence, sit down a minute. I want to talk to you."

I sat down on one of the folding chairs and she sat beside me, looking strained and tired, talking to me, but not looking at me. We had not spoken much during the past two weeks. She sat with her hands folded in her lap and then she said slowly, "Lawrence, George drinks occasionally. And when he starts, well, he just doesn't stop, as you can see. I don't think you had better plan on the summer tours . . . or any more tours at all. George and I are going back to Montana. To stay. We're leaving tomorrow." She paused and then said very softly, "I'm sorry."

I was still angry and upset and I felt that all George had to do was to make up his mind to stop drinking and everything would be all right again. I said as much to Mrs. Kelly.

She looked at me as she would a small child, and then she patted me on the arm. "Lawrence, some day perhaps you'll understand. For now, I can only ask your forgiveness." She picked up some props and her list of the night's receipts and quickly left the room. Mechanically I took down the green curtain and pulled out the wire and packed it away, and then I gathered the rest of the props and stacked them in Kelly's car. I didn't know what to say to Mrs. Kelly. I didn't know what to say to anyone. It was a bleak and cold night. Strangely, I can never recall the name of that little town where Mrs. Kelly and I had our talk. It is something I would rather forget.

I do remember walking up and down the main street of the town, bundled up in an overcoat with a scarf around my neck and my hands deep in the pockets of the coat, trying to keep warm. But it was not really the winds that chilled me that night. It was the thought of what had happened to all of us, and especially of what had happened to George. I thought then that I understood why he had never tried to go to Broadway or Hollywood, why he had deliberately chosen to stay in these isolated towns. But it was many years before I fully understood the real reason for his behavior, and came to realize how fine a man he truly was.

He had opened up a whole new world for me, undertaking the impossible when he tried to make an actor out of an awkward farm boy who couldn't even speak English, and he had been kindness itself to me. He had tried always to turn the spotlight over to me, to build me up, to give me the self-confidence I needed so badly. I remembered with a sudden twinge an incident of just a few months earlier, when I had been getting a shave in a small town. I was lying back in the chair, my face covered with hot towels. A couple of other customers came in and began discussing our show of the night before. "Oh, it's good," they agreed, "but it's really just a one-man show. It's all Kelly."

George had never made me—or any of us—feel that way. To him, each one of us was important, and he had given me more feelings of self-worth than any other person I had ever known. Now, when the situation was reversed, I couldn't help him.

It was one of the unhappiest times of my life because I loved the Kellys, and I felt lost. We had been planning on the summer tours, so I had no bookings in sight and I didn't know what to do or where to go. As it turned out, George had one last gift to give me. He had already given me invaluable training and more self-confidence than I had ever had in my life. Now, with the end of The Peerless Entertainers, he had just given me the chance which was to mark the major turning point of my professional life.

But on that cold and saddening night there was no way for me to realize this.

6

FERN

I WENT TO BISMARCK, NORTH DAKOTA. JOHNNY AND HOWARD came with me, and we began trying to get going again. It wasn't easy. We couldn't find many jobs and finally I decided to form an orchestra myself. I rounded up a fine pianist named Art Beal and the four of us managed to play a few dates in the vicinity, but we had nothing steady and the weather grew bleaker every day. When an unseasonal blizzard blanketed the city with several feet of snow and brought everything to a standstill, I suddenly decided I had had enough of cold and snow, and engagements that were few and far between. "Let's get out of here," I said to Johnny, "and head down south. We can work there just as well as we can here, and at least it will be warmer."

"Right," said Johnny instantly. "Let's go. The sooner the better. I don't care if I never see another snowflake again."

Both Howard and Art were more than willing to go, too, and we started out early the next morning. The tag end of the blizzard was still blowing and it was a miserable day. We drove behind a snow plow every inch of the way, at a maddeningly slow pace, starting and stopping, starting and stopping, and sliding and skidding in between. The snow on each side of the road was piled so high we had to twist our necks outside the car window in order to see the sky. It was bitterly cold, and we took turns driving and then trying to sleep, hunched underneath overcoats and blankets, and using our suitcases for pillows. But the constant jerking of the car made sleeping almost impossible. We drove all day and until almost four o'clock the next morning when suddenly Johnny sat up and said positively, "Lawrence, we've got to stop! If I don't freeze to death, I'll die from lack of sleep."

Howard and Art agreed with him. "Yankton is just a few miles ahead," said Art. "Let's stop there at a hotel and get a few hours' sleep and a good breakfast and then we can keep on going." I didn't want to stop and tried to convince them to drive straight through, but they were exhausted and won me over. At four-thirty in the morning we pulled to a stop in front of the Collins Hotel in Yankton, South Dakota, so frozen and travel weary we could hardly get out of the car, and we dragged our luggage into the deserted lobby and roused the desk clerk. He handed us a key, took instructions to call us at seven-thirty in the morning, and, almost before he had time to get back to his desk, we were all upstairs in our room, fast asleep, and warm for the first time in almost twenty-four hours.

The next morning, refreshed by three hours of sleep, I got dressed and went out to eat. Then I came back up and tried to shake the other boys awake. "Come on," I said to Johnny, "get up. It's time to eat."

He flung my arm away. "Are you crazy?" he groaned. "I just lay down. Go away." He rolled over and pulled the covers over his head. I didn't have much luck with Howard or Art either. They both lay as though they were dead and I couldn't even rouse them. Finally I got Johnny to agree to get up in half an hour and get all the boys into the coffee shop for breakfast. Just to be on the safe side I also left another message with the desk clerk. Then I went out to explore the city.

It was a beautiful morning. The skies had cleared completely and were a clear, bright blue. The sun sparkled on the snow-covered sidewalks and there were crowds of people on the streets, all smiling, happy to be out in the sun after such a long time. I strolled up and down, thinking over our prospects, trying to decide what was the best thing to do. Suddenly I had an idea. I knew there was a brand-new radio station in town, WNAX, and I decided to go over and take a look at it. Maybe there would be something for us there.

In 1927 radio was still something of a novelty, and the broadcasting studio itself was of great interest to me. It was located on the top floor of the Gurney Seed and Nursery Company—a name which was almost a household word in that part of the country—and it was a finely equipped studio, built with a soundproof glass front so that an audience could sit in the auditorium outside and watch the proceedings. The other three walls of the studio were hung with heavy gray soundproof drapes, and there was a small window cut into the rear wall for the engineer's booth. When I walked in that morning a man was standing in front of a large, round-headed microphone, announcing the news. Even at that early hour there were several people in the audience watching him.

"Who is that man?" I asked the girl at the reception desk.

"Mr. Gurney," she replied. "Chandler Gurney. The Gurneys own this station."

I watched him as he finished his broadcast. He was a handsome man, a little older than I, and in a few more years his name would be known all over the country as the new senator from South Dakota. I waited till the end of his program and then I went up to congratulate him.

He was pleasant and affable, so I quickly added, "I have an orchestra, Mr. Gurney. We're just traveling through town on our way to New Orleans, and it occurred to me that maybe we could play a broadcast for you while we're here."

He was interested. "How big is your band?"

"Four pieces. And our drummer Johnny Higgins is a fine singer. We specialize in polkas." He nodded. We were in the heart of polka country, a fact of which I knew he was well aware. "Well," he said, "bring the boys in and I'll give them an audition." He looked at the clock. "It's eight-fifteen. Can you have them here by nine o'clock?"

"Yes," I said casually, "I think I might be able to arrange that. We can make it by nine." I smiled, shook his hand, bowed to the girl at the desk, and strolled out of the studio. Once out on the street I ran all the way back to the Collins Hotel, skidding on icy patches, jumping over puddles, spattering snow all over myself. Near the Collins I tore into the coffee shop where the boys were sitting around a table, half asleep, pushing down eggs and bacon.

"Come on!" I yelled. 'Hurry up! We've got an audition!"

"Lawrence," said Johnny, in real annoyance, "will you cut this out! First you wouldn't let us sleep and now you won't let us eat!"

'We've got a chance for a job," I said rapidly, "that will give us some money so we'll be able to eat a whole lot better for the rest of the trip. Now hurry up. We have to be at the radio station at nine o'clock."

Their jaws dropped. "I don't know how to play on the radio," complained Art.

"Neither do I," I said flatly, "but now's the time to find

out." I left them stuffing down their breakfast and I ran upstairs and began dragging our instruments out. They came up to help me and then we all rushed downstairs, got into the car, and drove over to the radio station, discussing which numbers to play for Mr. Gurney. "You sing 'Mexicali Rose,' Johnny," I said. "I told Mr. Gurney we had a singer and he seemed to like that."

"Boy, I'm sure in great voice this morning," grumbled John, but I could see that all the boys were excited by our new adventure. At five minutes to nine we arrived at the studio and walked in as though we had all the time in the world. Mr. Gurney was waiting. "Right on time! Just go on into the studio there and you'll go on the air at nine o'clock."

I was flabbergasted. "On the air! Don't you want to hear us first?"

Mr. Gurney laughed. "I can hear you on the air just as easily as I can listen to you out here. Go ahead. I'll show you what to do."

We walked through the heavy double doors into the studio and arranged ourselves around the mike. By the time we got John's drums set up it was almost nine and Mr. Gurney suddenly turned to me and said quickly, "What's the name of your band again?"

"Lawrence Welk and his Novelty Orchestra," I whispered.

He nodded, and as the big hand on the clock swung around we heard him say, "Good morning, ladies and gentlemen! WNAX takes great pleasure in bringing you the music of Lawrence Welk and his Novelty Orchestra, direct from our studios in downtown Yankton. The boys will open the show this morning with 'Mexicali Rose,' Johnny Higgins on the vocals."

I stood where I was, hand raised and ready for the down beat, until finally Mr. Gurney jabbed the air violently in my general direction and hissed, "Go ahead. Go *ahead!*"

I nodded brightly and, as usual, began to pound on the floor with my foot to start the beat. At this the engineer clasped both hands to his ears, a look of agony crossed his face, and he disappeared from view behind his window. I wondered briefly what had happened to him, but then we all swung into the number and gave it everything we had. Johnny sang very well, in spite of no sleep and little breakfast, and during the number Mr. Gurney whispered to me again, "What do you want to play next?" I told him, and that was the way we conducted the whole show. Before we finished our second number the secretary appeared outside the window and waved a few slips of paper at us. She was smiling happily. Mr. Gurney went outside and got them. They were requests from people listening to our show. They had called to say they liked it and more than half the requests asked for Johnny to sing "Mexicali Rose" again. By the time the show was over, the secretary had a whole stack of such papers, and we all were excited by the reception we had received. In the middle of all the congratulations, the engineer came over to me. "Don't ever do that again," he said earnestly.

"Do what?" I asked him.

"Pound on the floor like that. You nearly knocked us off the air, and you nearly blew my head off."

"Oh I'm sorry," I said contritely. I tried not to pound hard after that, but it was difficult for me to overcome the habit, and finally, in desperation, the engineer threatened to put a pillow under my foot.

That morning, however, I had no idea that I would be staying around long enough to make any arrangements for a pillow to put under my foot. After the broadcast I expected Mr. Gurney to pay us, and then we'd be off on our way to New Orleans. Instead, he asked me if we would like to play again that afternoon and the following day too. "Well," I said hesitatingly, "I don't know. We're on our way to New Orleans. What do you think, fellows?" We looked at each other without saying anything, and finally Mr. Gurney said, "Suppose I give you a week's contract? That will give us time to see how we like each other." After a few moments' discussion we decided to stay for the week. New Orleans would still be there and we'd have a little nest egg. We didn't know it then, but that chance stop in Yankton and our impromptu "audition" were to change the future for all of us.

We got the same kind of flattering reception when we did our next broadcast, and at the end of the week Mr. Gurney offered us another week's contract. We were pleased but still eager to get to New Orleans, so we hesitated a good deal deciding to accept it. Then another astonishing thing developed. WNAX was an extraordinarily powerful station—in fact, it was the only station for miles around—and we began to establish the kind of reputation in a matter of days that ordinarily would have taken months or years to establish by making personal appearances. We began receiving requests from dance hall managers all around the countryside. When we turned down the first few, because we still intended to keep on going to New Orleans, they all upped the price they had offered us. Quite by accident we had fallen into a small gold mine. The more we played on WNAX, the more dance requests we received and the higher the prices we were able to command. For the first time I realized the power of the communications media, and this new thing called radio. When Mr. Gurney offered us a long-term contract, I had little difficulty in talking the boys into accepting it.

Yankton changed our lives. We found ourselves established as something of local celebrities, with a reputation that extended at least four hundred miles in every direction. When we went to play a dance we found a ready-made audience, anxious to see us as well as hear us, and each of us developed a fan following much like the group singers of today. There were always crowds of young people waiting for us whenever we arrived in a town, and by the end of a few months we had abandoned the idea of going to New Orleans entirely—at least for the time being. We were enjoying ourselves too much—and it wasn't just from the steady income from the radio and dance dates either. It was the girls.

I had long since gotten over my fear of sitting next to a pretty girl, and had managed to date quite a few of them, even during my tours with Mr. Kelly. And now that our

Yankton success gave me both the time and the money, I began to enjoy this part of my life even more.

Coming down to WNAX to watch us in action at the studio became more or less the thing to do in that part of the country. In particular, there was always a group of young student nurses from Sacred Heart Hospital who used to come in a group whenever they had time off. I knew almost all of them and had dated several, and sometimes I invited them to the dances we played in town. I greatly enjoyed all their company, but I never really got serious about any of them because I liked them all too much. One day, however, I looked out into the auditorium and there, sitting in one of the rows off to one side, was the prettiest girl I had ever seen in my life. She had great big brown eyes and very fair skin and dark hair . . . and she looked very unimpressed by everything that was going on around her. I smiled my best smile at her, but she didn't react a bit. All through the program that morning I tried to catch her eye, and whenever I did, I beamed widely. No response. I was intrigued, and the minute the program was off the air I ran outside to see if I could meet her. She had already gone. I described her to one of the other girls. "Oh, that's Fern Renner," she said. "You won't get anyplace with her. She's not only a nurse—she wants to be a doctor!"

Now I was more interested than ever, and I tried to find out some way to meet her. A week later she came back again, and before she could get away I dashed out to the audience during the program and managed a fast introduction.

"Could you have dinner with me tonight?" I asked quickly.

"No, I'm busy," she replied coolly.

I didn't have enough time to keep talking then, but I made her promise to wait till the show was over, and then I started in again. Fern was very difficult with me, but she finally agreed to go on a double date if I'd promise to get her back to her boardinghouse in plenty of time for her studies that night. I promised. I would have promised almost anything to get to know her better. True to my word, Johnny Higgins and I took Fern and her girl friend out that night and I took her home at eight-thirty. We had a good time and I thought I had made great headway, but I soon learned that Fern Renner was not about to be bowled over by a mere band leader.

This was in sharp contrast to a lot of the other girls at the time. In fact, there was a whole group of girls known as "band girls" who used to hang around the bandstand in every town we played, and they were about as different from Fern as night from day. Fern really didn't want to get involved in my life or with me. At first, though, I thought she was just playing games.

One day as I was driving down the street I saw her walking along with her girl friend. I screeched the car to a halt. "Would you care for a ride?" I asked hopefully. The other girl nodded. "Yes, sure!" And she rushed over and sat down next to me, leaving Fern on the outside. I didn't like that at all, so I said to the other girl, "How would you like to drive the car?" Then I got out and went around and sat next to Fern, but she never said a word.

She was much more highly educated than I, and she spoke English with very little accent, although she also was of German descent and had been raised in a small town, St. Anthony. She was Catholic too, and in many ways our viewpoints were similar. But Fern had a dream of becoming a doctor and her plans did not include a bandleader who spent most of his time traveling from one town to another. For a long time I despaired of even getting any dates with her; whenever I was in town it seemed she was always on a case, or taking a class, or due in surgery or something.

Finally I came up with what I considered a foolproof scheme. For years my friend Dr. Frank Abst had been urging me to have a small flap of skin, the result of a childhood tonsillectomy, removed. I had put it off. Now, I reasoned, if I could get Fern to be my nurse, if she could see me suffering in agony, maybe that would melt her heart. It was worth a try. I had put off that tonsil operation for years, but now I couldn't wait to have it done.

I went to see Dr. Abst. "Why the sudden rush?" he asked with a twinkle in his eye. (He knew about Fern.) "Well, never mind. I think I know. Check into the hospital tomorrow and we'll see that it's taken care of."

Early the next morning I set off for the hospital, but to my dismay I found that another nurse had been assigned to my case. Fern, who was still a student nurse, was not allowed to handle post-operative patients. It was too late to back out, so I went ahead and had the surgery performed, but I regretted every minute of it. Fern heard of my heroic gesture, however, and so she came to see me at visiting hours. As it turned out, I did get pretty sick at about that time and hemorrhaged, so she found a very pale and woebegone patient when she arrived. It always seemed to me that she was a little more friendly after that.

We began to see each other more and more often, but it was a funny kind of courtship in which I did almost everything wrong. Once I asked her to drive home with me to meet my parents. Instead of being flattered, she was insulted. "Strasburg is five hundred miles from here. I'm not going to drive all that way with you alone."

"But it's my *mother!*" I said, not understanding her for the moment. She just gave me a look. Another time I offered her a photograph of myself just before I left on a trip. I wanted her to have it so she wouldn't forget about me while I was away, but she just thought I was conceited. And so it went. But somehow over the next two years we got to know each other better, and the more I knew her the better I liked her.

Meanwhile our orchestra was growing. I added two new members and did then what I still do today, encouraged each one to develop his talents, with the result that each of the fellows could play at least one other instrument besides his own specialty. Practicing what I preached, I learned to play a little piano, saxophone, banjo, organ, and drums. One of our new members was Leo Fortin, a dark-eyed hot-tempered Frenchman from Waubay, South Dakota, and a fine trumpet player. He had one trick that used to fascinate our audience—he could play two trumpets at the same time, and for a while he even rigged up a gadget so that he could play three. He never failed to steal the show with his trumpet "duet." Rollie Chestney also joined the group and we had Cliff Moe, a saxophonist, and Homer Schmidt, who played drums. We all became very good friends.

It was a fine time for all of us. The whole country was riding a crest of prosperity in 1928 and 1929 and we felt it in Yankton too, playing twice daily at the radio station and crowding in several dances every week. I had established the pattern of dividing our radio salary equally with all the boys, and I did the same thing for our dance dates, after deducting operating expenses. Since we played on a percentage basis, we all earned very good money. With WNAX as a continuing source of advertising, we were booked solidly for months in advance and I got to be something of an expert at fitting bookings into place like a crossword puzzle so that we could use our time to best advantage.

I used all the tricks George T. had taught me and I learned a few of my own in those happy years. Generally we played all the ballrooms on a sixty-forty percentage basis, but as our reputation grew, some of the ballroom managers offered us seventy, eighty, and in some cases, ninety percent of the gross. And in a few rare cases they even offered us a hundred percent, figuring they would make some money from the sale of refreshments and establish their ballrooms in the mind of the dance-going public.

I enjoyed playing all the towns, but I had my sights set at that time on playing for Tom Archer's chain of ballrooms. He had seven of them through the Midwest—the Arkota and Neptune Casino in Sioux Falls, the Rigadon and Shore Acres in Sioux City, the Chermot in Omaha, the Frog Hop in St. Joseph, and the Tromar in Des Moines. They were all large well-run establishments that played only well-known bands. He stubbornly resisted hiring me for a while, because, he said, my band was too small. "I only use big bands in ballrooms," he told me. "Your six-piece band just isn't big enough." I was just as stubborn as he was; I was then billing us as America's Biggest Little Band, capitalizing on the fact that all of my boys could double or triple on their instruments, so that we were capable of putting on a show as good as a band twice our size. Finally Tom capitulated, after the other ballroom managers began to tell him how much money they made whenever we played, but he stuck flatly to the sixty-forty percentage arrangement. I was willing to accept those terms because I knew his ballrooms would open up new territory for us.

Both professionally and personally it was a good move for me. Tom became a close personal friend and helped me in many ways, spending time after the dances going over our performances with a fine tooth comb. I had asked him to tell me any comments he heard during the evening, and particularly any complaints. Even though I enjoyed hearing compliments as much as anyone, I knew it was from the complaints that we really learned. Tom was always blunt and to the point. If the audience got bored during any part of the evening and began to cluster around the refreshment stand or to leave the hall, he was quick to tell me. "Well, Lawrence," he'd say, easing his bulk into a restaurant booth somewhere, "I think I've got a little pointer here for you." Maybe we had played a tune too fast or too slow or had played too many of the same kind in a row. I learned a good deal about pacing a show during those years from Tom.

Those dance dates built up both our bank accounts and our stamina. We all got so we could sleep sitting up, and we enjoyed those long overnight drives. Leo in particular enlivened many a long trip with his sharp conversation, and we used to enjoy reminiscing about some of our adventures. The boys never let me forget about the time, early in our Yankton years, when we had played a dance date in weather so cold that we all sat on the bandstand with our overcoats and knitted caps on. It was thirty-seven below . . . and that's cold! Homer even played drums with his gloves on, and I would have worn mine too, if I could have played a note with them. At intermission time I braved the shattering cold to race out to that little house in the back, and it was so cold that I broke all records sprinting back in. I made a spectacular reentry. In my haste to get out of the icy air I had forgotten to pull up my suspenders, and they dangled loosely below the hem of my coat. Snickers and chuckles and finally roars of laughter followed me all across the floor and I was as red as my flannel shirt by the time I got to the bandstand. That was my most embarrassing moment!

One day when Fern was out in the audience watching our radio broadcast I pointed her out to Mr. Gurney. "See that girl in the first row?" I asked.

"I certainly do," he replied. "She's the prettiest one out there."

"Well, what would you say if I told you I was going to marry her?"

"I'd say congratulations," said Mr. Gurney. Then, after a moment's pause, he wheeled around in astonishment. "Do you mean to tell me some girl has actually got you thinking about marriage? You! You'll break a million hearts!"

"Well," I said, "I'm not doing a very good job of breaking hers." At just about the time I thought I was making some headway with Fern, however, I finally got my chance to make a long-awaited Eastern tour. I had signed with MCA earlier in the year—a contract that seemed like the end of the rainbow at the time. The contract was to be valid until the agency earned a million dollars in commissions, and if the agency earned that much, what would the boys and I be earning? It sounded too good to be true, and it was. MCA handled all the biggest bands in the country, all the top groups, and Lawrence Welk and his little Yankton outfit were so far down the list they had trouble remembering our names. But they finally did come up with an Eastern tour, and with Chan Gurney's blessing we started off to conquer the East—and make a dent in the world of the big-time bands.

We went down to dismal failure. For one thing, the country was beginning to slip definitely into the Depression and money was getting tighter. For another, the Easterners were not quite ready for our brand of polkas and waltzes. And, to tell the truth, we weren't quite ready for the big-time. At any rate, we didn't make it, and I was very disappointed. I was caught between unhappiness at having to return in defeat, and happiness at getting back to see Fern again. She listened philosophically as I told her about our failure in the big cities, but she couldn't stay around very long to comfort me because she had already accepted a job at St. Paul's Hospital in Dallas, Texas. I hated to see her go, but almost as soon as she left I got a six months' booking at Eddie Ott's Broadmoor Club in Denver, Colorado, and so would have been separated from her anyway. For the next few months we wrote to each other. It was a terrible task for me. I wrote with a dictionary beside me, looking up the words I didn't know or didn't know how to spell. It took me hours to write a letter that made sense and said what I wanted to say. I guess I must have said the right things though, because when she took her vacation a few months later, she went back to Yankton by way of Denver, which is not exactly the fastest way to get from Texas to South Dakota. It was in Denver in 1931, that I finally got Fern to agree to marry me. We were well into the Depression then, but I was doing fairly well in Denver, and I had three bookings lined up after that, so it seemed to me that my prospects were steady enough to ask her to marry me.

Fern went back to work in Dallas while I continued to play at the Broadmoor, and we wrote daily, making plans for our wedding. I had romantic visions of going to Niagara Falls for our Honeymoon. My next long booking was at the De Witt Clinton Hotel in Albany, New York, and I thought this would be a wonderful way to begin our married life. Fern agreed, and we finally settled on April 19, 1931, as our wedding day.

Our wedding was certainly different. For one thing, we were married at five-thirty in the morning. The boys and I were scheduled to play an engagement at Norfolk, Nebraska, on April 18, and Fern's train arrived in nearby Sioux City, Iowa, at four o'clock the morning of the 19th. We had to be on the road that day by ten o'clock in order to make that night's booking, so we decided on that early morning hour in order to give us some time for a small wedding breakfast after the ceremony. We asked Dr. and Mrs. Abst to be our attendants, and the four of us, along with the priest, Father Leo McCoy, were the only people in the Sacred Heart Cathedral that morning. It was quiet and still with only the candles on the altar to light the church. We all felt the solemnity of the occasion and we were all a little nervous—it was young Father McCoy's first wedding, too!—but it was a beautiful ceremony and meant everything to Fern and me. It had taken me a long time to make the decision to marry, and now that I had, I wanted to take care of Fern and give her the best life possible. After Father McCoy had finished the Mass and given us the Nuptial blessing, we started down the church aisle. Suddenly I heard footsteps pounding behind us. It was Father McCoy, red-faced and panting. "Come back quick," he said. "I forgot something." Fern looked horrified and I was a little worried myself, but as it turned out he had only forgotten to bless the ring. He went ahead and blessed it—a simple platinum band which Fern still wears today—and we were officially man and wife.

Once more we walked down the aisle and out into the early morning sunshine, where we were stopped short by what we saw. There were the boys—Leo, Rollie, Cliff, all of them—draped all over each other in attitudes of utter exhaustion, every one of them with a bag of rice clutched in his hand, and every last one of them sound asleep. They had been sitting on the steps waiting for the church doors to open at five that morning. Not knowing they were there, of course, we had gone into the sacristy of the church through the back door, and they had all fallen into a deep sleep in the meantime. We roused them. "You mean to say you're already married?" cried Leo in annoyance. "After we sat here all night? Well, that's a fine thing!" A little grumpily they threw the rice at us, but then we all burst into laughter and went on down to the Martin Hotel, where we had been staying, for our wedding breakfast.

It was a rather Spartan breakfast, with coffee instead of champagne, but there was a lot of love there. Rollie and Leo and Homer made a fine toast and I responded as best I could, and when I looked at my lovely wife I felt very very proud and very lucky indeed.

After breakfast we went up to get my luggage, and just as we were leaving the room the phone rang. It was MCA, and what they had to say effectively ended all thoughts of a Niagara honeymoon. The Albany engagement on which I had been counting so much had just been canceled, and they had nothing else lined up for me. All I could count on was my one-night stand in La Crosse, Wisconsin, that night, plus one in Milwaukee. That was it.

What a wedding present for a brand new bride! For the moment I had no real job at all. I didn't know what to say to Fern, and so I didn't say anything at all. Of course, Fern knew without my telling her that something had gone wrong, and when we were out in the car I finally told her what had happened. She just smiled. "That's all right," she said. "I'm not worried. You'll get something else." She gave me a very nice wedding present with those words.

We drove nearly all day long, and by the time we arrived in La Crosse the disappointment over losing the Albany job had faded and I was full of confidence again, sure that everything would be all right. Evidently I was in a fine and foolish bridegroom state of absent-mindedness. We went into the hotel where we planned to spend the night and I signed the register. Then I took Fern by the arm and started across the lobby toward the elevator, but the clerk called after me and his voice was pretty sharp. "Mr. Welk!"

I turned. "Yes?"

"Please come back here." He was very cool.

I turned and went back to the desk. "What is it?"

"I'm sorry, sir, but we don't allow this sort of thing here."

"What sort of thing?"

He turned the registry book around and pointed with his finger. There on the top line I had just written in my largest and boldest handwriting "Lawrence Welk and Fern Renner." "Oh," I said. "Is that all? Well I just made a little mistake!" I crossed out Fern's name and wrote "Mr. and Mrs." in front of mine. The clerk turned the book around, looked at the altered signature, looked over at Fern standing there looking beautiful and confused, and then winked at me very broadly and nodded.

"Oh, I see," he said, "I see!" Then he winked again.

Fern was furious and just about ready to leave me. "How could you do such a thing?" she demanded. She was so embarrassed she refused to leave our room all the time we were there, and she rushed out like a sprinter the next morning on the way to our car. I thought the whole thing was funny, but she didn't.

7

MY BAND WALKS OUT

AFTER OUR ALBANY BOOKING WAS CANCELED I THOUGHT OUR best bet would be Chicago because we would be able to find more chances to work there. But I was wrong. Chicago in 1931 was feeling the effects of the Depression even more than the smaller towns and cities. Jobs were just as hard to find there as anywhere else, and maybe harder. I tramped the streets daily looking for work, I bombarded MCA with requests to find us bookings, and I sent off letters myself trying to find engagements for us, but none of our efforts were fruitful.

Fern and I rented a tiny room in a dingy hotel on Wabash Avenue, close by the El, and tried to pretend we were just on a carefree honeymoon. I didn't have enough money to take her anywhere, so most of the time we just window-shopped or went down to Lake Michigan, where we strolled along the water's edge, holding hands and trying to reassure each other. "See that big pink building over there?" I said to her one night. She nodded. "That's the Edgewater Beach Hotel. And someday I'm going to play there." She just squeezed my hand. At the moment it seemed like the wildest of dreams.

My Band Walks Out

All the boys lived close by and I felt a terrible responsibility for them, as well as for my brand-new bride. I redoubled my efforts to find work, including sending off a letter to a friend of mine, a Mr. Rademacher, who owned a summer resort at Twin Lakes, Wisconsin. While I was waiting to hear from him I doled out pennies every day and all of us lived pretty close to the bone for a while. I didn't want Fern to know how worried I was, so one night I decided to throw caution to the winds and take her out. "Come on," I said. "Louis Armstrong is playing in town. Let's get all dressed up and go hear him."

"All right," she said, "Who's he?"

That should have been enough to stop me right then. Instead, I explained to her very carefully just who he was, and then I got out enough money to pay for our tickets and we set out. I might as well have saved the cash. Fern was just mystified by the whole evening. Armstrong was playing in a smoky basement club with low ceilings and recessed lights. The room was filled, on this particular night anyway, with an enthusiastic crowd of eager Dixieland jazz lovers. I was in seventh heaven listening to his artistry on the trumpet and I could hardly sit still. "Isn't this wonderful?" I shouted to Fern above the storm of applause at the end of one number. She just smiled, a little uncertainly, and shrugged her shoulders.

All at once I realized that what seemed like the greatest music to me was just a lot of noise to her. I realized also what kind of life I had put her into—one she would never have chosen for herself, but one she was determined to understand for my sake. More than ever I wanted to succeed so I could give her the things she really wanted. But toward the end of those dismal days in Chicago I could barely give her enough to eat. Finally I decided we'd better get back to Yankton. I talked it over with the boys.

"What do you think?" I asked. "We've always been able to earn a living there. I'm sure I can pick up a few dates with Tom Archer, too."

Leo nodded. "Yeah, I think so, too. We're well-known

around there. It should be a lot easier." The rest of the boys agreed, and we planned to meet in Yankton in two weeks. I said goodbye to Chicago, determined to return and play there successfully some day. But I didn't say anything about that part to Fern; instead I suggested that now might be a fine time for her to meet my family and she agreed.

On the way we stopped off to visit Max Fichtner, who was then living in Decatur, Illinois. We were delighted to see each other. He was just as erect and impressive as ever, and his tongue was just as sharp.

"My dear child," he said immediately to Fern, "don't tell me you've married this traveling accordionist here?" Fern was bewildered by his caustic tongue, but before she could say anything he turned to me and said bitingly, "Are you still hitting as many wrong notes as ever?" I laughed. He hadn't changed a bit.

"Max," I answered, "why don't we find out?"

I went out to the car and got my accordion and Max and I spent the next few hours playing all our old favorites—"Zu Strasbourg" of course, and all the other sentimental waltzes and polkas which we had played together so many times during our years in Strasburg. He played beautifully, as always, and as he finished a spectacular run on the piano he sat motionless for a moment and then turned quietly to me and said simply, "Lawrence . . . you're good." I started to thank him, but instantly he held up his hand and added, "However, there's great room for improvement!" Coming from Max that was still a compliment, and I was very pleased.

Agatha Fichtner served us a memorable meal that night. Fern and I were so hungry by then that almost anything would have tasted good, but Mrs. Fichtner had made meat balls with rich spicy gravy and the kind of homemade egg noodles which had been a staple of my diet on the farm, and I don't know when anything ever tasted quite so wonderful. Max watched us as we downed every last crumb, and later on when we were alone in the living room he said, "Things have not been going so well for you, Lawrence?"

"A little slow. But we're on our way back to Yankton and I'm sure we'll do better there."

He nodded. "You stay with us a while. The rest will do you good."

We stayed so long that Fern got uncomfortable. "Lawrence, after all, they have twelve children," she said. "It just isn't right to impose on them like this."

That was true, of course, and so we left the next day. But that interval of good music and good food and understanding friendship, coming at a time when we needed it so badly, was a kindness I have never forgotten. I doubt if Max realized how much it meant to us.

From the Fichtners we drove on to Strasburg and the farm, where my family loved Fern on sight, as I knew they would. We stayed for just a few days and then headed back to Yankton and the boys.

In Yankton things picked up immediately. Tom Archer arranged dates at some of his ballrooms, notably the Arkota in Sioux Falls, and I managed to book several dances at small towns in the surrounding area. Then, to top the whole thing off, I received word from Mr. Rademacher that he would book us for the entire summer at his lake resort. I was delighted. "Listen to this," I said excitedly to Fern. "We'll have room and board and three hundred dollars a week! It'll be just like a paid vacation. Isn't that wonderful!"

She smiled. "Very nice. Very good."

The boys were as pleased as I was, and not even the fact that I had to pay MCA a commission, although I had arranged the booking myself, could dampen my enthusiasm. However, I was a little taken aback when I realized that after I paid MCA their sixty-dollar commission and the Union their thirty-dollar tax, we would have only $210.00 a week left to divide among us. But at least it was a job and it was steady. In the middle of the Depression that was a rare piece of good luck.

Meanwhile we continued to play dances in and around Yankton. Fern and I had taken a small room at the Collins

Hotel; in fact, several of the boys stayed there, too, and the Collins was to be our headquarters off and on for many years.

One day we left to play several engagements in and around Dallas, South Dakota, but Fern decided to stay in Yankton and visit with the Absts. It was the first time we had been parted since our marriage, and I didn't know if I liked the idea!

When we arrived in Dallas that day I went over to check out the dance hall. On the way back I walked by the local pool hall, and through the window I could see all the boys grouped around one end of the green felt table, their heads close together, talking very earnestly about something—and they didn't seem to be talking about pool. I started to go in and join them, but then I stopped. There was something odd about the way they were talking with such intensity, and just as I peered in, Rollie looked up and saw me. Immediately he reached behind him and grabbed a pool cue out of the racks, and the rest of the boys did the same thing, waving casually as they did so. I waved, too, but there was something upsetting about that little scene and I felt vaguely uneasy as I walked back to the hotel.

That night, however, I put the whole incident out of my mind, because we played to an unexpectedly large crowd and made a good deal of money. In fact, when I divided the evening's receipts with the boys, it turned out to be the most we had made in some time. "Well, fellows," I said happily, as I handed each of them his share, "it looks as if things are really going to change for us now!"

"Yeah," said Rollie rather slowly, "I guess maybe they are."

The next morning I was up early, as usual, and I walked over to the restaurant for breakfast. I was astonished to see one of my boys already there, drinking coffee. "What in the world got you up so early?" I asked in genuine surprise, sliding into the booth across from him. "What's the matter, couldn't you sleep last night?"

He laughed a little self-consciously. "Well, as a matter of fact, I didn't sleep too well. Funny you should come in here,

My Band Walks Out

Lawrence. I was just on my way up to see you."

"Oh?" I gave my order to the waitress. "Well, fine. What's on your mind?"

He looked a little embarrassed, unhappy even, and finally he said, "Well, Lawrence, the other boys have asked me to be their spokesman and come and tell you that . . . well, we've been talking things over and we think the best thing to do is to . . . well, to leave."

For just a minute I didn't understand him. "Leave? Where do you want to go?"

"No no, I don't mean like that. I mean we want to leave *you*. We want to leave the band." He paused. "We're quitting!"

"Oh, no," I said instantly. "No, no no. Don't tell me that."

"Yeah, well, we've been talking it over as I said, and we just think it's the best thing for all of us. And for you, too, Lawrence. You won't have any trouble getting another band together, musicians are a dime a dozen these days. You'll be okay."

I hardly heard him, because I was still hearing him say, "We're quitting." "But what are you planning to do?" I managed to ask. "Where are you going? Are you sure you want to do this?"

"Yeah, yeah, we're sure. I think we'll probably go to Chicago."

"But we couldn't get anything in Chicago!"

"You mean *you* couldn't get anything in Chicago!" he blurted out. "Maybe we can. I'm sorry, Lawrence, but . . ." he shrugged, and spread his hands wide, "that's the way it is. So . . . thanks for all the good years and best of luck." He started to slide out of the booth. "We'll see you tonight."

"Wait a minute!" I caught at his arm. "Just a minute. I know things haven't been going too well, but we're doing better now and we have the whole summer booked up! So why would you want to leave me now?"

He looked very uncomfortable. "Just . . . we feel we can do better on our own, that's all."

I persisted. "But why? Why do you feel that way?"

Suddenly his face got red and he leaned across the table and said very tensely, "I'll tell you why. Because of you, that's why! We don't want to spend the rest of our lives out here in these sticks and, Lawrence, that's where you're gonna be for the rest of your life! You're never gonna make it in the big time! Let me tell you something . . . " he gestured angrily, "you still bounce around like you're playing at a barn dance . . . and you can't even speak English! So if you want to know the real reason we're leaving, it's *you. You're* the one who's holding us all back!"

I was so bewildered, so dumbstruck at his sudden attack, that I just sat there staring at him, and after a moment he said awkwardly, "Oh, Lawrence, I'm sorry, really I am. But you asked for it! You wanted to know. Okay, now you know!" He got up out of the booth. "We'll see you tonight." When I didn't answer him, he said sharply, "Okay?"

I nodded dumbly, "Yes . . . okay. Tonight."

"All right then." He waited a moment longer, and when I still didn't say anything he turned and walked out the door. The waitress came over with my pancakes, put them down in front of me, and then poured out a cup of coffee. "Is anything the matter?" she asked uncertainly. "You look kind of white."

"No. That is . . . I'm fine. Thank you." I forced myself to drink some of the coffee, but I couldn't get a single bite of the pancakes down and finally I pushed the plate away from me. "Don't you like them?" It was the waitress again. I looked up at her. She seemed to be speaking from a great distance.

"No no, they're fine. It's just . . . I don't feel very hungry." I paid her and got up out of the booth and was surprised to feel how unsteady my legs were. I realized I was shivering a little, and I walked out into the early morning sunshine and then went back to the hotel and did something I had never done in my life before. I got undressed and went back to bed in the daytime.

I felt sick, numb, almost paralyzed with shock, and I couldn't get those blunt words out of my mind. "You're never gonna make it in the big time . . . you can't even speak English. You're the one who's holding us all back!" And from farther back in my memory I could hear my father's voice saying clearly, "You'll never be a success in the music business, and you'll be back here begging for a good meal one of these days." Suddenly I swallowed hard and rolled over in bed and buried my face deep, deep into the pillow. But I couldn't get those words out of my head. I think it was the lowest moment of my lifetime.

It's curious how we act in moments of personal despair. When we met for the dance that night none of us mentioned a word about what had happened. We all spoke pleasantly about trivial things. "Got your music lined up, Leo?" "Yeah, all here." "Good crowd tonight." "Yeah, not bad." We all smiled and played as usual and the audience was not aware that anything out of the ordinary was going on. But I felt as if I were operating on three levels at once. On top I was smiling and playing the accordion and kidding with some of the dancers who stopped by the bandstand. In the middle I was wondering about what was the best move to make, whether I should try to get another band together, and what I could tell Fern. And at the bottom of my mind, like a dull persistent ache, was the recurrent thought, "You're no good. You don't have what it takes. You'll never make it."

The next few days were kind of a blur for me. The word got around very fast and I had several telephone calls from other small bands offering me a chance to lead them or to join their groups, but something kept me from accepting their offers. For one thing, I had the Twin Lake booking lined up and I felt an obligation to carry it out. But more important than that was my own inescapable conviction that music was my life, and that no matter what had happened I should get my own group together. In the light of what had just occurred that seemed almost idiotic, but somehow I felt very strongly about it and by the time I got back to Yankton I had made up my mind. I would try to start all over again with a brand-new band.

Telling Fern about what had happened was much easier than I had anticipated. "I thought so," she said quietly. "Some of the boys' wives came up to the hotel to see me and they asked to see my wedding dress . . . and they talked then as if they were planning to leave."

"Did they tell you why?"

"No. Lawrence, don't feel so bad. I know you'll be all right."

I took her in my arms. I loved her so much.

Some of the bewilderment and pain began to lift the moment I returned to Yankton, and a day or so later when I dropped into church for some quiet reflection I had a sudden flash of insight which helped me very much at the time and has helped me greatly all my life. I realized that we are all vulnerable human beings, and whenever we put our love and faith into another human being, we are open to hurts and disappointments. That's just part of life. We all hurt each other, completely unintentionally at times. The only one to trust completely is God, and once you can understand that, and learn not to bear any malice or bitterness in your heart, your life will be much happier. I never again took anything quite so personally. I realized that the only important thing in life is to live it as well as you can. Everything else is secondary.

I came out of church that day feeling much better, and completely able to function again. Obviously, the first thing I needed to do was get another orchestra together, and I got out the show business magazine *Billboard* and began combing the ads, looking for the best musicians. During the following days I hired the Reed brothers, singer Bob Cromer, Merle Lawrence, and Chuck Coffee, among others. We weren't able to get together for two weeks, however, and in the interim I hired some local musicians to fill the few dates I had already booked. I was in a panic because one of my temporary trumpet players had just acquired a brand-new set of dentures and they clacked against his horn like a rivet gun. The audience just thought it was funny, however, and I learned something else—the power of a good reputation. The audience just accepted us on the basis of our past performances. They wouldn't have accepted us long if we hadn't improved pretty fast, however, and when I got my new group together we set right to work rehearsing extra hours. By the time we were ready to leave for Twin Lakes I had gotten my sense of perspective back. The shock of losing my own orchestra had begun to wear off and life suddenly began to look very hopeful again. I had a brand-new bride. And I had a brand-new orchestra. And we had a brand-new booking that would at least get us through the summer. We started off for Twin Lakes with high hearts.

8

MAKING ENDS MEET

OUR FIRST LOOK AT THE PLACE WAS EXCITING. IT WAS A PRETTY resort set among the Wisconsin pines and the air smelled so fresh and clean. We had traveled caravan style, all the way, in two cars, and we all jumped out eager to explore our new summer home. The manager took us into the ballroom first, a typical summer pavilion built of rustic pine logs. Like most ballrooms it looked pretty dreary in the daytime, and nobody said much. But it was our living quarters which really stunned us into unbelieving silence.

The manager first showed us where the boys would stay, a sort of shed built up against one side of the ballroom and fitted out with bunks. It looked like a cross between a barracks and a barn. Fern turned a little pale but the manager said quickly, "Oh, this isn't for you, Mrs. Welk. I have a private room for you and Mr. Welk." He led us through the ballroom and into a sort of closet built onto the other side. That's really the only way I can describe it . . . it actually wasn't much bigger than a clothes closet. Almost the entire floor space was taken up by an ancient double bed which sagged deeply in the middle and was covered with a tattered bedspread. A chest of drawers with most of the knobs pulled off was jammed into one corner and a wooden chair in another. That was it. No rugs, no closet, no curtains—in fact, no windows at all except for one tiny opening about twelve inches square, located so high on the wall that you had to stand on the chair in order to see out of it. The whole place smelled terrible and was covered with dust.

Fern looked around desperately. "Where's the bathroom?" she asked faintly.

"Oh," said the manager expansively, "Mrs. Welk, you just feel free to use the ladies' room in the ballroom. And you've got that whole wonderful lake to take a bath in. You're just going to love it here!" And he dashed out the door before we could say anything.

I set down the suitcases and Fern stood looking at the room. Then she turned right around and looked at me. Her lower lip began to quiver, and then Fern, who never cried, who wasn't the type to cry, sat down on the edge of the dirty bed and cried as if her heart would break. She sobbed so hard I was panic-stricken. "Oh, Fern, please," I said, "please don't do that. I can't stand to see you cry. Now look," I dried her tears, "look, it's really not as bad as all that." But I couldn't go on with that statement, because it really was the worst place I'd ever been in, and I'd been in quite a few. Fern cried so much I almost joined her, and I sat on the edge of the bed patting her on the shoulder and wondering anew at all the things that were happening to us. I wouldn't have felt so bad about the room if I'd been alone, but I saw it through new eyes now that I had my wife with me. I was ashamed to put her in such a place. Unfortunately, there didn't seem to be much I could do about it. I finally got her to dry her eyes and we went for a walk in the fresh air, but when I left her to begin rehearsal the tears welled up and she started to cry all over again. Those were three of the worst days for us that I can recall. She cried the whole time, which was so unlike her that I seriously considered borrowing enough money to send her home to my family on the farm.

Suddenly, on the third day, she stopped crying and started cleaning. Everything in that little room got thrown out into the sunshine. She got out soap and scrubbing brushes and cleaning powders and scrubbed the room from top to bottom, ceiling included. She climbed up on the chair and polished the one little window until it sparkled and then she hung a white ruffled organdy curtain she bought at the dime store. The mattress got a thorough beating and airing, and then she scoured and polished the bed and the bureau, and lined the drawers with fresh paper and arranged our few belongings carefully. We had brought our own bedding, so at least that was something she didn't have to clean, and she spent our last few pennies on a bright new bedspread. When I came in that afternoon after rehearsal I found a quiet room with the floors polished and gleaming, a little rug on the floor, some pictures tacked on the walls, and even a few wild flowers arranged in a vase on top of the bureau. Everything was spotless, and somehow it seemed comfortable and warm. It was a home. Fern had made us a home out of a broom closet. It seemed like a miracle, and from then on our engagement actually began to seem like a real vacation.

At first we spent a great deal of time rehearsing, but after the first few weeks, when we had gotten on to each other's tricks of playing, we didn't have to spend quite so much time at it, and occasionally we went swimming in the afternoon. One day Bob Cromer began diving and showing off for everybody else. Not to be outdone, I jumped in, too, and after I came up I noticed with real dismay that my ring—my George T. Kelly diamond ring—had slipped off my finger. I was heartsick. That ring meant a lot to me, not only because of its value, but because it marked the day when I had felt like a real professional and it reminded me of the link I had with George. All the rest of the afternoon the boys helped me look for it, diving, prowling through reeds and brush which grew in a tangled mass at the edges of the lake, diving again and again. It seemed a hopeless task, and finally, as the sun started to go down, we decided to give up. Suddenly Bob Cromer gave a shout and plunged beneath the water again. When he came up he was spluttering with excitement, tossing his hair out of his eyes, and holding his hand high above his head. "Your ring," he shouted, waving his arm, "I found your ring. Look!" It had slipped over a small twig of a bush growing beneath the surface of the lake and Bob had seen it sparkling brightly as the last rays of the sun penetrated the water. We were all very excited, and it seemed like an omen of good fortune ahead. That night my diamond seemed to sparkle brighter than ever before.

And it was an omen of good news. For several days I had been noticing that Fern had been in unusually high spirits, and sometimes I caught her looking at me as if she had an especially delightful secret to share. One day, as we were sitting on a log in the sunshine beside the lake, she told me the reason for all the smiles and dimples. "I think I know why I cried like such a baby when we first got here," she said. "It's because . . . well, it's because we're going to have a baby."

We were both joyful at the news, but I was almost overwhelmed! To have a child—to become a parent—this was a responsibility that meant the world to me and I was filled with a kind of determination I had never known before. For my wife, my child, I could do anything! I felt very humble, very thankful to God that we were going to be blessed with a baby. Then I lay awake all night long trying to figure out the best way to take care of my new responsibilities.

I wrote another letter to MCA urging them to explore every possible avenue for future bookings, and I got busy with letters and phone calls myself. Between my efforts and theirs we managed to get a very good booking at the El Mirador Ballroom in Phoenix, Arizona, at $425 a week, and that news, coming on top of Fern's announcement, capped the summer like a rainbow at the end of a driving thunderstorm.

Fern felt very well as we got ready for our departure and she helped load the car for our long cross-country trip. By now she was wise in the ways of travel accommodations, and she loaded down the car with a mop, a scrub bucket, and stiff brushes, in addition to my accordion and our suitcases.

We had just about enough money to make the trip and had budgeted ourselves very carefully for meals and motel accommodations along the way. But even though we were living very close to the bone, we looked as if we were rolling in wealth because we were traveling in a beautiful white Cord car. Years before, when we first came to Yankton and were making such good money, I had bought my first "big" car. I remember walking by a showroom late one night while we were playing a date at the Rigadon Ballroom in Sioux City and seeing that car. It was an Auburn, gleaming and sleek under the lights in the window. I wanted that car almost as much as I had wanted the accordion back on the farm, and I spent most of the night trying to decide whether to buy it or not. I could well afford to at the time, and I knew I wouldn't have to kill myself playing every possible date in order to pay for it as I had with my first car, but still it was a big investment for me and I hesitated about buying it. On the other hand, I've always had a weakness for sports cars—I think I've been rather a spoiled child when it comes to that—and I've always been able to figure out some reason why I should have one. That night I finally remembered George T. Kelly's advice about always looking as prosperous as possible. "Put up a good front, Lawrence," he had told me. "If you look as though you're doing well and you're happy, other people will be happier, too." I decided he was absolutely right, and the next morning I was waiting at the door of the auto agency when the dealer arrived to open up the place. Later on, I traded the Auburn in on the Cord, and still later I bought a Pierce Arrow to follow along and help carry our band instruments. So the boys and Fern and I made a very impressive sight as we rolled grandly through the corn fields and desert sands on our way to Arizona.

Fern traveled very well, but as we drew closer to Phoenix she began to tire. And then, like most expectant mothers, she began to dream of something she wanted to have—and she wanted to have it right then. "A nice big, juicy, cold, crisp dill pickle," she said dreamily. "Wouldn't that be nice?"

After a while she dozed off and my heart melted as I glanced at her, looking so young herself and soon to have our child. I would do anything for her, and all she wanted was a pickle.

Out of nowhere, at just about that time, appeared a small gas station with a grocery store attached to it and I drove in and got out of the car. Fern slept on. I went into the store and Fate smiled again. Just as the diamond ring had waited patiently to be found, glimmering beneath the waters at Twin Lakes, so now stood a big glass jar of homemade dill pickles, waiting, apparently, just for my wife.

"How much for the pickles?" I asked the owner.

I must have sounded pretty anxious because he asked for a dollar. And I guess I *was* anxious, too, because it took almost my last dollar bill to pay for them.

I got back in the car just as Fern woke up. "Fern," I said, so pleased with myself I could hardly stand it, "what do you think I have for you?"

"I don't know. What?"

I held up the jar. "This!"

She took one look and turned as green as the pickles. "Oh . . . please . . . put them away. It makes me sick just to look at them."

"But you said you wanted them," I protested, bewildered.

"I know I did. I don't know why. I certainly don't want them now."

Crestfallen, I put my prize away. I had just about enough money left to buy gas, oil, and one decent meal a day for

Fern, so I practically lived on those pickles, but I was hopeful that once we arrived in Phoenix I could draw an advance on our salary and we would all be able to have some good food for a change. I had figured our time and money very closely, and we arrived in Phoenix just as we got down to our last few nickels and dimes.

The city seemed to appear suddenly, rising up out of the desert almost like a mirage, a toy city that looked very white against the blue sky. We were all impressed with the clean buildings and crystal clear air, and looked with interest as Fern called off the names of the streets while we drove down the main thoroughfare looking for the ballroom. "There it is," she called excitedly at last, "right there, up ahead of us." The boys in the car behind honked to indicate they'd seen it, too, and we all pulled up in front of it with a flourish and got out.

It was closed—closed, shuttered, and barred. There were heavy planks nailed across all the windows and a chain padlock hanging from the front door. The El Mirador Ballroom looked as though it had been closed for good.

Nobody said anything for a while and then Chuck Coffee said dryly, "Maybe they heard us play somewhere else already." We all laughed a little hollowly. I went up and rattled the front door fruitlessly and looked the place over. A torn sign advertising the last band that had played there fluttered in the warm, dry air, but there was nothing else—no signs to indicate we were coming. Nothing at all.

Fern waited quietly in the car. The air was just as clear and the sky just as blue as they had been a few seconds ago, but somehow everything seemed dimmer. I got back in the car and drove to the nearest drugstore and called the manager of the ballroom.

"Well, I'm sorry, Mr. Welk," he said. "We tried to get in touch with you but you were already on the road and we had no idea where to reach you. We've had to cancel your booking. The ballroom has gone broke."

I was desperate, but at the same time I was furious with myself for having been so dumb as not to notify MCA where we would be en route. "Dummer-Esel!" I thought, "can't you ever do anything right!" The idea of being stranded in this town so far from home when Fern was going to have our first baby very nearly made me sick with anxiety, and I begged the manager to reconsider.

"Please! You've got to give us a chance! We drove almost two thousand miles to get here and we're counting on this booking. Can't you open the ballroom for just a night or two so we can earn enough money to get out of town?"

"I'd like to help you," he said sympathetically, "but it's not up to me. The ballroom is owned by twenty-two people and they've all agreed to close it up. I'm sorry, Mr. Welk, but there's nothing I can do."

The fellows stopped joking when I came out of the drugstore. I didn't say anything and I didn't have to. They knew by the expression on my face that I hadn't been able to save the booking.

After a while Bob said pensively, "I'm hungry, Boss. You haven't got a pickle on you, have you?"

In spite of myself I laughed.

"No," I said, "and I haven't got any money either. Have any of you?" Nobody did. There wasn't enough among the eight of us to pay for a good dinner or a night's lodging. I took my diamond ring and looked up the local pawn shop, and although it hurt me to do so, I pawned it for seventy-five dollars. It was a tenth of what I'd paid for it, but I was in no position to argue and I took the seventy-five dollars gratefully. At least we would all have a roof over our heads and some food, and I could begin to think out some plan of action.

By morning I had decided what to do. I went back to the ballroom manager and I told him what I had in mind. He was agreeable but not very optimistic. "Well, go ahead and try if you want to," he said, "but I don't think you'll have much luck." Nevertheless, he gave me a list of the twenty-two stockholders who owned the ballroom and I got busy on the phone. I called them all, and by the end of the day I had arranged a meeting for the next evening in the manager's office. The note of desperation in my voice must have convinced them of the urgency of my mission, because all twenty-two showed up, curious, I suppose, to hear what I had to say.

My proposal was simple and direct. I pleaded with them to open the ballroom, if only on a night-to-night basis, to let us show what we could do for them. They refused. I offered to forego our usual salary and play on a percentage basis, heavily weighted in their favor. They turned me down. I told them about our style of music, and the show we put on, and how much our audiences always enjoyed it. They were not impressed. "You don't seem to realize, young fellow," said one man irritably, "that we have lost money on every single band which has played here lately. We just can't take a chance."

"But my boys and I have just played a very successful engagement at Twin Lakes," I told them, "and we certainly didn't lose money for the management. We *made* money for them! And I know we could do the same for you!"

"No . . . no . . . I'm sorry. That's what all the other bandleaders said too. If that's all you've got to offer, I think we're just wasting each other's time. I think we can just conclude this meeting." He got up to leave, and some of the other men began shoving back their chairs, ready to go along with him. I was in a panic. We were right down to our last penny and I knew I had to do something and I had to do it fast, if there was to be any hope at all of saving our booking. "Wait a minute," I called feverishly. "Now just wait a moment, gentlemen, please! I . . . I think I might have an idea that could help us both."

They turned to look at me. "Well," said one of them, "what is it?"

I took a deep breath. "If you will just open the ballroom and give us a chance to play, I personally will take the loss . . . if there is any."

There was utter silence for a moment, and then the man who had started to leave said, "Say that again, please."

I repeated my words slowly. "If you gentlemen will open

the ballroom and let us play for you, and if you lose any money, any money at all, I will pay you back. Every penny."

They began to look at each other and to talk among themselves, while I waited, my heart pounding. At last one of them said, "Well, it's all right with me. I think you're a fool to make such a crazy offer. No other band has been able to make a go of it here. But if you're willing to open on that basis, I'm willing. What about you fellows?" The rest of the group finally agreed, and by the end of the meeting I had permission to proceed and I felt as though I could breathe again!

I couldn't wait to get back to our motel and tell Fern and the boys the good news. "It's all right!" I told them exultantly. "We're okay! We can go ahead now. They're going to open up the ballroom."

We all swung into action, living on a minimum of money and spending most of our precious seventy-five dollars on advertising and publicity. I had some posters printed up, which I distributed all over town, and I visited the local newspaper office and radio station and called on all the merchants in the city, telling them about our dance. I promoted it as heavily as I could in the next two days.

Meanwhile the boys steamed and pressed and brushed their band jackets and shined their shoes to a high gloss. I had long been telling them, "Even if our jackets aren't new we can look good as long as we keep clean and neat and keep our shoes shined and our hair combed. And keep your fingernails clean, too. And be sure you smile! If *you* look like you're having fun, the folks will, too.

We drew only a fair-sized crowd on opening night, but we played the best we had in months. I'd never seen such enthusiasm in a band! We knew how much depended on it. And by the time the evening was over, I was hopeful that word-of-mouth advertising would help us meet our promises. Almost always throughout my career I have found a similar pattern repeating itself. My first appearance, the first time I try anything, invariably is not very successful. I tend to grow slowly, but solidly, I think because I try to learn everything I can as I go along. I have never been an innovator, a creative genius. Rather, I have had a tremendous desire to learn, and to grow, and to develop whatever I have that will make for any kind of improvement in me or my group or the people around me. I try with everything that is in me to do the best I can.

I certainly tried everything in Phoenix! The boys and I played every kind of music the folks wanted, and we played with smiles from ear to ear. I danced with the ladies and continued to call on the local station and appear with my accordion wherever I could, to help publicize the band. But of course the most important thing of all was the music. We rehearsed constantly, and we played well enough so that the dancers kept coming back. By the end of the first week the ballroom was comfortably full every night.

It stayed that way, to our great joy and to the joy of the twenty-two stockholders. In spite of the Depression, or maybe because of it, folks were hungry for a good time and an evening of dancing seemed a good way to have it. They crowded into the ballroom—now the site of Del Webb Enterprises in Phoenix—where for forty cents they could dance and see our show. We did our best to give them their money's worth.

From our near-disastrous beginning, we managed to work our way through an engagement that lasted a full three months and, with the percentage basis I had worked out in the beginning, we made more than we had originally bargained for. The whole engagement was highly successful, and I got my Kelly ring back! I got it with the first seventy-five dollars I was able to put aside, and I never had to pawn it again. It always gave me a comfortable feeling of security in some of the up and down days that followed, and I still have it. There are a good many memories which flash back to me from that ring.

We spent a very happy three months there, but as our Phoenix engagement drew to a close I flew to the MCA office in Los Angeles to try to arrange some more bookings. I was very nervous about my first plane flight. As luck would have it, we had to turn back because of stormy weather. For a farm boy from North Dakota that was a pretty frightening experience, but I immediately got back on another plane and tried it again, determined to get some future dates. MCA had nothing at all for me, however, and I returned to Phoenix empty-handed. I set right to work, writing letters and making phone calls, and I managed to land us a series of engagements playing for room and board and tip money at luncheon and dinner in the restaurants of the Hilton Hotel chain in Texas.

We played in the cafeteria at the Baker Hotel in Dallas, the Hilton Hotel in Lubbock, the Hilton in Abilene, and the Texas Hotel in Fort Worth. We also managed to play a good many dance dates at ballrooms in the outlying territory, but we had nothing steady, so I was delighted when MCA wrote to advise me they had arranged a return booking for us at Eddie Ott's Broadmoor Country Club in Denver.

"C'mon, Fern," I said happily, "everything's fine! Go get your scrubbing brushes. We're on our way to Denver." But after thinking it over, Fern decided not to come. She wanted to stay in Dallas to wait for the birth of our child there, because she knew so many of the doctors and nurses at St. Paul's Hospital where she had worked previously, and she had great faith in one of the obstetricians, Dr. McLeod. It was a hard decision for me to accept, because I didn't want to leave her alone, but she felt she would be better off if she stayed. And so we parted for a little while.

It was now early spring, and when the boys and I arrived in Denver we found the weather unpredictable, as always. One day was clear and blue and sunny, and the next was gray and raging with a wild rain or snowstorm. The weather could change in five minutes, but I loved it. Colorado, with its towering rugged mountains and icy streams, in such sharp contrast to the flat endless prairies of my childhood, seemed very exciting to me.

We began a pleasant engagement at the Broadmoor, and I wrote to Fern daily, getting back daily letters from her with news of her condition. Our mutual friend Gladys Hambrick, a nurse, promised to call me the minute the baby was born. I roomed at that time with John and Dan Behr, and they waited out those last few anxious days right along with me. I'm afraid my music wasn't uppermost in my mind those days!

Later, one of the Behr brothers told me, "You know, the night your baby was born, we didn't know what had happened to you, Lawrence! You can't imagine the uproar you caused." Gladys had called our rooming house at five in the morning, and John had stumbled downstairs to answer the phone. "Get Lawrence quick," said Gladys. "Fern just had a baby girl and I want to tell him."

This galvanized John into action, and he tore up the stairs to my room and burst inside without knocking. I wasn't in bed. In fact, he could tell at a glance that the bed hadn't even been slept in. He ran all over the house, looking for me, and finally went back to tell Gladys he couldn't find me. Gladys was a little surprised. "Well, when you do find him, tell him he has a daughter who weighs five pounds twelve ounces and that Fern is just fine and the baby is beautiful."

She hung up and John roused his brother and the two of them combed the house again. "We thought you were kidnapped or something," said John. They never did find me and they finally left notes all over the house before they left for work that day—one propped on my pillow, one on the phone, one stuck on the front door, all saying "Call Operator 21 in Dallas. You just had a baby girl."

And where was I? Right there, the whole time. It never occurred to John to look out on the sleeping porch off my bedroom, because it had snowed during the night and it was still snowing at five o'clock in the morning. But there I was, sound asleep under four inches of Denver snowflakes, unaware of all the commotion. We had played late the night before, and I was so tired that I slept until the warmth of the sun's rays finally awakened me. Sometimes, when I tell this story, people are incredulous, and I suppose it does sound odd to those who have never slept out in the open. But I had been used to sleeping outside since my earliest days on the farm, and I enjoyed it. Besides, it hadn't been snowing when I went to bed that night. I had just rolled up warmly in my blankets, pulled one corner over the top of my head, and gone soundly to sleep. When the snow began to fall gently during the night it never disturbed me at all.

I burrowed out of my snowy tunnel in the morning— April 29, 1932— shook out my blankets, and strolled into my bedroom to get dressed. But the note I saw on my pillow made me fly downstairs fast and get on the phone. I had misread the note in my anxiety and haste, and when I got through to Gladys I blurted out hopelessly, "Oh, Gladys, do you think she will live?"

Gladys laughed. "Oh she's fine! Fern's wonderful."

"No, I mean the baby . . . she's so tiny. Do you think she has a chance?"

Gladys was amused. "Lawrence, for heaven's sake, all babies are tiny. She's fine. In fact she's beautiful. One of the prettiest babies I've ever seen."

"But . . . only five ounces!"

Gladys burst out laughing. "Five ounces! Oh, Lawrence, she weighs five *pounds* twelve ounces, and she's in very good shape. Everybody is fine. Now don't worry."

I nearly floated upstairs. Fern was fine. My daughter— how wonderful, how unbelievable those words sounded to me!—my daughter was fine, too. I wanted to shout with happiness and I got dressed and ran all over town telling everybody the good news.

Shirley was almost six weeks old before Fern was able to travel and bring her to Denver, and I will never forget my first glimpse of them. They both looked beautiful to me. Shirley seemed so tiny, so fragile that I was almost afraid to hold her. She had Fern's eyes—all our children have inherited those big brown eyes—and to me she was the loveliest and sweetest child any man could have. I immediately wrote a song in her honor, "You're My Home Sweet Home." I thought it was beautiful but I couldn't convince any music publisher to share my enthusiasm and I finally paid four hundred dollars to have it published myself. It was worth it to me. The birth of my daughter was one of the biggest events of my life.

As we finished up the Broadmoor Country Club engagement, Eddie Ott offered us another booking at a club in Estes Park, a resort not far from Denver. It was a lovely place, and Fern and I rented housekeeping-motel accomodations in common with Izzy King, our trumpet player, and his wife. We had separate sleeping quarters, but shared kitchen facilities. As usual, Fern scrubbed the place from top to bottom before we moved in. "Your wife is the cleanest person I have ever met," Izzy whispered to me, awed. I laughed, but I had to agree.

Those were happy days, and we were made even happier when a new booking agent, Bill Fredericks, called to tell me he could set us up at the Muehlbach Hotel in Kansas City. We were all overjoyed. The Muehlbach was one of the top hotels in the country and to play an engagement there was a real accomplishment. We all began planning in great excitement, but just before our Estes Park engagement closed the booker called to say that the deal had fallen through. Once more we were left with no future bookings lined up, which came as a real disappointment after our hopes had been raised so high. It seemed like a very good time to go home. I wanted my family to see Shirley, and Fern was anxious to see her mother again, too. So once again we headed for South Dakota.

I had always thought my mother was beautiful, but she looked especially so to me as she held Shirley for the first time. She settled down in her old rocking chair, cuddling Shirley close, murmuring soft German phrases to her, singing some old-country lullabies, as Shirley nestled contentedly in her arms. Suddenly the years melted away and I could remember her doing the same thing when I was a small boy. I realized with a pang that my mother was growing old. I didn't like to think about that. Instead, I wanted to tell her how much I loved her. But, as usual, I couldn't quite get the words out. I sat down beside her, and she stopped rocking and reached out and brushed my hair back in the old way, and then she smiled at me, her eyes warm and tender as always.

I smiled, too. I loved her so much. But I couldn't seem to tell her.

From Strasburg we went to visit Fern's mother in St. Anthony, and then we headed back to Texas for more one-night stands. It was a difficult trip and, for the first time, the question of the travel involved in my work loomed as a serious problem. When there had been just Fern and I, our trips seemed like vacations. But traveling on the road was no way to raise a child, and the very instability of this profession I loved so much made me think seriously about giving it up. I spent many sleepless nights, after we settled temporarily in Dallas, thinking about it, trying to decide the best thing to do.

"Would you rather I gave up the music business?" I asked Fern one evening, as I packed my bags, ready to leave for some more one-night stands.

She stood holding Shirley, without answering for a while, and finally she said, "Yes, I think I would, Lawrence. It might make a better home life for Shirley if you got a job and stayed in one place. At least . . . I would like to see you try."

I nodded. I felt much the same way myself. "All right. I'll try. I'll really try."

And I did. But I couldn't seem to find anything. I wasn't trained for any other line of work, except farming, and my lack of education hampered me, too. And I had to fight off the continual attraction of music. I combed the papers daily, looking for business opportunities of some kind, and one day I found an ad for a thirty-room hotel going at a rock bottom price. I went out to take a look at it. It needed a little repairing and some paint, but it was in fairly good condition, and when I discovered I could buy it without a down payment and very low monthly installments, I bought it. "I think it may be just the thing we've been looking for," I told Fern. "We can live in the five-room suite on the top floor and have a real home for ourselves. We'll rent out the rest of the rooms on a permanent basis. I know a lot of musicians who would be glad to rent clean rooms like these, and the rentals should more than take care of our payments and give us a monthly income besides. And maybe I can keep on with the band business too . . . just as kind of a sideline."

Fern gave me a look, but then she laughed a little. She knew before I did, I guess, that the band would never be the sideline. The hotel would. And she was right. Not only that, but she got stuck with most of the work of running it.

Our experience in the hotel business was dramatic from start to finish. We changed the name of the hotel from the Maine Peak to the Lawrence. And we had no sooner moved in than one of the tenants knocked on our door and said nervously, "Come along with me. There's something funny going on downstairs." I went with him and as we turned the corner into the downstairs hallway we both could smell the strong odor of gas. "It's coming from that room at the end of the hall," he said. I tried the door but it was locked. With the fumes pouring out I knew there wasn't time to run back upstairs and get the keys, so I pulled back and hurled my 185 pounds straight at the door and managed to bash it open. There on the floor, with her face close to the deadly fumes pouring out of the wall gas heater, lay a woman completely unconscious. I grabbed my handkerchief and held it over my nose and dragged her out into the hall, while the other fellow quickly turned off the gas and ran to call the police. By the time I got the woman out into the fresh air the police had arrived, and fortunately the ambulance did, too, in time to revive our would-be suicide and whisk her off to the hospital. So everything turned out all right, but it was hardly an auspicious start. I had to leave town right after that on a short tour, and while I was gone Fern discovered that some of the old tenants were running a bootlegging establishment from their rooms. They were highly indignant when she called the police. "We've been doing this for years and nobody else ever complained before!" cried one of them bitterly. "What's the matter with you anyway, lady?"

By the time I got back, Fern was a little shaken by a few

other experiences as well. She wasn't at all sure we should stay in the hotel business. It meant far more work for her than it did for me in some ways, and I found that I could not really keep my mind on it. I was always thinking about my music and the best way to improve it—what we could do to make it sound just a little better, make people smile just a little more, make them a little happier. My mind was filled with musical figures and sounds almost constantly; even when the front of my mind was talking radiator leaks and repairs and monthly rentals connected with the hotel, the back of my mind was busy with the band and bookings. Fern realized this, and when I was offered a chance to sell the hotel, she agreed. Financially, it had worked out quite well for us. I made a seventeen-hundred-dollar profit, which was more than I had made with the band in any of the preceding three years. But it had not been the home we wanted. So once again we decided to go back to the place that had always seemed like home to us. We decided to go back to Yankton.

9

HONOLULU FRUIT GUM

I WENT RIGHT UP TO SEE CHAN GURNEY AT WNAX. "I can certainly use you and the boys, Lawrence," he told me. "The only trouble is I can't pay you very much."

"How much can you pay?"

He considered. "Sixty dollars a week would be the very best I could do."

That was about ten dollars apiece, and even in the middle of the Depression it wouldn't stretch very far. "Chan," I said after a moment's reflection, "I think I have an idea that could help us both."

He burst out laughing. "I thought you would. In fact I knew you would! All right, what's your big idea?"

Honolulu Fruit Gum

"Why don't the boys and I play a half-hour program for you every day at no cost to the station? You could give us a half hour of free air time for ourselves, and there wouldn't be any money involved at all. How does that sound?"

Chan regarded me speculatively from across the desk. "Lawrence," he said at last, "that's probably one of the best ideas you've ever had." He grinned again and reached across the desk, and we shook hands on it.

The idea worked well right from the start. Chan used his half hour to advertise hog tonic and chicken feed, or whatever specials the Gurney Company was advertising that week, and we used our half hour to publicize our dates for forthcoming dances. After a few months at the station we even attracted an advertiser—the Old Home Bread Company—so that we earned a little extra money in addition to what we got for our dance dates.

Encouraged by this slight prosperity, Fern and I took our windfall from the sale of the Lawrence and made a down payment on a tiny house, and invested in an electrical and hardware store in town. I felt, rather cautiously, that we were on our way again.

We loved our little house. Shirley was growing into an enchanting little girl with big dark eyes and a mind of her own. As she grew older she also developed an unfortunate habit of biting other children, especially the little girl who lived next door. We tried everything to stop her. Fern talked, I talked, but nothing worked. Finally, in desperation, I built a fence around our house, not so much to keep the other little girl out as to keep my own daughter safely penned in. But the very first day the fence was up, Shirley coaxed her little friend to stick just one finger through the lattice work at the top, and then she promptly bit it! I gave up, and Shirley finally got over the habit on her own.

One day, as I looked up from the small desk at WNAX where I kept all my music and route cards, I saw Leo Fortin standing in the doorway, regarding me with that familiar twinkle in his snapping black eyes. I hadn't seen him since my band had quit on me that night in Dallas, South Dakota.

"Hi ya, Lawrence," he said. "Can I come back and work for you again?"

I burst out laughing. He was the same old Leo—right to the point as always, without any preliminaries. "Well, I don't know, Leo," I said. "Come on in. We'll talk it over. How've you been anyway?"

He shrugged. "Aaaaah . . . up and down. We couldn't make a go of it in the band. It just didn't work out."

"The band?"

"Yeah. That's the real reason we left, you know."

I waved him in a seat beside the desk. "No. No I didn't know. Tell me."

"Well, I know one of the guys gave you a lot of baloney about you and your accent and all, but the truth is that Mr. King—you know that promoter in Dallas—he was the one who talked us into it. He told Rollie and me and the rest of the fellows that he could get us a lot more bookings and more money if we started our own band. He wanted Rollie to lead it and he made it sound so wonderful that, well I guess we just didn't know a good thing when we had it. Anyway, Lawrence"—his dark eyes were very serious—"it's over, and I'd like to come back. How about it?"

Of course I took him back. He was still the best trumpet player I'd ever had, and we'd always had a deep friendship. Leo stayed with me—off and on—for a good many years.

I was happy to have him back of course, and not just because he was a good musician, but also because his explanation confirmed the truth of something that had been gnawing at the back of my mind ever since the boys had left. And that was that anyone who is determined to break up a business, or an organization, or a family—or a six-piece band—can do so if he puts enough effort into it. Whenever people can be made unhappy enough, and restless enough with their jobs, they will leave, whether they have any real plans in mind or not. It's just human nature, and it has been demonstrated to me over and over again through my years in the music business—the Lennon sisters probably being the most famous case of all. It has nothing to do with the relationship between employer and employees. It has to do with human nature itself. Over the years I learned to become very philosophical about it; whenever anyone wants to leave, the best thing to do is accept their decision and help make the transition as easy as possible. It is always difficult, especially when there is real affection and regard involved, but it is just part of life.

By 1934 I had added Jerry Burke to our orchestra and he continued to play piano and organ with us for many years. We played countless one-night stands—the Corn Palace in Mitchell, South Dakota, the Glovera in Grand Island, Nebraska, the Japanese Gardens in Flandreau, South Dakota, the King's Ballroom in Norfolk, Nebraska, all the Tom Archer rooms. No matter where we played, in a tiny, rundown, splintered dance hall or a fancy place with balconies and attached restaurants, there was always a great excitement in the air, caused partly from the dance itself and partly from the element of suspense. Would she or wouldn't she dance with you? I can't speak for the girls—I suppose they worried about being asked—but I can remember what an ordeal it was for me when I first started going to dances in Strasburg. It took me twenty minutes to get up enough nerve to ask a girl to dance, and if she turned me down I went right out and jumped on my pony and galloped straight home. It didn't take much to shake my self-confidence in those years. I got over that gradually, but I always felt a twinge of sympathy when I saw a boy grin nervously and approach a girl, ready to ask her for a dance, and I always hoped she'd say yes.

All of us got so we could drive in our sleep in those years. One of my friends, Bill Wilson, who worked with me closely later on in Chicago, says, "We'd be driving along some dark night out in the middle of nowhere, on our way to some engagement, and Lawrence would be in the front seat, head propped against a pillow, apparently sound asleep as we sped across the prairies. I'd slow down at some cowpath crossing, unmarked with any kind of sign at all, wondering what to do next, and Lawrence would rouse up out of sleep, say clearly, 'Turn left here, Bill,' and go right back to sleep again. The funny part is he was always right. I used to think he had some kind of divining rod in his foot."

Even though we took turns driving it was a very rugged routine, and frequently the boys would arrive so tired they were not in the best of condition to play. I began to give some thought to working out a system so that things would not be so hard for them, and I came up with what I think may have been one of the first of the sleeper busses. I contacted the Wilson Body Company in Sioux City, Iowa, and together we worked out a design. It didn't look exactly like a Cord Cabriolet—in fact it looked more like a cattle carrier—but it worked, and gave us many added hours of needed sleep. We fitted it out with six bunks—two double deckers on each side and two more across the rear, and there was enough room to set up a card table between them, so the boys could enjoy a game or two as we rolled along. I hired a full-time driver, Morris Knutsen, and he drove from a cab attached up front. The idea worked out very well.

But I was still a long way from being satisfied. I continually looked for ways to improve our situation, and one day I decided that what we really needed was a full-time sponsor. All the big-name bands of the day—my real goal, all the time was to be a "big-name band," of course—were sponsored by some big company or hotel, so I approached several businessmen with the idea of sponsoring us. None of them was at all interested, however, and finally I decided that if no one else would sponsor us, we would do the job ourselves.

I contacted a dealer on the West Coast and bought wholesale lots of a chewing gum called Honolulu Fruit Gum. That had an exotic ring to my Midwestern ears, and the Honolulu Fruit Gum Company promptly became our new "sponsor." I had the gum wrapped in fancy colorful paper and I sold it in all the ballrooms and drugstores and restaurants in the Midwestern states. Since I bought it for just a fraction over a penny per package and retailed it for a nickel, we made a very nice profit. Then I had the outside of our new bus painted with big flowers and garlands and a large flowing inscription which read "Lawrence Welk and

His Honolulu Fruit Orchestra." All the boys hated that name, and Chuck Coffee almost quit. "I am *not* going to play in any orchestra which calls itself the Honolulu Fruit Gum Boys," he announced flatly, but he finally gave in and stayed.

The boys also hated the white full-sleeved shirts and paper flower leis we wore in keeping with our new tropical islands background. Leo, in particular, complained bitterly about the leis. "The darn things make us look like a Honolulu sunrise," he muttered. That was true, because in those days, long before the advent of air conditioning, the atmosphere in some of the ballrooms got so hot and sticky that the color in the leis started to run, and the boys often ended up the evening dripping wet and every color of the rainbow.

Despite these drawbacks, the idea caught on like wildfire. I began to promote contests in all the towns we played, to elect a Miss Fort Dodge or Miss Grand Island or Miss Pierre as preliminary events for the big state-wide final contests later on for Miss Honolulu Fruit Gum. In order to vote for your favorite, you had to buy a pack of chewing gum and mail the wrapper in with her name on it. As a result our chewing gum sales soared. In each of the towns we played we found crowds of pretty young ladies eager to be contestants, and in many of the cities, they were sponsored by the service clubs or the Chamber of Commerce. The boys and I began to appear at all kinds of lunches and dinners and parades held in connection with the events. Business boomed.

I contacted electrical manufacturers asking for prizes, in return for free advertising, and all of them were more than happy to jump on the bandwagon. One distributor of farm battery radios donated $1,758 worth of prizes. All the local radio stations took up the idea enthusiastically, too, and they were waiting to interview us wherever we appeared. The whole thing became highly successful. When I first started "sponsoring" us we were established as a $65 per night band. Within a few weeks we had made a hundred percent jump in our price and our minimum guarantee went up to $125 plus, of course, the usual percentage. The fact that the chewing gum business itself became wildly successful seemed almost like an added bonus. I had to hire extra salesmen to handle all the business, and eventually I had nineteen of them working for me.

While I was thinking about the best men for the job I remembered my old friend George T. Kelly. I hadn't heard from him in years, but I knew he would be perfect if I could induce him to come out of retirement. I wrote to him, explaining the idea in detail and asking if he would be interested. He was. He wrote back to say he would join me immediately.

I was delighted to see him. He still had the same understanding twinkle in his eye, the same courtly good manner, the same easy friendliness. We threw our arms around each other. "Lawrence, it's so good to see you! And I'm so proud of you. I knew you'd be a success the day I hired you."

"If I am," I said, "it's because of you."

"Nonsense. You'd have done it anyway. I just happened to be there when you got started."

But nobody knew better than I how much I owed George. I had a sudden vivid recollection, as we stood beaming at each other, of the day he gave me some advice which literally changed my life. I had been so shy, so ashamed of my accent when I first joined his troupe that I could barely look at anybody, and I just mumbled some kind of greeting with my head down whenever I was introduced. George soon put a stop to that. "Lawrence," he said to me one day, his blue eyes very dark and his face serious, "now I want you to cut that out. Whenever you meet somebody new, look them right in the eye and shake hands firmly. Remember," he tapped me on the shoulder for emphasis, "in the eyes of God you are just as good as anybody else. Don't forget that." I never did, and I began to get over my feelings of inferiority. George was the first person who ever believed in me. He helped me to believe in myself, and I have tried to do the same thing for other people ever since.

Neither of us referred to our last sad days together, and

George plunged wholeheartedly into his new job. He was a superb salesman, of course, and within a matter of days the sales in his territory far exceeded those of anyone else. Before long he was in charge of the entire operation. He was with me when we finalized the deal for the battery radios, and both of us were in high spirits as we began the long drive back home to Yankton from Sioux City. George sat beside me, cap on the side of his head, arms folded, long legs crossed, chuckling as he reminisced about the old days. "Well, I always knew you'd be a big success," he said, "as long as you kept your mouth shut. What an actor you were! Remember that first acting job you did? I tell you, Lawrence, I thought you were going to faint!"

I laughed. "So did I! And remember the night the curtain fell down and you were just standing there in your. . . . "

"I do. I do indeed. I was ready to fire you that night!"

"And the time—where was it?—that little town near Enid, Oklahoma, when we had just one lady out in the audience?"

"Ah yes. One of our greater triumphs. Oh my, the world lost a lot when The Peerless Entertainers folded!" He grinned over at me.

"George," I said impulsively, "we work so well together; it's so wonderful to see you again. I . . . tell me . . . I've wondered so many times. Whatever happened that time back in North Dakota?"

George sat quietly for a moment and then he took his cap off and twisted it round and round in his hands. After a moment he sighed and said, "Well, Lawrence, I've often wanted to tell you, but . . . we people who have that sickness . . . we just don't like to talk about it."

"Sickness?"

"Yes, sickness. That's what it is, you know. You see, I'm fine as long as I don't touch liquor. I don't even want a drink. But if I somehow get just one drop it sets up some kind of craving in me that I just can't control. I have to have another drink. I have to have it. If it meant I had to smash open a store window with my bare fist and grab a bottle and run, I'd do it. I think I'd even kill for it." We drove on in silence for a moment and then he said softly, "Lawrence, it's been the devil of my life. I just can't touch it—ever."

I had never heard of such a thing and I said so.

"Well it's true," said George slowly. "I don't know what the real reason is. Maybe there's some kind of medical explanation, some kind of chemistry involved. I just know that one drink, and I can't stop. I can't stop until I'm so sick I can't drink any more." He paused. "That's what happened to me back there that time. I couldn't explain it to you then, and afterward . . . well, you were doing so well in Yankton it seemed kind of pointless." He grinned at me again, that old Kelly grin, and added almost shyly, " I didn't do it on purpose you know. I just want you to know that."

I looked at this good man who had fought such a tremendous battle all his life and had never mentioned one word about it. It's one thing to have the kind of nature that allows you to live an orderly and decent and quiet life without too much struggle. It's another thing altogether to fight the battle of strong passions and desires and win out over them. George had done so. Time and again he had conquered his own personal enemy, and I respected him more than ever now that I knew. I understood at last why our troupe had fallen apart during those dismal days in 1927. "Why didn't you tell us, George? Why didn't Alma explain?"

"It's not that simple."

"But we would have understood. We could have helped you."

George smiled at me. "That's one battle a man has to fight for himself, Lawrence. Nobody else can do it for him."

We drove home the rest of the way in silence, but closer, I think, than ever before.

With George's help the chewing gum business turned into a highly successful operation. We made more money with it than we did with the band. "If I were you I'd cut out this music racket and stick to selling gum," George joked one night. "I think you'll do better at it in the long run."

We were, indeed, making a good deal of money, but we

were also running into some trouble. The Wrigley Chewing Gum Company claimed that I was infringing on their rights because my spearmint gum was wrapped in colors similar to theirs, and my brand name, Welk's, began and ended with the same letters as Wrigley's. Some of the ballroom managers began to complain, sometimes bitterly, that the job of cleaning up after Lawrence Welk's Honolulu Fruit Gum Orchestra was just too much. The floor was always knee deep in wrappers after we left, necessitating a major cleanup job. Then too, the gum stuck to the walls and the floors, which often had to be resanded and repolished. Some of the great interest in the contests began to diminish a little also, and all in all it seemed wiser to close down the Great Chewing Gum Experiment. It had achieved its real goal anyway. I had been "sponsored"—and our name was a little better known.

10

DOUBTS

BACK IN YANKTON WE PICKED UP THE PATTERN OF ONE-NIGHT stands and radio shows. But now we were unsponsored. We played often at the Chermot Ballroom in Omaha, and I became friendly with the local union man there. He began to work on me to move the orchestra to Omaha. "This town is ten times the size of Yankton," he explained. "You'd have a much bigger base of operations. And you could settle down and play steadily at one of the hotels. You wouldn't have to be on the road so much."

That was a real inducement. I hated to leave Fern and Shirley alone so often, but up until then it had seemed to be the only way we could make a living. I thought about the situation and talked it over with Fern. Omaha had several big hotels, the Paxton and the Carpenter among them, and a big amusement center, Joe Malec's Peony Park. If I could land a steady engagement at any one of those places Fern and I could have a much more satisfactory home life. I also talked it over with Vic Schroeder, my new agent-partner and good friend. Vic and I had established our own booking agency in Yankton, trying to book small bands throughout the Midwest area, and we figured we could do a much better job for them if we worked out of Omaha. We decided to make the move.

We put our little house up for sale, sold it almost immediately and moved bag and baggage to Omaha. When we got there we had a rude shock. My union friend had been right on several counts. Omaha was certainly larger and offered wider scope for our musical activities, but there was just one drawback. I couldn't play there without an Omaha Musicians' Union card, and I was told by the union that I would have to wait at least six months before I could get one. "Why didn't you tell me?" I exploded to my friend.

"Well," he shrugged, "I don't know. I guess I thought you knew."

Since none of us could work steadily in Omaha for at least six months, and there were no guarantees that we would get a card even then, I found myself right back in the routine of driving hundreds and thousands of miles on one-night stands again. I was deeply disillusioned, and when Fern suggested it might be a good idea to get out of the music business entirely, I was very willing. We bought a house on the outskirts of Omaha on a five-acre plot of ground on Miami Street, and went into the chicken raising business.

Both of us knew a great deal about it, of course, from our farm backgrounds, and we worked very hard at our new project. I think we could have made a real success of our new project, except for two factors. One was that Fern and I continually urged friends to drop by our "farm" for a chicken dinner, or a free chicken, or both, and I saw our profits eaten up right in front of our eyes many a night. And then, too, without my having to say anything, Fern could see that I was edgy and discontented. I missed the music

Doubts

terribly. Raising chickens might be a good way to earn a living, but there was no real joy in it for me. I did the best I could, but I realized I was just counting the days until I could say "Goodbye chicken and hello music" again.

At the end of six months I went back to the union office. No card. They were sorry, but there was no vacancy for me and they had no idea when I could be admitted. I continued with the one-night stands since I could not arrange anything steady for us in the Omaha area, and I kept after the union, but they always had some excuse. Finally I went back to my friend and asked him if he could help.

"Well I'm sorry, Lawrence," he said, "but frankly, my hands are just tied. There isn't a thing I can do about it."

"Why not? What's holding it up?"

He looked unhappy. "The officials of the local union here are also musicians," he said, "and I guess . . . well, I suppose they feel you are a threat to them. If they give you a card, you may take some of their jobs away from them. That's the real reason."

I never got a card in all the years I lived in Omaha. Eventually I was forced to leave.

But there were other events in Omaha which were exceedingly pleasant. One of them was the birth of our daughter Donna, on February 13, 1937, another dark-eyed little girl, and a sparkler right from the beginning. Donna loved animals as much as I did. Today she has a horse, and she's always had at least one dog around her house. That was a great bond between us, because I've always had a deep affection for dogs, too. I remember one time, years ago, when I was playing in a very small town, I spotted a beautiful springer spaniel hunting dog wandering down the street. I inquired around and found that he belonged to a local man who had fallen ill and wasn't able to take care of him. When I asked the man how much he wanted for his dog he shrugged and said, "Oh, five or ten dollars I guess."

"No no!" I said, "that dog is worth much more than that."

I finally gave him twenty-five dollars and took the dog along with me in the car, and he and I developed an almost mystical relationship. I called him Rex. He went hunting with me whenever I got the chance and he seemed to understand what I wanted even before I gave him any orders. Fern liked him as well as she liked any dog—which wasn't very much—and Rex understood that he was never to come in the house. The minute I went away on tour or even for a one-night stand, he would just disappear. "When you drive away," Fern told me, " Rex goes away, too."

She never found out where he went and neither did I until years later, when a man came up to me at the Palladium Ballroom in Hollywood and told me that Rex always came to his house while I was gone. "The wife and I always knew when you weren't home," he told me, "because Rex showed up right away at our back door." But in those days I never knew where he was. I just knew that the moment I drove in the driveway Rex would bound in out of nowhere, happy to see me, licking my feet and doing everything but say, "Welcome home, Boss."

Eventually I had to give him away, because I had to make a long Eastern tour and I gave him to a farmer friend named Neal Bretz. I missed him very much. It must have been at least three years later that I stopped by to visit Neal one day. We sat chatting in his living room. "How's Rex?" I asked him.

"Well, he's just fine," said Neal. "A great hunting dog, every bit as good as you said."

Suddenly there was a terrible commotion at the kitchen door and then a huge red brown whirlwind burst in, skidded across the linoleum floor, paused momentarily at the door of the living room, and in one huge leap sailed twenty feet through the air and landed plop on top of my chair, his paws on my shoulders, licking me all over my face and ears, whining and shivering with delight. Neal was astonished. "That dog has never been allowed to set foot in the house even once," he cried. "He stays half a block away out in the barn! Now how'd he know you were here?"

I didn't know, but I was very glad to see my old friend again.

Donna had much the same feeling for animals, and loved

to visit farms where she could play with them, but as she grew older she didn't like to see me going away on tour. Whenever she saw me starting for the door with my bags packed, she would clutch me around the knees and beg, "Don't go, Daddy, please! Why do you have to go?"

I tried to explain to her that I had to travel in order to make enough money to take care of her and her mother and Shirley, but that didn't make her like it any better. "I have money, Daddy," she said. "I have thirty-five cents. Don't go." Those big eyes got very solemn and her chin started to quiver, and it was so hard for me to leave. Whenever I came home she was always waiting for me at the front window, ready to fly outside into my arms, full of a thousand questions, anxious to tell me everything that had happened since I had been away. I loved my family so much that the tours became harder and harder for me to undertake.

One bright fall day I went to visit my parents. They had moved into town, in Strasburg by then, leaving Mike and Louie to run the family farm, and whenever I was within driving distance I stopped by to see them. My father stood beaming as he opened the front door. "Come in, come in," he said. "What a nice surprise! Your mother is at the store, but she'll be home soon."

He padded out to the kitchen in his house slippers and got down the bottle of schnaps for my welcome-home drink. He never failed to offer it and I never failed to take it, even though I never liked the taste and got it down as fast as I could. "Gesundheit," he said in the familiar low-German toast, and "Gesundheit" I responded, clinking his glass with mine. We sat and talked idly for a while, catching up on all the news, but soon he sighed. "I'm a little tired," he said. "Come in the bedroom, please." We went in and he stretched out carefully on the bed, propped up against the big down pillows, with his hands clasped behind his head. I pulled up a chair and sat beside him. He looked at me and his eyes twinkled. "I am just remembering what a clumsy boy you were. You never could learn to work the blacksmith bellows for me. Or did you do that on purpose?"

I laughed. "I don't know, Father. I really don't. I think I tried, but . . . you know."

"Yah, I know. Your head was always on the music." He sighed again, and taking his arms down he gazed thoughtfully at the backs of his hands where the blue veins bulged thickly. "Lawrence," he said, "there are things we must talk about. I have been making out my will . . . no, no, I don't expect to die tomorrow, but these are necessary things. I am leaving the farm equally to you boys. You'll each get a quarter share."

"No, Father, please." I shook my head. "I . . . thank you, but I'm doing all right in the music business now and I'd like you to give my share to Mike and Louie and John."

He looked at me appraisingly. "You're sure?"

"Yes. I want you to do it that way."

"All right." He paused, seeming ill at ease somehow, something most unusual for him. Then he said, almost formally, "Lawrence, there is something else."

"Yes, Father."

"Will you . . . take care of Mother, if she ever needs any help?"

I swallowed. "Yes, of course, Father. I . . ."

"And the rest of the family, too, if they need it? You will take charge of things?"

"Yes. Yes, you know I will."

"I know. I know." He smiled gently. "I have been so lucky. A fine wife. Such good children. To live in this country."

I was very moved. My father rarely spoke to me at such length, and never on such personal terms. I realized that by asking me to take care of the family, he was really telling me I had done the right thing to leave the farm and make music my life's work. Never once had he said this in so many words, although I had heard from others that he was really rather proud of me. Whenever I played in Strasburg he would stroll up and down outside the hall, stopping passers-by to say, with a nod of his head, "Hear that music? That's my son, the leader of the band." I was deeply touched at his request and I wanted to say something, to thank him again for getting me my accordion in the first place, but as usual I couldn't quite get the words out. Then his mood changed anyway, and he said in his familiar gruff manner, "Well, no doubt you're a big success today, Lawrence, but I'm the one who taught you how to play! And I could still outplay you if I wanted to."

"I'm sure you could, Father."

"But I'll let you do it now."

We sat in silence for a moment. His eyes closed and I thought he had drifted off to sleep, but then he said very softly, almost to himself, "You were so stubborn. The most stubborn boy. You surprised me. But I think I knew when you came home from the Hague dance that you really meant what you said about leaving. I knew you'd never stay on the farm after that."

"But you tried to talk me into staying."

"Yah, yah, I know. But I knew the music was inside you that night. I just prayed you could have your music and still keep your faith."

We heard footsteps on the front porch then, and his eyes lighted. "There's your mother." He got up immediately and we started back to the living room, but in the doorway he stopped and said loudly enough for her to hear, "Well, it's a nice surprise for you to come by, Lawrence, but you should do it more often. Your mother misses you. You know how women are." He winked and grinned at me and I winked back. I felt so very close to him. And I have always been grateful for that visit. Because I never saw him again.

The one-night stands and sleeper jumps continued. One day just at dusk, the boys and I were traveling along in our bus to Estherville, Ohio. I sat working on some bookings as Morris drove along the familiar highway. Some of the boys were taking advantage of the long haul to take a nap; two of them sat quietly playing pinochle. Suddenly, without warning, the bus lurched crazily and plunged over the side of the highway, rolling over and over until it came to a stop with a sickening crash at the foot of a rock-strewn gully. All of us lay for a moment, too stunned to comprehend what had happened. Then, to my horror, I could smell the fumes of leaking gas and I knew we had to get out of there fast. I struggled up to my hands and knees and looked around. I was sickened at what I saw. Leo Fortin and Terry George lay pushed against the sides of the berth, their faces gashed and streaming blood, both of them moaning in pain. The other boys lay in a tangled heap in the middle of the aisle, dazed and unable to move.

After a moment I became aware of Morris outside, crawling over the rocks and brush toward the broken window, his face white in the darkening gloom. "Lawrence, for God's sake get them out! Gas . . . it's leaking!" He picked up a rock and bashed in the remaining pieces of glass in the window and we managed to lift both Leo and Terry through and carry them as far away from the bus as possible. The rest of the boys managed to get out under their own power and we all tore off our coats and made pillows for Leo and Terry while I tried to wipe the blood from their faces.

We stood together in a shaken little group, shivering with cold and shock, looking back at the pile of rocks and boulders where the bus lay on its side, its wheels still spinning slowly in the fading light. The whole scene took on a nightmarish quality. I became aware that I was praying constantly—praying that the boys were not badly hurt, praying for help, praying for guidance as to what to do next. Time seemed to telescope for me; it seemed that the ambulance arrived almost immediately to take the boys to the hospital. The state police had already arrived, and Morris and I stayed behind while they filled out their report. "You guys are lucky to be here," said the policeman soberly, as he looked over the battered bus. "It's a wonder you weren't all killed."

I was still shaking. I couldn't wait to get into town and see how the boys were. Finally the police took us into the hospital where Morris and I discovered, almost to our surprise, that we had several cuts and bruises, too. To my great relief, it turned out that neither Terry nor Leo was critically injured. They both had suffered facial cuts, which always bleed profusely, but neither of them required much more than some expert bandaging.

However, we were all badly bruised and shaken-up, and for once in my life I took some aspirin, while the other boys had some stronger pain killers. I arranged for a garageman to pick up the bus and see about repairing it; it developed later that the spindle had broken. Then we rented another car and continued on to Estherville. By then we were in that almost hysterical state of high good humor which sometimes follows a near-disastrous accident. We were all so happy to be alive and in fairly good health that we were delighted to perform that night, even though we were all covered with bandages and held together with adhesive tape.

Nevertheless, the whole incident bothered me terribly. Many times during the preceding years I had wondered if I were truly carrying out God's plan for my life. I often thought that my almost miraculous escape from death as a boy on the farm, when I had been struck by peritonitis, meant that perhaps there was some special plan for me, and I longed to do the right thing. The times when Fern had been forced to sleep in ramshackle buildings; the times when we didn't have much to eat and no steady job to look forward to; the precarious nature of the music business itself had sometimes given me pause, and I had often spent hours wondering if I were really doing the right thing. This accident somehow brought everything into sharp focus for me. True, I was fairly successful, but I was a long way from realizing my real dreams. I was providing well for Fern and the girls, but not as well as I wanted to. I could not count myself an overwhelming success, except for the fact that I enjoyed every minute of the time I spent with music. But maybe the very fact that I enjoyed it so much was a sin. I was confused, disturbed, unhappy, and the fact that I had indirectly been the cause of so much pain and potential tragedy for my band members upset me deeply.

For weeks after that I couldn't sleep. Ordinarily I fell asleep the minute my head hit the pillow, but now I tossed and turned for hours before I could fall asleep, and then I had a recurring nightmare. We were back in the bus again, plunging over the side of the embankment again, falling, falling into endless space. I would wake up, drenched in perspiration, my heart pounding. I could not seem to get that incident out of my mind, and finally I decided I had to do something about it.

I went to a priest in Omaha and poured out the whole story to him. "I can't seem to forget it, Father," I told him, "and now I am wondering if this was some sort of signal from God—something telling me that it's wrong for me to stay in the music business. I would never want to hurt anyone, but I have, and I can't seem to forgive myself."

The priest listened closely and asked me a few questions, and then he looked at me sharply. "In the first place," he said, "an accident like that could have happened anywhere, anytime. It could have happened while you were driving down a farm road on your way to a threshing job. No one was killed. No one was even seriously injured. So get that thought out of your mind.

"And as for music being a sin—it isn't. Music is a joy. It's a decent kind of pleasure that has brought happiness to men for hundreds of years. I'd just count myself lucky to have found the kind of work you like so much. I cannot believe that God wants you to deny yourself and give it up. On the contrary, I believe He wants you—He wants all of us—to use our talents to the fullest. Go back to work. Stop worrying. Just play the best music you can."

His talk relieved me enormously and I was able to get back to work with my usual energy. And the terrible nightmares finally stopped.

I have tried to follow his advice all my life. Sometimes, when the band plays so well that I get goose bumps, or people come up to me at one of our concerts and tell me how much our music has meant in their lives, I do feel almost sinful at the tremendous pleasure it gives me. To be granted some kind of usable talent and to be able to use it to the fullest extent of which you are capable—this, to me, is a kind of joy which is almost unequaled. I have found it in music, my father in farming. I know others who have found it practicing medicine, or running a bakery, or driving a truck—in running a bakery which makes the best kind of bread there is, or in driving a truck better than anyone else.

That's the kind of achievement which makes a man happy.

11
CHAMPAGNE MUSIC MAKERS

IT WAS THE TAG END OF THE THIRTIES AND THE BIG-NAME BANDS were in their prime. And how I loved them! I could never get enough of their music, and even when the boys and I were playing dance dates of our own somewhere, I would slip out to my car at intermission and try to tune them in on the radio. Even today the names of those big bands ring through my ears like music—Glenn Miller, Tommy Dorsey, Jimmy Dorsey, Guy Lombardo, Isham Jones, the great Paul Whiteman, Duke Ellington, Hal Kemp (I loved his band so much I once drove over four hundred miles from Big Springs, Texas, into Dallas just to get a close-up listen to his brass and reed sections, which played with almost machine-like precision), Benny Goodman, Artie Shaw, Jan Garber, Orrin Tucker, Russ Morgan, Woody Herman, Glen Gray and his Casa Loma Orchestra.

All the orchestras of the day had descriptive names. Guy Lombardo and His Royal Canadians were known for " The Sweetest Music This Side of Heaven," and, generally speaking, the American dance public agreed with him. Wayne King, The Waltz King, had the Lady Esther Radio Program and was one of my favorites. Henry Busse played Shuffle Rhythm, and when you heard it you couldn't sit still, you just had to dance. Shep Fields had Rippling Rhythm, an effect he achieved by blowing through a straw into a glass full of water. Every one of those bands had a distinctive sound, something so special you could tell which band you were listening to long before an announcer identified it for you.

I particularly loved Red Nichols and His Five Pennies, with his great trombonist, Miff Mole. I literally wore out every record his group ever made, playing them over and over until there just wasn't any music left in the tracks. My heart nearly fell out when I listened to them, they played with such purity and drive, and I longed to have Red play in my own orchestra. I never quite got up the courage to ask him, however, but years later, when I was in Los Angeles with our television show and Red was playing a stand at the Town House Hotel on Wilshire Boulevard, I went to hear him, and I told him how much I had wanted him in my band. Red's eyes crinkled in that nice grin of his. "Is it too late now?" he asked. "No!" I cried, and so Red played a few solos on our program while I stood in the wings beaming, as another dream came true.

Two other great bandleaders of those years were Duke Ellington and Cab Calloway, both of whom had superb orchestras. The Duke was famous for his very original harmonic patterns. Whenever one of those bands played in a Midwestern city, the whole town turned out to hear them. Where other orchestras played three-or four-minute arrangements, the Duke and Cab would play for eight, nine, or even ten minutes at a time, and the more they played the more enthusiastic the crowds became. They really put on a tremendous show for the dancing public, and dancers and orchestra set each other off until, between the two of them, they generated enough excitement to blow the roof off.

Louis Armstrong, then as now, was one of the greatest trumpet artists of the day and had a tremendous following. George Thow, who played lead trumpet with Jimmy Dorsey before he joined our band, remembers the time when he was a Harvard undergraduate and went up to New York City just to hear Louis. By the time he arrived at the famed Connie's Inn in Harlem, where Louis was appearing, George didn't have enough money left to get into the club. Nevertheless, he waited around until Louis drove up in a long black limousine and got out, wearing a full length fur coat.

George approached and explained his predicament. "Boy," said Louis, flashing his famous friendly grin, "don't you worry about a thing. You just come along with me." And he grabbed George by the arm and sat him up onstage all evening where he could get a close look at Armstrong's technique. Whenever George complimented him, Armstrong would grin and say, "You ain't heard nuthin' yet!" Most top band leaders of the day gave the same friendly consideration to up and coming young musicians, and there was a great spirit of camaraderie among them in spite of the intense competition.

Whenever those great bands and performers appeared, they drew enormous crowds, hungry to listen and dance, crowds which appreciated the fine musicianship of each of the players. In most cases they knew the names and specialties of every musician in every band. They were the musical heroes of the day, much like the rock groups of the fifties and sixties.

I loved to watch and listen to them, and I just ached to get into that big league myself. I thought about it all the time, and I knew I had to figure out some way to join them.

One night when we were alone at dinner I put down a forkful of chicken-baked-in-cream, one of Fern's specialties. Her eyes widened; if I didn't eat that chicken, she knew something was wrong. "What's the matter, Lawrence?"

I pushed my plate to one side and looked across the table at her, trim and neat as always, in a pink housedress. "Fern, I . . . there's something I want to talk to you about. Do you remember when I tried to make a go of it in the big time, a few years ago?"

She nodded and made a little face. "I certainly do! How could I ever forget it. Why?"

"Well," I said, a little taken aback at her reaction, "I want to try it again. I just feel I should make one more attempt."

"Oh, I see." She looked at me rather searchingly for a moment. "And the boys don't want to go along with you? Is that the trouble?"

"No, no, that's not it. They want to try it. But in order to make an all-out attempt to get into the big time, it will mean that we'll probably have to give up our home here, and you and the girls will have to come along on the road with me while I try to get some long-playing stands at the big hotels in the East, or in some big city. It's just about the only way to establish a big name." I paused. "Fern, I know it's a lot to ask of you, but . . . will you go along with me on this idea?"

She looked unhappy. "Why do we have to leave here? Why can't you just go alone?"

"Because I can't keep coming back here every few nights and establish any kind of nationwide reputation. And I don't want to go away and leave you for any length of time. I want us all to be together. And I have to know that you are behind me in this decision."

"Oh, Lawrence! Why can't we just stay here? Shirley will be starting school soon. Why do you feel you have to do this?"

"Because I think this is the last good chance I'll have. I think I owe it to the boys. They've worked just as hard as I have."

She sighed. "It seems like a terrible chance to take."

"I don't think so," I told her. "I believe we can do it. Fern . . . will you at least think this over for me?"

She nodded, slowly. "Yes, of course, Lawrence. Let me think about it for a few days."

We said no more about it then, but the very next evening she came to me and, her brown eyes very serious, said, "Lawrence, do you really want to do this?"

"Yes, I do. At least I want to try."

"You're not afraid to give up our security here?"

"No, I'm not."

"All right." She said it reluctantly but firmly. "All right, Lawrence. If that's what you want then, of course"—she smiled and touched my arm—"of course I'll back you up." I think I knew right then that some day I would make it.

The next step was to tell Vic Schroeder, and he reacted much as Fern had. "Now why do you want to take a chance like that? The woods are full of big-name bands. You've got a good thing going right here for you. You're probably the top band in the Midwest territory. And our other five bands are doing well too, so why take a chance and give it all up?"

I told him the same things I had told Fern. "I just feel I have to, Vic. It's been on my mind for a long time. I think the boys are ready for it and I just don't think I could ever forgive myself if I didn't at least make the effort."

He nodded slowly as I talked. "Yeah. Yeah. Well, I can understand that. Okay, if you've made up your mind then I'll just wish you the best of luck."

We set to work dividing our business interests and settling accounts. "Why don't you just take the other five bands, Vic," I suggested, "and I'll just leave? Do you think that would be fair?"

Vic shook his head. "Welk, you old . . . of course it would be fair! It would be more than fair. I just wish I could keep on handling you, too, but you'll have to get a national booking agent now." I nodded. Suddenly Vic got up from behind his desk and came around and took both my hands in his. "Lawrence," he said gently, "I hate to lose you. But just the same, I hope I never see you here again—except on tour, leading a big-name band. He smiled warmly.

Our first real break came in 1937 when we were playing in Chaska, Minnesota, a little town about thirty-five miles outside of St. Paul. Will Osborne was being featured at the Lowery Hotel in that city. I had long been impressed with the style and ability of his slide trombones, and I wanted all the boys to hear him. "Come on," I told them, "I'm going to take you into St. Paul and treat you to lunch. Let you listen to a real artist at work. Maybe you can learn something from him."

"Gee," said one of my boys, impressed, "if *you're* going to treat us all to lunch that guy must be good!" And he was good. Osborne had a wonderfully smooth trombone section. I used to think it sounded something like cows mooing—only very artistic cows! He and his orchestra were featured at the hotel during the lunch hour, and then again from ten till one at night, standard practice in those days. We all listened intently as he played to the big luncheon crowd.

Afterward, as we walked back to our car which I had parked about a block away, we discussed his superior technique. On the way we passed the big St. Paul Hotel. "Wait a minute, fellows," I said on the spur of the moment, "I think I'll just run up and say hello to Mr. Calhoun, the manager. Maybe I'll have him book us in here for a while."

They all laughed. "Yeah! Sure! Have him book us into Carnegie Hall while you're at it."

I grinned and pushed open the revolving doors to the St. Paul. It was "the" hotel in St. Paul, well-known for booking top-name bands, and I walked across the thickly carpeted lobby floors, admiring the dark red overstuffed furniture and walnut tables and the air of quiet luxury, thinking how wonderful it would be to play in a place like this some day. I wasn't sure Mr. Calhoun would remember me. I had met him once before at Tom Archer's Chermot Ballroom in Omaha and he had casually suggested that I visit him if I ever got out to St. Paul. He did remember me, however, and was very cordial, inviting me into his inner office. "Well, Mr. Welk, how are things going for you?"

"Very good," I told him. "The boys and I are busy with one-night stands. But we'd like to settle down for a while." I smiled. "How about booking us in here?"

"All right," he said casually. "When would you like to start?"

I was so startled I could hardly answer him. "Uh . . . well, anytime you say! I'm booked up pretty far ahead, but if you'll give me a day or two I think I can telephone the ballroom owners and rearrange our schedule so we can open for you in two weeks." I looked at him again to make sure he wasn't kidding. "Are you serious, Mr. Calhoun?"

"Of course I'm serious. I'm looking for a band right now."

I jumped to my feet. "Then I'll get busy on the phone and get back to you right away. By noon tomorrow. Will that be all right?"

"Fine," he said, smiling a little at my excitement. "Just let me know as soon as possible."

I shot out of his office, ran down the stairs, and tore through the lobby, but I slowed down as I saw the boys waiting impatiently for me beside our sleeper bus. Jules Herman, my trumpet player, eyed me suspiciously. "What are you looking so smug about?" he demanded.

"Oh, nothing," I said airily, polishing my fingernails on the lapel of my jacket. "Only we're not going to do any more one-nighters. We're going to start playing at the St. Paul!"

They couldn't believe it. "You're kidding!" "The St. Paul!" "Really?" "How much?" "How'd you do it?" All of them were just as excited as I was, because the St. Paul was a prestige place to play, and all of them waited anxiously as I telephoned the ballroom managers and explained our situation. Every one of them agreed to postpone our bookings until a later date, in order to give us a chance to make this important location-job appearance, and by the end of the following day the deal was all set.

Fern and the girls and I moved into a house on the edge of White Lake outside of Minneapolis, and she scrubbed and polished while the boys and I worked overtime on new arrangements and novelty numbers. All of us were thrilled at this unexpected piece of good luck, and we could hardly wait for our big-time debut.

The night before we were to open, I dropped into the hotel to hear Les Brown's closing performance. He had a group called the Duke Blue Devils, and they were good. I mean they were good, they were solid! I could hear the rhythmic throbbing beat of their music clear out into the lobby which was filled with people. The Casino Room itself was so crowded I couldn't even get my coat checked. "I'm sorry, sir," said the hat check girl, shrugging her shoulders, "but there's just no more room for any coats."

"Has it been this crowded every night?" I asked, fighting down a sense of panic.

"Yes, just about. Of course, it's more crowded than usual tonight. It's his closing night."

I nodded and, holding onto my coat and hat, pushed and shoved until I could get inside the ballroom. The place was so packed there was hardly any room for dancing. In fact, most of the couples were pressed solidly against the stage, listening raptly to Brown's powerful band. He was, and he still is, one of the few top band leaders who can do his own arrangements, and he is an expert. Looking around at all those excited, absorbed faces, and the great numbers of listeners jammed into the room, I had a sinking feeling. I hoped we could do half as well.

I didn't say anything to the fellows, but I was worried about keeping up with Brown's record. It seemed as if my worst fears were justified the next night, when I looked out into the room at about ten-thirty and saw that it was only three quarters filled. I was dismayed. Opening nights were always crowded, if only with press people and friends of the management in on free passes. But here we were with a house not quite full, and if it was this way on opening night, what were our chances for the rest of the run—if we got any run at all? I put George Kelly's acting advice to good use and smiled widely, but inside I was very worried and I didn't sleep much that night. Early the next morning I went up to Mr. Calhoun's office, expecting to hear the worst. Instead, he grinned as I entered his office and said, " Well, Lawrence, that was a very good opening night last night!"

"Very good?" I was dumbfounded. "But we didn't have nearly the crowd that Les Brown did."

Calhoun laughed. "No, I know you didn't. But *your* crowd spends money. Brown's doesn't—at least not very much."

"What do you mean?"

"Brown pulls a lot of college kids. They're great kids but they don't have any money. Don't you know what they do?"

I shook my head. Calhoun was amused. "Well, they dash across the street to the drugstore and buy a coke, and then they come back in here and have a free listen—no cover charge, you know. Now, you didn't pull as big a crowd, that's true. But your crowd got all dressed up and sat down and ordered full-course dinners and drinks and champagne and . . . well, you did just fine, Lawrence. As a matter of fact, last night you pulled one of the biggest grosses we've ever had."

The relief was almost overwhelming. "Then we're all right? Everything is okay?"

"Yes, everything's okay! Settle down for a nice long run. Everything is just fine."

Calhoun was right. I had learned something about the difference in crowds and the way different music appeals to different types of people. It helped us to develop and refine our own style, and it also helped to make our entire run very successful. Sometimes we filled the big Casino Room and sometimes we didn't, but we always managed to make a profit for the hotel and the booking gave us a tremendous boost in our name value.

What made things even better was coming home at night and finding my three girls there, sleeping peacefully, and not hundreds of miles away from me. Donna was still a baby, of course, but Shirley and I spent hours together every day, talking about anything and everything. We often went fishing together. The first time I took her out on the lake with me I put all the worms on her line, and then explained patiently just exactly how to catch a fish. I was a wonderful teacher. She promptly caught six fish in a row, while I sat on my side of the boat and caught exactly nothing. Shirley thought this was a great joke and for years afterward she would confide to friends, "Daddy's not a good fisherman. But he's very good for putting worms on your line."

Those were some of the most wonderful days we ever enjoyed together as a family but, as so often happens in life, in the midst of our joy came a time of sorrow. We received word from Strasburg that my father had died of uremic poisoning. Fern was almost as upset as I, because she had grown very close to him, sensing the warm love that lay beneath his gruff exterior.

I drove home for the funeral services, but on the way the roads became so slick and icy my car skidded wildly and turned over and over, landing in a ditch at the side of the road. I was not hurt, just dazed and shaken, but the car was almost demolished. The whole episode of my father's death remains a sad memory for me.

But I was grateful for two things. He had lived long enough to see me established in a good hotel, with my orchestra beginning to make something of a name. And we had reached an accord, a mutual understanding over my leaving the farm. He hadn't liked my aims in the beginning, and it had long been a touchy point between us, but he had gradually come to understand and accept them, as he had expressed with such gentleness the last time I had seen him.

I loved my father deeply, and always had. More that that, I respected him. I would miss him very much.

We had a nightly radio broadcast from the hotel over KTSP, and our announcer was an up-and-coming young man named George Putnam, who went on to become the famous Los Angeles newscaster. He was just beginning his highly successful career at that time, and even then I knew that his strong and friendly personality would take him places! From many points of view our engagement at the St. Paul was highly rewarding, and it led directly to another booking at the William Penn Hotel in Pittsburgh, one of the truly outstanding hotels in the country. We were all delighted at this news. My new booker, Bill Fredericks, of Fredericks Brothers in Chicago, had arranged the booking on Calhoun's recommendation to his friend Jerry O'Neill, the manager at the William Penn. Not only did he land the booking for us, but we were set to open on the stroke of midnight on New Year's Eve in 1938, in the exclusive Italian Terrace, the finest and most expensive room in the hotel. We were scheduled to follow Dick Stabile into the Terrace Room, and it seemed to all of us that we were really on our way, with nowhere to go but straight up. I guess it was just as well that none of us could see too far into the future. If we had, we would have probably packed up then and there and gone back to Omaha.

For the time being anyway, we were delighted. Fern and I rented an apartment in Pittsburgh after a diligent search for one which took children. We learned to our chagrin during those years that most apartment-hotels would take adults, and they would take dogs, but they wouldn't take children. Then the boys and I all invested in full-dress suits for our big occasion. We looked so grand when we got all dressed up that we hardly recognized ourselves. But anything else would have seemed out of place in the Italian Terrace Room.

It was huge, with lofty ceilings and great mirrors outlined in curved and gilded frames, and crystal chandeliers and paintings and frescoes on the walls. Thick carpeting covered the floors, and all the tables were set with heavy white damask tablecloths, a great deal of silver and crystal, and centerpieces of red roses. The place was almost overpowering in its beauty. It was by far the most luxurious place in which we had ever appeared . . . and a long long way from the farm.

I used to watch people as they walked into the room. Many of them would stop dead in their tracks at the door, looking around nervously, almost overwhelmed with all the plush decoration. And a great many of them would just turn around and walk right out again. Only those who were very wealthy and used to this sort of grandeur all the time seemed able to relax in the place.

New Year's Eve went very well. Dick Stabile introduced us and everyone was in a festive mood. There were toasts of champagne and we played lots of waltzes and romantic dance music, while the lights from the chandeliers reflected in all the mirrors and the whole room seemed to sparkle and glow. It was an auspicious beginning, made even more so by the glowing review of Si Steinhauser which appeared in the Pittsburgh *Press* the next day. Steinhauser was a highly popular columnist, locally famous for accurately predicting success or failure for various bandleaders, and when he gave us such a favorable review we were almost in heaven. The next night there was a continual parade of people coming up to the bandstand to ask, "Did you read what Si Steinhauser said about you? He says you're going to be a hit!" It seemed to me we had finally made it. We were solidly in the world of the big time at last!

A few days later something else happened which had a profound effect on our career. We were playing three nationwide broadcasts a day from the hotel over WCAE, the Mutual-Don Lee Network outlet in Pittsburgh, and before long we began to be inundated with fan mail. One day our announcer, Phil David, came striding into the dining room with a whole stack of letters in his hands and an excited gleam in his eyes. "Lawrence, I want you to take a look at some of these letters," he said. "See if you notice the same thing I do." I took the mail and began to run through it, and almost immediately I saw what he meant. All the letters had nice things to say about our music, and in addition almost every one added words to the effect that it sounded "gay," "sparkling," "light," "effervescent" (I had to ask Phil about that one), "bubbly," "happy."

"You know what these letters are saying, don't you?" Phil demanded. "They're saying that dancing to your music is like sipping champagne. Lawrence, you've got yourself some Champagne Music!"

The moment he said it, I knew it was right. Suddenly everything fell into place! From America's Biggest Little Band to the Hotsy Totsy Boys and The Honolulu Fruit Gum Orchestra, we had finally found the name which seemed to really suit us—the Champagne Music of Lawrence Welk. It led naturally to a Champagne Lady later—Lois Best was actually the first girl to wear that title—and all the boys became Champagne Music Makers. In many ways it marked a real turning point for us. Phil Davis had done us a great favor when he found that name.

With our new title came a real flash of inspiration. I dug out the song I had written years before to celebrate Shirley's birth, "You're My Home Sweet Home." Originally I had written it as a slow, sweet legato ballad, a kind of hymn to my daughter, but now I began to play the same tune at a much faster tempo, with a few added runs and frills. The result was a light, frothy piece which seemed to suit our musical style perfectly, and I began to use it as our theme song. When people asked me what the name of it was, "You're My Home Sweet Home" just didn't sound right to them, and so one day I decided to have a contest to give the song a new name. The winner was to have a free dinner and evening of dancing at the Terrace Room. Within a matter of days we had found the name we wanted—"Bubbles in the Wine." It was suggested by a local Pittsburgh lady who promptly came in to claim her prize. At last we were established in a big hotel with a fine new title and a theme song to match. I almost exploded with happiness!

But for a while we had trouble trying to get the sound of a champagne cork exploding out of the bottle, which we needed to go along with our new theme. At first we tried opening a real bottle, but we never got the same effect twice, and it was almost impossible to get it opened at the exact moment required in the song. I finally solved the whole thing by sticking my finger in my mouth and popping it out with a "whoosh"—something I still do today and something the boys tell me I have developed into a real art form. I may not play the accordion as well as Myron Floren, but I play a champagne bottle much better than he does.

Everything about our new name seemed to develop quite naturally, almost as though it had been planned all along, but actually the champagne music style itself came about almost by accident. In the beginning I couldn't afford to hire the kind of musicians who were skilled enough to sustain long musical notes. I always managed to have good key men, of course, but some of the pick-up musicians I was forced to hire on the road were so bad they could barely play on key, let alone hold a note any length of time. In desperation I had worked out arrangements where they wouldn't have to hold any notes too long. This resulted in short, light, delicate musical figures which, combined with an accordion which is a bright-sounding instrument anyway, led to the sparkling "bubbly" kind of sound that had intrigued all the letter-writers so much.

One of those letter writers had a lasting effect on my life. Her name was Edna Stoner, and she wrote to us from her home in Beresford, South Dakota, to tell us how happy she was that we were playing from such a fine big hotel. "I used to dance to your music when I was a teen-ager and you were playing in Yankton," she wrote, "and you were always my favorite band. I just wish you all the luck in the world." She went on to tell us that she had been bedridden ever since 1928, when she was struck down by crippling arthritis. But she didn't complain at all, and I was so impressed with the quality of happiness and sweetness in her letter that I wrote right back to her and we began a correspondence which lasts to this day.

With all our fan mail and our fine reviews from Mr. Steinhauser, with our brand-new name and our regular radio broadcasts, I felt we were secure at last. I should have realized, I suppose, from an incident that occurred during our opening night that I—for one—had maybe come too far, too fast. Even today I shudder with embarrassment whenever I think about it.

I had been standing on the stage that night, leading the band and enjoying myself hugely as I watched the beautifully dressed crowds swirl around the floor, when suddenly I saw one of the waiters scurry across the room and beckon to me from the foot of the bandstand. "Hurry up," he whispered as I bent over to hear him, "Mr. O'Neill wants you to come over and visit for a while with his guests."

If he had invited me to jump in and swim the Atlantic Ocean, I couldn't have been more terrified. I knew that O'Neill had the cream of Pittsburgh wealth and society at his table that night, and the thought of meeting all of them and trying to make small talk was almost more than I could stand. I was sure I would do or say something to embarrass us all. But I had been commanded to appear by Mr. O'Neill, and appear I would, no matter how painful it might be.

I thanked the waiter, stalled around for a while playing the accordion, and finally got down off the bandstand and threaded my way across the dance floor, smiling nervously, while my Adam's apple threatened to choke me to death in my unfamiliar new finery. I wished I had my accordion strapped on. I wished I were back in my overalls. I wished I were anywhere but walking through that glittering assemblage on my way to meet famous names I had been reading about in the world of finance and high society for years.

However, all of Mr. O'Neill's guests were so gracious and charming to me that it turned out to be much easier than I expected. I managed to make my way clear around the table, bowing to the ladies and shaking hands with the men, without making any serious mistakes at all—at least none of which I was aware. I was so thrilled at this accomplishment that I beamed with joy and relief as I prepared to escape back to my home on the bandstand. But just as I turned to leave, one of the guests reached out and said in a kindly tone, "Oh don't go, Mr. Welk. Sit down and have a drink with us."

"Yes, do, Lawrence," said Mr. O'Neill immediately. There was nothing to do but sit down, although I was overwhelmed with panic again because I didn't have the faintest notion what to order. In spite of the fact I had been on the road for years arguing with my boys about liquor, I had never paid any attention to *what* they were drinking— only how much—and now I couldn't think of a thing to drink except the spiked beer and schnaps which my elders used to favor on the farms in Strasburg. Somehow I didn't think that was the thing to order at the Italian Terrace. I strained my ears to hear what the other guests were asking for, and I heard a few murmurs of "Scotch and soda," so when the waiter got to me that's what I ordered, too. He nodded gravely and wrote it down and once again I was saved.

But not for long. When he returned he set down two glasses in front of me instead of one, and once more I was in trouble. I knew the Scotch was in the smaller glass, and I also knew the Strasburgers would have tossed that down in one gulp, but I wasn't sure that was what one did in polite society. I sat frozen miserably, sneaking little peeks out of the corner of my eyes, till I noticed several of the guests casually pouring their Scotch into the big glass of soda. Vastly relieved, I did the same thing. But I still had one more hurdle to jump. A tall glass swizzle stick was protruding from the top of the soda glass, and I was just mystified by the thing. I didn't know what it was or what to do with it, and again I tried sneaking looks at the other guests to see what they were doing with theirs. Unfortunately, every time I peeked they weren't doing anything, and so I finally took the plunge myself. The thing looked like a very fancy glass drinking straw to me, in keeping with all the glass and glitter in the Italian Room, I reasoned, and that's what I used it for. Or tried to. After the first few fruitless sips I realized it wasn't a straw at all and I was supposed to stir my drink with it, not try to drink through it. I went scarlet with embarrassment and thought, "Well, dummer-Esel, you've done it again!" I don't know whether anybody saw me or not. I was too mortified to look up. I just put the glass down quietly on the table, and after that I stopped trying to be something I wasn't. Nobody will ever know how happy I was to get back up on the stage where I belonged.

Glass swizzle sticks notwithstanding, nothing could dampen our enthusiasm that first week. We managed to attract fairly good crowds every night, although they seemed lost in that vast and formal room, and we got a great deal of favorable newspaper and radio publicity, plus continual sacks of fan mail, and so I was stunned, really stunned, to receive our notice at the end of a month. I just couldn't believe it. "But why, Bill," I said desperately when he told me the news. "Why? I thought we were doing so well here! What's the reason?"

Bill shrugged. "I dunno, Lawrence. O'Neill didn't say. He just said, 'That's all for a while.' Lawrence, it's not the end of the world, you know. We'll get some other bookings. Don't worry."

His reassurance didn't help. I was just sick about it, even though the same thing had happened many times before. But we had made such an apparently successful debut that this very public failure was almost more than I could take. For the first time I realized some of the pitfalls of being well-known; it was nice if you were successful, but it made it just that much harder to take when you failed. It seemed to me that we were right back in that old barnstorming seesaw of up one day and down the next. Only now the stakes were much higher.

Fern didn't say anything and neither did the boys. All of us were constrained and unhappy. Fortunately, Bill Fredericks arranged a booking for us at the Normandy Ballroom in downtown Boston almost immediately, and that helped a good deal. We left Pittsburgh at once, and I wondered soberly as we drove along if I were doing the right thing in trying to crack the walls of the big-name bands. Maybe I just didn't have what it took after all.

In Boston, however, our demoralized spirits began to pick up. We were back in the kind of territory we knew best, playing to crowds that loved to dance, and within a week after we started the place was jammed to capacity every night. Lois Best came out to join us as our very first Champagne Lady. I had heard her when she was singing with Benny Burton's orchestra in Pittsburgh, and had asked her to join us at the first opportunity. Her arrival helped make the engagement even more successful. Fern and the girls and I settled into a pleasant, old-fashioned apartment house, which even boasted a small grassy yard where the girls could play, and all of us were quite pleased. I began to feel a little better. We were in good shape again. Financially we did well because we were playing on a percentage basis, and gradually my abrupt firing from the William Penn began to seem less severe. Cautiously, at first, I started to dream a few more big dreams.

We had played at the Normandy only a few weeks when Bill called me from Chicago one night in great excitement, and told me he had wonderful news for me. "Hold on to your hat, Lawrence," he said. "You're going back to the William Penn again."

"Oh now, Bill," I said, annoyed, "why do you tell me a story like that? You know they don't want me back there."

"But they do! O'Neill himself called and asked for you!"

"Oh come on. He fired me after just a month. Cut it out, Bill. Don't kid me."

"I'm not kidding you. O'Neill wants you back. The

orchestra they brought in after you left did much less business than you. Besides, he plans to use you in a new room."

To Bill's surprise I got obstinate. "Well, I don't want to go. We like it here and Fern is happy and I don't want to go back to that place for just a couple of weeks. I'd rather stay here."

Bill was amazed. He had been sure I would be thrilled. "Well, Lawrence, this puts me in a hell of a spot. I didn't know you felt that way! I've already committed you. If you back out now it could mean a lawsuit. Come on, I'm sure it will work out."

Naturally I didn't want to become involved in a lawsuit—although I'm not sure to this day that Bill wasn't bluffing when he told me that—so I finally agreed to wind up our Boston engagement and come back to the William Penn. But I didn't want to go and I had grave reservations.

Bill was right, however, and I was wrong. The new room was perfect for us. O'Neill put us in the Chatterbox Room, a much more comfortable and informal place, with a warm and cozy feeling about it, and we were an almost instantaneous success there. The ropes were up even on Monday night, traditionally the slowest night of the week, and our original engagement was extended again and again. It was a wonderful feeling—one of our happiest times—made more so, perhaps, because it was such a contrast to our Italian Terrace fiasco. By the time we finally wound up our successful appearance there we were getting offers for $500 a night, which was quite a jump from our Honolulu Fruit Gum days at $125. The future began to look very very good again, and it looked even better when Bill arranged the booking I had been dreaming about almost as long as I could remember.

"Say, Lawrence," he said to me almost casually one day as we were going over some business, "I have your next booking arranged."

"Oh?" I looked up at him. "Where?"

He grinned, knowing how much it meant to me.

"The Edgewater Beach Hotel in Chicago."

12

I TALK!

For years the Edgewater Beach Hotel had been a kind of symbol to me. Back home on the farm I used to lie on my bed at night with the radio held close to my ear, listening to broadcasts from that hotel. "And now," the announcer would say, "we bring you the music of Danny Russo and his orchestra, direct from the Edgewater Beach Hotel in Chicago . . . the beautiful Edgewater Beach, on the shores of Lake Michigan, where there is dancing under the stars!" I had it pictured in my mind as a sort of palace with moonlight shining on the water and the dancers whirling around under the stars. Years later, when I got my first glimpse of the place during my days with Lincoln Boulds' orchestra, I was not the least bit disappointed. It was a very impressive structure of pinkish stone, built right along the water's edge, and, true to my dreams, there was an outdoor terrace for dancing which overlooked the water. I was determined to play there some day.

Now, at last, that dream was coming true. I walked around in a daze for hours after Bill gave me the good news. In my mind's eye I could see my name up on the marquee: "The Edgewater Beach proudly presents Lawrence Welk and His Champagne Music." All the biggest bands of the day were associated with leading hotels—Guy Lombardo at the Roosevelt in New York, Freddie Martin at the Cocoanut Grove in Los Angeles, Orrin Tucker at the Palmer House in Chicago. Now maybe Lawrence Welk would be established as the permanent band at the Edgewater. It was a thrilling thought. I remembered our "honeymoon," when Fern and I had wandered along the edge of Lake Michigan and I had promised her I would play there some day. Now it was happening, and I couldn't have been happier.

A few days later the bubble began to burst a little. L. A.

Fredericks, Bill's brother, had me come up to the office to sign some papers, and while I was there he said, almost too casually, "They want you to make a little speech opening night, Lawrence,"

"Oh now, L. A., I can't do that!" I cried, instantly in a panic. "You know how bad I talk!"

"Oh, this'll just be a few words. I wouldn't worry about it," he said, trying to make it sound insignificant.

But worry I did. I had put off talking for years because I was so ashamed of my accent. Once in a while I had worked up enough nerve to say "We will now play 'Sweet Sue'" or something like that, but almost always I had relied on my accordion and a smile, and hired a master of ceremonies to do any necessary announcing. Now, however, it looked like the moment of truth had arrived and I went over to the hotel to make absolutely sure that I would have to talk. The manager, Mr. Dewey, seemed surprised when I asked him about it. "Well, yes, certainly you'll make a little speech of welcome on opening night," he said, "and then I think you should make every effort to chat with the audience during your run here. Work out a little patter for yourself. You'll find it will add a great deal to your show." He smiled as if it were all settled, and I found myself smiling weakly and nodding agreement although I got sick to my stomach just thinking about it. "I have a couple of newspaper friends," Mr. Dewey went on, "and they'll write out a little speech for opening night. After that, you can just sort of talk for yourself."

I thanked him and walked out of the hotel, scared to death. That night I went in to watch Orrin Tucker, and I came out feeling worse than ever. Tucker looked so handsome in his white tie and tails; he joked and laughed so easily with his audience that I was in despair and ready to go back to the farm. "Oh, what am I doing here?" I thought. "I can never do that. I can't even speak good English!"

Nevertheless, I went back to the hotel the next day, picked up the promised speech from Mr. Dewey, and read it through, ready to start practicing. It was just a few short lines, as I recall now, but it might as well have been the Gettysburg address as far as I was concerned. I could not seem to get it memorized. It was peculiar. From my earliest childhood I could hear a piece of music just once and then play it immediately from memory. But words—that was a different matter. I had never really learned the basics of English grammar. George and Mrs. Kelly had helped me a great deal, of course, and I had taught myself by studying German-English prayer books. But even though I had learned enough to get along, I was never really absolutely sure that I was using the right words. What's more, I hated the sound of my voice. Try as I might, I couldn't seem to get rid of that extra "ah" syllable at the end of so many words, and I had constant trouble with "th" sounds. A word like "telethon," for example, would come out "tellatawn."

Nevertheless, I plowed doggedly ahead. I made several copies of the speech and put them everywhere—one in my car, one in my briefcase, one stuck up in the bathroom mirror where I could see it when I was shaving—every place I could think of. Finally I got the thing down letter perfect, and by opening night I felt I was as ready as I ever would be.

The Terrace looked beautiful that night. Completely out in the open, it was set up with small tables topped with vari-colored umbrellas. The balustrade that encircled the dance floor was strung with leaves and flowers and twinkling lights, and there were big tubs of flowering shrubs set all around the edge of the floor. Again, true to my youthful dreams, the waters of Lake Michigan shone darkly in the background, although there were no stars out that night. It was hot and humid, typically sticky Midwestern summer weather. About eight o'clock the Terrace began to fill up rapidly with girls in their pretty summer dresses, and their escorts wearing the white jackets and dark trousers that were popular then. A hum of excitement began to fill the room, but backstage there was an air of barely controlled panic.

I think the boys were almost as nervous as I was. They all knew how worried I was about talking, and I think they may

The Road

have been even more worried. Leo paced up and down, as Jules Herman and trombone player S. K. Grundy stayed cool, running a few practice scales. Bob Cromer kept clearing his throat, while I stayed in the corner going over my speech again and again. All too soon Mr. Dewey came backstage, rubbing his hands together and nodding brightly to everyone. "Well," he said cheerfully, looking at us, resplendent in our white ties and tails, "you look fine. Just fine! All set, Lawrence?"

I nodded and gave him a sickly grin. "All set," I said. I sounded a lot more confident than I was.

Finally the moment to start the program arrived and the boys filed out and took their places. Mr. Dewey strode onstage after one last reassuring smile and I waited while the curtains parted and he made a short speech of introduction. My stomach was so tied up in knots it really hurt, and the palms of my hands were wringing wet. Over and over in my mind I kept saying, "Ladies and gentlemen, it is a great honor." Then, as if in a dream, I heard Mr. Dewey announce my name, followed by a polite smattering of applause.

I clutched my baton, walked out to the center of the stage, smiled nervously, and opened my mouth to speak. "Lady . . . and gentlemens," I said, and thought "Oh *no!*" But that's as far as I got. A terrible clap of thunder exploded directly overhead with such force it nearly knocked me off my feet, and then the skies erupted with a drenching downpour such as I have never seen before. I felt like I was drowning, standing up. All the girls began screaming and clutching at their hair, and their escorts whipped off suit jackets to protect them and rushed them into the hotel lobby inside. After about two seconds of indecision my boys picked up their instruments and fled, too. Jerry had the presence of mind to unplug the electric organ as he ran off and one of the other fellows grabbed a piano bench on the run. Everybody left—except me! I stood right where I was, frozen to the spot, and went right ahead and delivered that speech to an empty terrace, while the rain plastered my full-dress suit to my body and ran down my face like tears. Thunder rolled and lightning flashed, and still I went on. It was as though I had programmed myself to speak and couldn't stop until I had finished. I did everything but take a bow at the end.

Afterward, when I walked offstage, soaked to the skin, the boys looked at me sympathetically but not one of them said a word. I think they felt almost as bad as I did. I had worked so hard and so long on that speech, and now it seemed as if even the heavens themselves were protesting. All of them watched soberly while I stood and dripped sadly into an everwidening puddle, and suddenly the whole thing struck us as uproariously funny. We laughed until we were almost sick, and by the time the shower cleared up we had laughed ourselves out of a bad case of nerves. We all combed our hair and pulled our suits into shape as well as we could, although I walked back on stage looking as though I had slept in mine for at least a week. Somehow we managed to get through the rest of that opening night fiasco.

Even though it seemed funny in a way, it was a very disheartening debut and it weakened my already shaky self-confidence. I tried hard to talk every night after that, but it was always a terrible ordeal and I was always worried for fear I'd forget my lines or say the wrong words or the audience would laugh in the wrong place—or it would rain again. A few weeks later something else happened that makes that whole engagement at the Edgewater stand out in my mind with painful clarity. The management had thoughtfully hired twelve beautiful girls to ride twelve milk-white horses around the edge of the dance floor as part of the evening's entertainment, and one of the horses promptly disgraced himself in the middle of the opening parade. Howls of laughter greeted this performance, and I remember thinking disconsolately, "Well, even the horse is trying to tell me to go back to the farm. They really didn't have to go to that much trouble."

I was in a strange state of indecision during those weeks at the Edgewater. Opening night had shaken me a good deal, of course, but what was more important was that I felt I was in unfamiliar territory where I wasn't at all sure of myself. I realized things were not going as well as they should, even though we attracted large crowds, and a few weeks later Bill Fredericks gloomily confirmed my worries. Some of the most influential patrons of the hotel just didn't like me or the music we were playing. I was given to understand that unless I pleased these people, and one couple in particular, our engagement would end a whole lot sooner than I had anticipated. I was heartsick, especially since I couldn't pinpoint exactly what our problem was.

Slowly I began to suspect where part of the difficulty lay, and as things turned out I was correct. Being new in town, I had been besieged by song pluggers. I was so anxious to make friends with everyone that I tried my best to help them, and it never once occurred to me that they were using me. They'd come to me with sad stories and beg me to play their songs, "just once, only once," during our nightly radio broadcasts. I remember one fellow who actually got down on his knees and with tears in his eyes begged me to play the song his publishing company had sent him. "If you don't play it I'll lose my job and my family will starve," he sobbed. He even had a telegram delivered to himself to back up his story. So I played his song. Later on I found out that the song pluggers got together and cooked up heartbreaking stories among themselves to try out on me. "Just cry a little for Welk," they said, "and he'll do anything for you."

Of course, I didn't know this at the time, so I naïvely tried my best to include all their numbers. Once we played twelve songs during our coast-to-coast radio program, which ran only fifteen minutes, and sometimes there were so many new and unfamiliar orchestrations stacked up on the music racks that the boys would get them mixed up, and one or two of them would be playing different songs at the same time. But that didn't seem to matter because they all sounded alike anyway. I realized dimly that I shouldn't be doing this, but I didn't want to offend anyone, and once I had promised a song plugger that I would play his number, naturally I always did.

Things got so bad, however, that one night out of sheer desperation I decided to put the situation squarely up to the couple who were so dissatisfied with me, and ask for their help. At intermission I walked over to their table and introduced myself. I had just read Dale Carnegie's new book, *How to Win Friends and Influence People,* and now I would see for myself if any of his advice worked. They were cordial and asked me to sit down. "I wonder," I said, "if you folks would help me out."

"If we can," the man said pleasantly.

"Well," I said, plunging right in, "as you can probably tell, I'm a farmer and I'm still in overalls, in a lot of ways. I want to please all you folks but I'm not sure exactly what you want. Are there any suggestions you have? Any ideas?" (That had been one of Carnegie's main points: "If you want to make a friend of someone, ask for his help or advice.")

Immediately the man leaned forward and said very positively, "Yes, I *do* have a suggestion. Start playing songs we recognize, like 'Margie' or 'Whispering.'" He gestured impatiently. "You've been playing a lot of tunes that don't make sense to my wife or me. We can't dance to them." I nodded and mentally decided to limit the number of plug songs from then on. "And then," he continued, "loosen up a little. Be more friendly and talk with the audience. We like that." I thanked him with genuine feeling and we parted with smiles as I went back to the bandstand after intermission.

Later, as they danced around the floor to our newly-inspired version of "Margie," we beamed at each other, and I had a sudden flash of inspiration. Leaning down, I said to the man, "I wonder if you would care to lead the band for a while, and let me have a dance with your good wife here?" He looked delighted, and immediately hopped up on the bandstand and flailed away in front of the orchestra while I waltzed off with his wife. I have since discovered there's a little ham in most everyone, and most people enjoy leading the band. Sammy Kaye adopted the idea for a national radio program, but I believe we were the first ones to do it back in those Edgewater days.

As it turned out, that was the right thing to do. Carnegie was right. My new friends stopped by the manager's office that night to say that since I was trying so hard I really ought to be given more of a chance; the manager wasn't in, but they wrote a note and slipped it under his door. Our engagement was saved—at least temporarily.

From then on I concentrated on playing the kind of music we had been used to playing. I found out all over again that people everywhere who liked to dance had one thing in common, whether they danced in an empty garage in Coldwater, Kansas, or in the most ornate ballroom in the country. They wanted music with a good strong rhythmic beat and a tune they recognized. They did not want a mixture of second-rate melodies which were unfamiliar to them. It was a costly lesson for me to learn, however. When we opened at the Edgewater we had been established as a $500 per night band. Those first few disastrous weeks of floundering around with the song pluggers weakened our reputation so badly that I felt lucky to get $250 by the time we left.

Something had to be done, and it had to be done fast if we were to reestablish our reputation. I told Bill and L. A. to get us booked into the Chicago Theater, even if we had to play there for nothing. They finally arranged the booking at our regular salary of seventeen hundred and fifty dollars a week and we opened to tremendous crowds, because the Chicago was also playing a highly successful Bette Davis movie! People waited in line clear around the block to see the movie, and Bill took pictures of the crowds outside in such a way that my name on the marquee was also displayed, and it looked as if they were pushing and shoving to get in to see us. Those pictures helped set up many a future booking.

That Chicago engagement in 1939 was a breathing spell for me. It gave me time for a reassessment of our progress,

I Talk!

and I got some of my old self-confidence back. We went back to playing our own style, the thing we did best, and I retreated again behind the accordion and hired a master of ceremonies to do the announcing chores. I realized that some day I would have to talk, but with the miserable experience at the Edgewater still fresh in my mind I felt I wasn't quite ready.

One afternoon, however, I had a caller backstage. He introduced himself as Eddie Weisfeldt, the manager of the Riverside Theater in Milwaukee, Wisconsin.

"I like your show very much, Lawrence," he said, as he sat down in my dressing room. "But tell me something. Why do you sit up there in the back row playing your accordion with the rest of the band? That just doesn't make sense to me. Why don't you come down onstage and be your own master of ceremonies?"

"Well," I said, "just listen to me. That's why I don't do it. I can't talk. Nobody can understand me."

"I can understand you," he said quietly. "And the audience likes to hear a bandleader talk. Now look," he added, "Henry Busse talks. Phil Spitalny talks. And you can't accuse them of speaking the King's English."

"Yes, but . . . my accent is so thick . . . and I'm not always sure of my words. Besides," I told him, "I already tried it at the Edgewater Beach. It didn't work."

He grinned. "So I heard. But Lawrence, I really think you should try it again. It would add a great deal to your show. In fact I think you'll have to do it, if you expect to become an established personality." He looked at me searchingly. "I think you should give it one more try."

I shook my head regretfully. The Riverside was a top house, and I knew it would help us to appear there, but I just didn't have enough confidence in my ability to speak, and again I told this to Mr. Weisfeldt.

He nodded. "All right," he said. "But think it over. Think about what I've said." He put on his coat, picked up his hat and started to leave, but just at the door he stopped, half-turned, and then said casually, almost over his shoulder, "And Lawrence, if you do change your mind, let me know. You're worth thirty-five hundred dollars a week to me—if you'll talk."

My jaw dropped. "What did you say! Did I hear you right?"

He was smiling broadly and his eyes twinkled. "You heard me! I said thirty-five hundred a week."

"Mr. Weisfeldt," I said, with sudden overwhelming resolve, "for that amount—I'll talk!"

And I did. It was agonizing for me at first and I made mistakes constantly. One time I introduced my orchestra as the Shampoo Music Makers, instead of the Champagne Music Makers, and it was not unusual for me to bring singers up to the "microscope" instead of the microphone. That didn't bother me nearly so much as the times I said something which made perfect sense to me, but everybody in the audience burst into laughter. Those were times when I wanted to crawl under the piano with embarrassment. But somehow I got through that week and managed to introduce all the numbers, and as the days went by I got a little better. Not much, but I kept at it and things did get a little easier for me. The relief I felt whenever I had finished speaking was overwhelming, and I think I played the accordion better then, than at any other time in my life. It was such a wonderful feeling to get back to doing what I did best that I practically danced across the stage when I played.

Mr. Weisfeldt was a great influence on my life. He helped me in many ways, not only by encouraging me to speak, but also by teaching me how to dress better and learn some of the manners and niceties of everyday living. For years I had been dressing in the flashy clothes I had worn in my Peerless Entertainers days. I look at pictures of myself in one suit I particularly enjoyed wearing, and I marvel that I ever had the courage to wear it. It had broad blue and gold stripes nearly three inches wide—and I wore a fancy vest and bowler hat to go with it. I had had a dressmaker in Yankton make it up for me, and I thought it was really something. Mr. Weisfeldt diplomatically suggested that I tone things down a little, and wear sports clothes in the daytime and dark suits at night. "And get your clothes fitted, Lawrence," he told me. "It will pay you in the long run to get your clothes tailored. You have a nice physique. Show it off a little."

He tried to build up my self-confidence in speaking by having several ladies call and compliment me on my "thrilling" voice. I was very flattered and it did help my morale until a lady called and overdid it a little. "I just saw your show and you have *such* a manly voice," she gushed. "I love it!"

"Why thank you very much," I smirked. "But really, I don't think I can compare with those other band leaders."

"Oh, yes you can!" she cried. "Honestly, you're just as good as Jan Garber!"

Well, I liked and admired Jan Garber, who is still a good friend of mine, as well as anybody, but even he would be the first to admit he didn't sound much like Richard Burton. I was disheartened all over again, but by then I had started talking—and I haven't stopped since.

The Edgewater engagement had a profound effect on my life. It reaffirmed my basic instincts as to what constituted good entertainment and made me realize again that the true goal of any performer should be to perform what the audience wants to hear, and not what the performers—or song pluggers!—want to perform. It spurred me into doing something I had been putting off for years: it made me talk. And in spite of our disastrous opening, it established our name firmly in the world of big-name bands. Sometimes at night, when the last show at the Riverside was over and I had gone to my dressing room to pack my briefcase full of the music and memos I carry constantly, all the lights backstage would be going out one by one, till just the work light on stage was left shining. The theater would be dark and empty as I walked out, full of shadows at the back of the house, where an hour earlier there had been crowds of people laughing and applauding. And suddenly I would think to myself, "I did it. I talked!" And I would remember the days on the farm when I hid behind a chair whenever company came to call, and the times I danced around a hayloft with an imaginary partner and pretended to be leading a big orchestra while all the people in the audience laughed and applauded. I realized with a kind of wonder that dreams do come true. Even for someone who couldn't speak English and never had a music lesson or much of an education, dreams do come true. I wished that my mother could see me.

PART THREE

Chicago

13

THE TRIANON

FOM THE RIVERSIDE THEATER WE WENT ON TO PLAY EXTENDED location jobs at various hotels around the country, and while we were playing at the Adolphus Hotel in Dallas, Texas, our son Larry was born on my birthday, March 11, 1940. What a birthday present! Lawrence LeRoy, Jr., was born in the same hospital where Shirley Jean had been born eight years earlier, and we were all delighted. I think I spent every penny I had on me that day sending off wires and phone calls to spread the word. I had been thrilled and happy when the girls were born, of course, and I think there is a special kind of relationship between a father and his daughters, but I must confess that Larry's birth was not quite like anything I had ever felt before. A son! All of us were very happy, and Donna and Shirley were most impressed with their baby brother.

But Larry's birth posed a real problem. I had been aware for some time that traveling on the road was not the ideal way to bring up two little girls. Shirley had already been forced to change schools several times, and every time we packed up and moved, it meant Fern had to drag along all kinds of extra clothes and equipment. Now with an infant son the problems would just be tripled. It wasn't fair to them, and I knew the time had come to settle down somewhere.

I tried to decide what to do about it, and it seemed to me the best solution would be to live in some big city where we could play long engagements at leading hotels or ballrooms and still be able to fulfill one-night stands within an easy traveling radius. New York seemed to offer the most opportunities in some ways, but it also seemed too big and impersonal. I considered Pittsburgh for a while, and also some of the big Southern cities, but I finally decided that Chicago would be the best choice. It was centrally located, it had several big hotels, and the people in the surrounding states had always enjoyed our music. I aimed for a permanent berth in Chicago and I knew just the place I wanted to play. I went in to see Bill Fredericks about it.

"Bill," I said, "I want you to book us into the Trianon."

Bill snorted with laughter. "Forget it! Andrew Karzas has his place booked up solidly for months ahead; he wouldn't give you a tumble.

"Why not?"

"Why should he? He's got every top band in the country playing there whenever he wants them."

"Bill," I said. "I want you to get me a tryout. Let Mr. Karzas hear for himself whether he wants us or not. You can do that, can't you?"

"I don't know," he said doubtfully. "I don't think he'll meet your price."

"Then we'll meet his. I'll play there for nothing for one night if necessary. Just get me the chance to play at least once."

Bill did. In fact, he managed to book us in for one night at our regular price. Mr. Karzas liked what he heard and signed us to a twelve-week contract. I was very happy about it, and hopeful that by the end of that time he would like us well enough to sign us to a permanent contract. I moved Fern and the girls and the baby into a small apartment on the South Side of Chicago, and the boys and I went to work with everything we had to secure the engagement. If Mr. Karzas liked us, the future looked limitless.

He liked us enough to offer us a permanent, year-round job which permitted us to play for months at a time at the Trianon, or its sister ballroom across town, the Aragon, with time out for a yearly cross-country tour. For the first time in a long time we had real security and a chance to settle down and live a normal home life, plus the prestige of playing in a top ballroom. I felt as if I had just scaled a mountain or gotten safely across a wild and dangerous stream. All of us in the band could relax for a while now and enjoy our music and our life and our own families. In many ways, the next ten years in Chicago were the happiest ones of our lives.

It was a pleasure to play at the Trianon, which was probably the most beautiful ballroom ever built in America. The owner, Andrew Karzas, a dark-eyed man of Greek extraction, had spared no expense in decorating it, and I often thought that even the original Trianon Palace in France couldn't have been any prettier. The huge dance floor was oval in shape and constructed of the finest hardwood. Columns of imported Italian marble surrounded the floor and swags of heavy satin, outlined in silk braid and gold tassels, hung between the pillars. The wide promenade surrounding the dance floor was covered with a thick carpet woven with a sort of fleur-de-lis design in it, and there were hundreds of gilt armchairs set along the wall. Narrow mirrors hung between each of the windows, which were draped in satin to match the stage curtains, and the whole room was lighted by recessed spotlights set into a carved and gilded ceiling. There were even box seats in an upper gallery, also covered with Italian marble and decorated with gold leaf. It was a truly impressive sight. Actually Karzas was a hard-headed businessman who understood that all of this was merely trappings, and that the important thing was the music and the feeling of personal communication between the orchestra and the audience.

He explained all this to me one day not long after I had started playing there. We had lunch together, and afterward Mr. Karzas set his cup of coffee down decisively and said, "Lawrence, I want to tell you something. You've often mentioned how beautiful this ballroom is. And you're right, it is. But that's not the important thing." He leaned across the table and tapped slowly to emphasize his words. "The important thing is that the kids who come in here to dance will go home and tell their friends the next day that they got your autograph." He peered at me sharply from under his thick brows. "You can establish more goodwill, and build up your band more quickly, by spending a little time out there autographing and talking with your audience, than you can in any other way. It's important for you to understand that." He leaned back in his chair and went on to explain some of the other fine points in the music business, and I listened intently, because he was by all odds the most successful ballroom operator in the country. Everything he said made sense, and when I went home that night I said to Fern, "I had lunch today with one of the smartest men I've ever met."

I followed all of his suggestions, making a point of signing autographs from then on. Before I had felt that maybe it was egotistical of me even to think anyone would want my autograph, but after Mr. Karzas had explained how much everyone enjoyed that personal touch, I was more than happy to sign. I've spent hours ever since scrawling my name on programs or cocktail coasters or books of matches or even beer-stained napkins, . . . and I can honestly say I have enjoyed it. It seems like very little to do for people who have spent both time and money to come and see you, and I have never been able to understand those who refuse to sign autographs.

Karzas was right about most things, but occasionally even he made mistakes. He didn't like the Champagne Lady I had at the time—Jayne Walton—and, for some reason, he didn't like Jerry Burke either. "That organ he plays sounds too tinny," he complained. "A piano would be better." He told me to let both of them go, but I felt very strongly about them myself. Jayne had a beautiful voice. I had heard her originally on my car radio, singing over Station WOW in Omaha, and had been so impressed I had wired her an offer to join the band. And I felt that Jerry and his musicianship added a great deal to our group, too. So when Mr. Karzas gave me his ultimatum, I decided to try a little strategy of my own.

Karzas had given me two weeks to make the change, but during that time I used both Jerry and Jayne on every radio broadcast we had. I believe we were doing twelve a week at the time over WGN in Chicago. I had Jayne sing a song which she sang especially well in Spanish, "Marie Elena," on each broadcast. She had been born in Mexico and had lived there the first eight years of her life, so her accent was perfect. Before long people were clamoring for her to sing it every night. Her version had a lot to do with the song's popularity in those years. I also featured Jerry in several solos during that time, and he got much the same reaction. Just before the two weeks were up, Karzas called me into his office.

"Welk," he said quickly, "did you fire those two? Jayne and that organist fellow?"

"No I didn't, Mr. Karzas," I said, waiting for the explosion to follow.

"Well, don't," he said grinning. "Keep them on. They're both good. I must have made a mistake."

Right there I had learned the value of exposure, and it was a lesson that would come in handy during our television days ahead. By simply allowing people to hear more and more of a good talent I had built up a definite desire for it, and both Jayne and Jerry remained great favorites with our group.

Jayne didn't fit in with the popular notion of the glossy girl band singer of the day. That had been one of Karzas's main objections to her. When he first told me to fire her, he curved his hands through the air, drawing a feminine outline and said, "She just doesn't *look* like a girl singer." But she had great charm. She was Irish, with sparkling eyes and a ready wit, and of all the Champagne Ladies we ever had she was the one who was closest to my family. I used to describe my ideal girl singer as "A sweetheart to all . . . a sweetheart to none," and Jayne fit that to perfection.

She could tell instantly when somebody in the band was feeling blue. "Come on," she'd say, "you haven't taken me out to dinner for a long time. Let's go!" And before he knew what had happened, some lonely saxophone or trumpet player would find himself pouring out all his troubles into Jayne's sympathetic ear. Even without his being aware of it, she had cheered him up for the evening. Sometimes she would quietly pay for the dinner herself.

She and I joked constantly. When she first joined the show, she used to fall for some of my teasing, but she soon got on to my tall stories and would just say wearily, "Okay, Welk, cut it out. I've heard that one before. You'll have to come up with something better than that." She did a good deal of driving from one town to another on our one-night stands. "I really love to drive," she told me one time. "Listening to all you guys snore is so much better than listening to you yakking all the time." She was joking—I think—but all of us felt that same kind of magic when we took our turn driving through the quiet countryside in the middle of the night, with time to reflect while everyone else in the car was sleeping soundly.

I was a great one for marking out shortcuts on road maps, and I used to give Jayne all kinds of instructions just before I dozed off. "Oh you!" said Jayne furiously one time, "you and your shortcuts! How come we always land in town hours after everybody else in the band has arrived?" I was convinced that my shortcuts made sense and so I kept trying to use them; on the nights I felt especially exhausted I'd mark the map very carefully with all kinds of notes and directions and then say to Jayne, "Now if I get sleepy, would you please drive for a while?" The minute I said that, Jayne would reach silently for her cosmetic bag and begin rolling her hair up on curlers, "So I won't look dead when we arrive in the morning."

One time after I had turned the driving over to her and gone to sleep, the car came to a sudden stop, jolting me awake. I turned, rather dazed, to see Jayne sitting reflectively behind the wheel, gazing at me with a "Well-Welk-you've-done-it-again," look on her face.

"What's the matter?" I asked, trying to wake up.

"Oh, nothing," she said airily. "Only I just don't feel like swimming right now."

"Swimming? What do you mean?"

"Don't you hear anything?" she asked rather tartly.

"Like, say, the waters of Minnetonka? You don't? Well, open up your big dumb ears and listen!"

I listened. Sure enough, I could hear the slap of waves outside, and when I looked I saw a heavy chain strung across the roadway in front of the car, and a dimly lighted sign which read, "Next Ferry: Seven A.M." I looked at my watch. It was then four o'clock.

"Oh my," I said. "Jayne, I'm sorry."

She burst out laughing and slid the car into reverse. "Some shortcut! Well, never mind. I'll just cut back to the main highway. Maybe we'll beat the rest of them into town this time."

She was always a wonderful sport about our traveling, even though she complained that MCA, who booked our tours, must do so by throwing darts blindfolded at a map on the wall. "Wherever it lands, that's where we play, just so long as it's only three hundred miles from nowhere." One time, after a particularly long haul, we were nearing Norfolk, Nebraska, at about five-thirty in the morning. I was driving and Jayne was trying unsuccessfully to sleep against the rising crescendo of snores from the back seat. "Oh, how did I ever get into this silly business," she moaned. "I'm *so* exhausted! What I wouldn't give for a nice soft bed right now."

"Oh, is that all you want," I said expansively. "Well, I know this farmer right over here. We'll just stop in and he'll probably be glad to let you sleep in the spare room for a while."

Jayne looked annoyed. "Oh, for goodness sake, stop it! You think every farmer in the world is your friend."

"Well they are! And besides, I know this farmer. Really I do."

"Uh-huh. And I know the Queen of England." She settled down lower in the front seat and tried to go to sleep on the back of her neck. She *did* look exhausted, and on a sudden impulse I wheeled the car around at the next intersection and headed back up the road to the farmhouse we had just passed.

Jayne sat up straight. "Now what are you doing?"

"I'm going to ask this fellow to let you sleep for a while."

Jayne exploded, "Lawrence! You can't just go driving into some farmer's yard and ask . . . "

Before she got the words out of her mouth, I had turned off the highway and up the dirt road toward the barn, where a farmer in striped overalls was busy milking cows. He straightened up as I approached and peered through the early morning gloom. "Why, Lawrence," he shouted, "for goodness sake! What a nice surprise! What are you doing here! Come on in. Mary will fix you some breakfast."

Jayne's jaw dropped. "What do you know," she muttered. "You do know him!"

Harry Kirstein of Hooper, Nebraska, was an old friend of mine who had come to hundreds of my dances over the years. He didn't dance himself, but he was a good critic (and a blunt one, too) and he always told me what the folks really enjoyed. He promptly offered Jayne a chance to sleep if she wished, and then we all went into the house where pretty Mary Kirstein was busy fixing breakfast. She was just as friendly and gracious as Harry was, and Jayne couldn't get over our pleasant reception, especially at that hour in the morning. After a while she asked Mary where the ladies' room was. "Well, it's just where it's always been," said Mary lightly. "Right out there behind the barn!" Jayne thanked her and trudged off, throwing me a dirty look over her shoulder as she left. She never did like "privies," as she called them.

When Jayne returned she went off to the spare room, and a couple of the other fellows and I drove on into town to attend early Mass. By the time we had returned and helped Harry with a few of his chores it was noon, and Jayne got up feeling much refreshed after her long nap. Mary Kirstein insisted we stay for lunch—and what food! Chicken, pork, and homemade bread and fresh-churned butter along with preserves and all kinds of fresh vegetables. Jayne was sparkling with wit and good humor by then and she began to eat a chicken leg with great relish. Suddenly the wind changed, blowing in right over the open hog pens outside and straight through the open screen doors and windows right to where we were eating. Jayne got one whiff and stopped chewing, practically in mid-bite. Then she put her chicken leg back down on her plate and sat there turning greener and greener as the heady fumes from the hog pens filled the room. She had her mouth full and I could see she was having a terrible time trying to get that chicken down, but finally she did, giving me one agonized, accusing stare as she gulped and swallowed. She continued to sit there looking very small and quiet for the rest of the lunch; and she never said another word until after we were back in the car and some of her normal color and spirit had returned. Then she said thoughtfully, "You know, Welk, you told me when I joined your band that I would be the Champagne Lady. Hah! Some Champagne Lady! Listen. I will stay in this glamorous orchestra of yours under two conditions only. No more outside plumbing. And *no more hog pens.*"

Of course I couldn't guarantee that, as Jayne well knew, but she stayed with us for several more years. She often came to visit us at home and we spent many happy times together.

Fern and the children and I all enjoyed our new home, a two-story brick building in the River Forest section of Chicago. I had selected it originally because it was within walking distance of a grammar school, a high school, and Rosary College, but true to her independent spirit, when Shirley reached college age, she decided to go to Marquette University instead. During their growing-up years, though, the children were able to attend St. Vincent Ferrer's grammar school and Trinity High regularly, without a break of any kind—a record for the Welk family.

Fern loved it. At last she was able to put down roots and decorate and keep house to her heart's content. I began to enjoy being a father-in-residence, too. I became very good at mowing the lawn and working in the yard, but I managed never to master things like fixing leaky faucets or repairing broken light fixtures. Years before, my father had finally given up on my ever learning how to work a blacksmith forge, and Fern finally gave up expecting me to become a handyman. The simplest household repairs always seemed to baffle me, and they still do. On the other hand, Fern got to be an expert at them.

The children were a great joy to me as they grew up. Fern was the disciplinarian in the family, because it was almost impossible for me to mete out justice very strictly. I always "talked" to the children, and I remember Donna once rolling her eyes to heaven and imploring, "Oh Daddy, please! Just spank me instead!" But I could never do that. I always gave them a warning the first time they misbehaved, pointing out exactly why what they had done was wrong, and explaining that they could expect a stiffer punishment if they repeated it. I gave them a second warning, too, but the third time I clamped down and punished them by taking away some privilege they particularly enjoyed. I always gave them their choice of punishments, and they were scrupulously fair about picking a punishment to fit the crime, frequently choosing a much stiffer penalty than I would have. This system of talking nearly always worked with me and I rarely had to go beyond the second warning—although I do recall one time when my patience snapped and I actually spanked two of them.

I was out mowing the lawn, trying to work out a musical arrangement in my head at the same time, when Donna and Larry got into a noisy argument behind me. They kept it up so long I finally stopped mowing, turned around, and gave them lecture Number One. They promised to stop, but two minutes later the fight was on again, with much shrieking and shouting and threats of terrible reprisal. I was very irritated and did a little shouting myself. "Donna! Larry!" I said sternly. "Stop that fighting this minute. If you don't stop, I'll be forced to spank you!" Since that had never happened before this didn't impress them very much and I barely had time to turn around and start mowing before they were at it again.

Now I had to carry out my threat, and so I spanked them, although, as my daughter Donna reminds me, "Spanked! Dad, all you did was have us hold our hands out, and then you slapped them a teeny little bit." Nevertheless the fact remained that I had struck two of my children, and all three of us were so appalled at this unusual behavior that we very nearly all burst into tears. Donna and Larry went sobbing and screaming into the house, straight to the kitchen where Fern was working. "Mother, Mother, Daddy hit me, he hit me!" shrieked Donna, sobbing as though her heart would break, and Larry was bellowing loudly, too. I stood outside listening to all the sobs and chokes, and the comforting, "There . . . there's" from Fern, and I felt terrible. I couldn't believe I had lost my temper to the extent that I had actually struck my own children, and the louder and longer they cried, the worse I felt. I couldn't stand it. I called to them to come back out into the yard. "Here," I said, wiping Donna's tear-streaked little face with my handkerchief, "here's fifty cents for each of you. Go buy yourself some goodies. And please, don't cry like that!"

Their tears stopped instantly, and Donna hurled herself into my arms. "Oh, Daddy, you're the best Daddy. Oh, I love you," she crooned, clutching me tight around the waist. Larry beamed like the sun and dashed back to the kitchen where, Fern told me later, he informed her that from then on he wanted to be punished by me instead of her. "Boy, Larry and I thought we had really stumbled onto a gold mine that time," remembers Donna. "But it never happened again. We couldn't get Daddy to spank us anymore."

I just couldn't do it; Fern was in charge of that department. She did a wonderful job with all the children. She was always so gentle and loving with them, but they knew she meant what she said, and there was never any question in their mind as to what was the right or wrong thing to do. Actually, the children were always extremely cooperative with us, and gave us many hours of deep pleasure, as they and their own children still do today.

14

MOTHER

It was in Pittsburgh that I got the telegram. "Come home at once. Mother is dying." I stood holding the telegram in my hands, sick at heart, remembering a thousand things all at once. How gentle she was, how kind, the way her hair curled around her face when she was flushed from dancing, the way she sat so straight in church holding her prayer book, the soft way she called me "Lawrencell." I felt so guilty, because I knew she had been ill with diabetes for some time, and even though I had tried to get home and see her as often as I could, I knew I hadn't gotten there often enough. The last time I had talked to my sister Agatha she had said, "Mama wants to see you, Lawrence. Come home as soon as you can."

And now maybe it was too late. But I felt I had to try and see her. We were playing on tour at the Kennywood Amusement Park at the time and I went in to the manager and explained the situation to him. He was sympathetic. "Go ahead, Lawrence. You can fly in and see her and probably be back for the show tomorrow night."

I threw some things in a bag and drove quickly out to the airport. The weather was bad and the fog blowing in from the Ohio River grew progressively heavier as I drove. When I arrived, the man at the ticket desk said, "I'm sorry, Mr. Welk. All the planes have been grounded for a while. There'll be an indefinite delay."

I sat down to wait, and in spite of myself my eyes filled with tears. I longed to see my mother one more time and tell her how much she meant to me. None of us in our family had ever been very good at expressing ourselves verbally; instead, we had shown by our actions how we felt about each other. My mother had shown us more love than any human being could rightfully expect. I loved her, and I wanted to tell her so.

I paced the floor of the airport for a while, watching the fog grow thicker and thicker, clustering around the dim lights on the runway until they were blacked out entirely. Finally the manager came over to me and said, "There's no use staying, Mr. Welk. All the planes are grounded for the night. You can't possibly get out of here now."

I got into my car and drove slowly back to town, much of the time with the door open so I could see more clearly where I was going. I had just gotten into bed in my hotel room when I heard the telephone shrill. And I knew before I answered, what it was.

It was my brother John. "Mother just slept away very peacefully," he told me. "We were all here with her."

I couldn't answer him. "Are you there?" he asked me finally.

"Yes. Yes I am, John. I tried to come home, but all the planes are grounded here."

"Yes, I know," he said. "We heard about the weather. Don't try to come home, Lawrence. It's too dangerous. I'll keep in touch with you."

He hung up, and I felt like a small boy again. Both my parents were gone, and even though I hadn't seen either of them very often in the past few years, I felt as if a whole piece of my life had died with them. My childhood, all the things they had spent so many years teaching me, all the kindness and goodness they had shown me, was all gone now. My mind was full of memories that night and I was very lonely.

I was unable to get home for the funeral services. I knew they would be held at St. Peter and Paul's Church, which had been such a big part of my mother's life. I knew that my brothers and sisters and all the grandchildren would be there, and the priest who knew her so well would speak the words of the Faith she loved so much. I could not truly weep for my mother, whose whole life was a living testimony to the faith she believed in, but I did weep—I guess for myself—for the next three days. I stood on the bandstand at the amusement park and smiled and played the accordion while the tears just rolled down my face. I couldn't seem to stop them. I could not help remembering that if it hadn't been for my mother I would never have gotten an accordion in the first place. I would never have been able to realize so many of the youthful dreams which had seemed so unattainable to everyone else but her.

I owed so much to her, and I hadn't been able to tell her at the end how much I loved her. And now I never would.

15

EXPENSIVE UNDERWEAR AND A LADY DRUMMER

THE TRIANON BECAME OUR HOME BASE DURING THE FORTIES, and one of the features I recall most vividly there was the "Battle of the Bands." The Trianon had a side stage in addition to the main bandstand, so that two bands could take turns playing, vying for top honors from the crowd. Each band played a set of three numbers, and the winner was decided by applause. Dick Jurgens used to win almost all these contests hands down, until Guy Lombardo came along and unseated him with a particularly cunning trick. Lombardo would play the first two numbers with his usual great style, but on the third one he would go all out, playing with great rhythm and excitement and building to a rousing climax. He would start to wind up just as the curtains began pulling to a close, and invariably the crowd would start screaming "No! No! More! More!" The curtain would have to be pulled open again to thunderous applause and cheers. "I can't compete against that!" said Jurgens ruefully, shaking his head after Lombardo disposed of him that first time. Over the long haul, though, Jurgens was an easy winner, particularly where I was concerned. I rarely won those band battles. During my years in the Midwest as a territory band, I had frequently played against Tiny Little and His Toe Teasers. Mr. Little was the father of Big Tiny Little,

My mother, Christina Schwahn Welk, and my father, Ludwig Welk. Pictures taken about the turn of the century.

The farm, where I first discovered I would rather work the bellows of the accordion than those of the blacksmith forge (center building).

I don't know which was the worst title: "Lawrence Welk and his Hotsy Totsy Boys," "Welk's Novelty Orchestra," or "Lawrence Welk and his Honolulu Fruit Orchestra"! The boys complained about all three.

George T. Kelly, of The Peerless Entertainers . . . and my peerless friend and teacher.

"America's Biggest Little Band." (You can see why they quit me!)

Advertising poster for my first big job with Lincoln Boulds. "Sensational Lawrence" looks scared to death . . . and to tell the truth, I was!

Featuring America's Foremost Dance ACCORDIONIST presenting New Rhythms

Known from Coast to Coast Through the Presentations of His "America's Biggest Little Band"

Now! Offers You the Biggest and Best Band of His Entire Musical Career

LAWRENCE WELK·

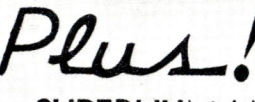

Plus! SUPERHUMAN Instrumental Performance Acts Rendered by the Accredited Originators Thereof

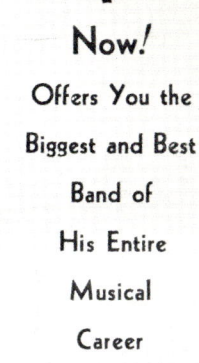

—ADDRESS ALL COMMUNICATIONS TO—
MIDDLEWEST BROKERAGE CORPORATION
GENERAL OFFICE
· YANKTON, SOUTH DAKOTA ·

That's Leo Fortin playing two trumpets at once and Terry George doing a rousing version of "Nola" with his foot. These two always stopped the show.

My first "location" job, at Eddie Ott's Broadmoor Club in Denver, Colorado. After that, the one-night stands seemed much harder. Left to right: Charlie Coffee, Merle Lawrence, Gordon Mayley, Al Storer, and Izzy King.

On a state highway near Yankton, South Dakota, with Cliff Moe, standing on top of our sleeper bus. You can see why those one-night stands weren't always pure pleasure!

Lois Best, who was the first official Champagne Lady . . . and obviously one of the "best"!

Tom Archer, the famous ballroom owner, who kept pulling me out of the hole all during the thirties. A dear friend.

On the stage of the Italian Terrace Room in the William Penn Hotel in Pittsburgh, Pennsylvania, in 1938 . . . the place where Champagne Music was born. Jerry Burke at the organ, Jules Herman second from right, back row.

The beautiful Trianon Ballroom in Chicago where we played for almost ten years. (The side stage, barely visible at the left, is where visiting bands would engage us in a "Battle of the Bands." We usually lost!)

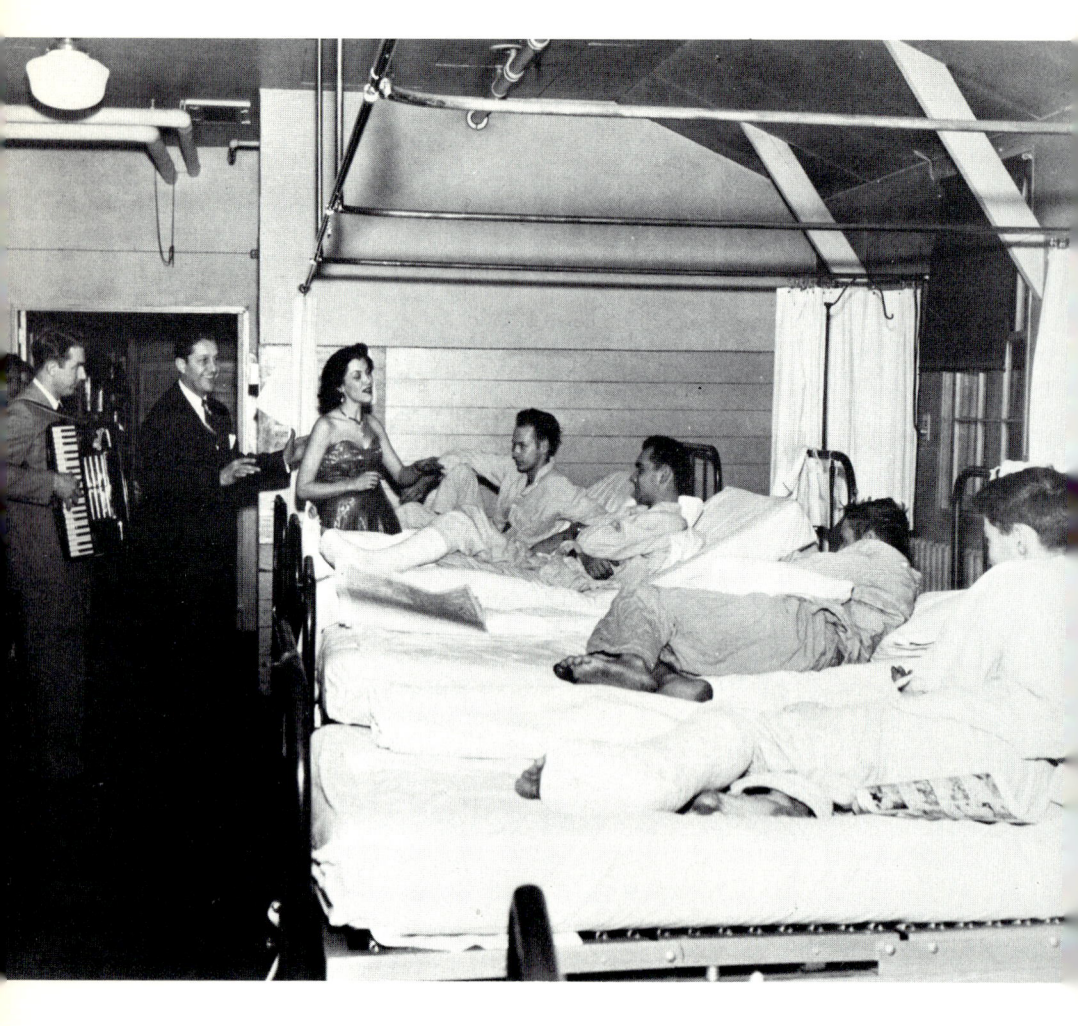

Myron Floren, Roberta Linn, and I entertaining at an Army Hospital near Denver, during our years touring for the Miller High Life Revue.

Champagne Lady Alice Lon and I cutting capers at the Aragon during our very early days of televising. That's Bob Lido, Dick Kesner, and Aladdin in the string section at my left.

With Fern and the children when we were living in River Forest, Illinois, in 1945.

Our lovely Irish Champagne Lady, Jayne Walton, with pianist-comic, Tommy Sheridan, at the Trianon in Chicago. The Irish and the Germans got along very well!

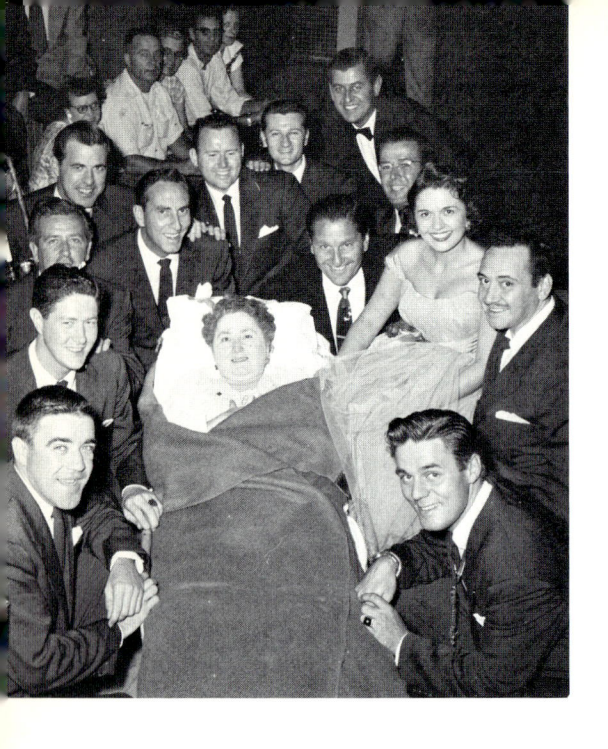

Edna Stoner, my pen pal from Beresford, South Dakota, with the Champagne Music Makers. . . . after a performance at the Corn Palace, in Mitchell, South Dakota.

A surprise appearance on "This is Your Life" in 1957. Ralph Edwards at left, The Lennon Sisters, Kathy, Dianne, Janet, Peggy, my son Larry, and my daughter Donna. Chuck Coffey, who played in the band during the thirties, is visible at rear.

who later played rag-time piano on our television show, and he had one of the best and most popular bands in the area, playing with a pounding, powerful, irresistible kind of rhythm. He always beat me. In fact, he was so good I almost gave up my own band and went to work for him. One time when the Music Makers and I played a personal appearance at the Arcota Ballroom in Sioux Falls, Tiny came to visit us. I introduced him to the crowd and told them how he always used to beat me. "Yes," said Tiny, "I always won. But look at Lawrence now. I'm beginning to think I lost."

So many memories come flooding back to me from those Trianon years. Jayne continued to sing Spanish songs; "Noche De Ronda" was one of them. The combination of Irish Jayne singing Spanish songs with a German bandleader in melting-pot Chicago turned out to be a good one. Trianon audiences loved her. But mainly the Trianon audiences came to dance. Some of those dancers were good enough to be of professional caliber. It was the custom, during those years, for groups of boys and girls to come separately, as well as on dates, and many a lifetime romance began with a tag dance at the Trianon. Some nights we had a predominantly Polish audience, and how that big room would come to life then! The Polish polka is very fast, very quick, and requires tremendous endurance. Watching from the stage as the dancers bobbed up and down, it used to look to me as if the whole floor were on springs.

By 1941 the whole country was involved in World War II, and we began to play a great many shows at the army and navy bases around Chicago, in addition to our Trianon dances. The army liaison man in charge of these performances was a slim and energetic young fellow named Sam Lutz. Sam, who is just as energetic but not quite so slim today, says, "Lawrence and the Music Makers never turned me down, and I could always count on him if one of the other stars backed out at the last minute. And he never asked me for Kleenex or butter or anything else which was in short supply or available only at army supply houses. He just did the best he could to help."

I was surprised when Sam mentioned this to me. It never occurred to me that anyone would want to barter off a performance in return for some of the things which were rationed in those years. I was past the age for being called into service and felt that entertaining was the least we could do.

Whenever we had a spare moment, Jayne and I would go alone to entertain at the hospital wards. This was always so hard to do, and it was particularly hard for Jayne. We'd go through a ward with me playing the accordion while Jayne cracked jokes and sang. The minute we finished, she'd rush out into the hospital corridor and double up with sobs. "Oh, I can't help it," she wept one day. "All those boys keep telling me about when we played at dances in their home towns, and half of them will never even walk again. I just don't think I can *do* this!" It was very difficult for her, but after a moment she'd dry her eyes and straighten up, and then breeze into the next ward, smiling brightly and telling jokes and singing. None of the boys would ever know she'd been in tears a moment before.

We began to work out a schedule of playing for most of the year at the Trianon, and then traveling cross-country for a month. A 1942 schedule I've kept in our files gives some idea of the kind of touring we did. We opened at the Ritz Ballroom in Bridgeport, Connecticut, on March 8 of that year, played March 9 and 10 in New York, opened March 11 in Altoona, Pennsylvania, March 13 in Milwaukee, March 17 in Dubuque, Iowa, March 18 in Sioux City, Iowa, March 20 to 26 at the Tower Theater in Kansas City, March 27 to 29 at the Iowa Theater in Cedar Rapids, April 1 to 4 at the Crystal Ballroom in Coloma, Michigan, April 5 for one night at the Trianon in Chicago, April 6 at the Modernistic Ballroom in Clinton, Iowa, and back April 7 to begin another long run at the Trianon again. No wonder Jayne said MCA threw darts at the wall. Connecticut to Kansas is a long haul.

Every time I look at that particular schedule, it seems to me that the words "Tower Theater, Kansas City" leap at me in great big letters. Of all the engagements we have ever played, I think the Tower Theater must rank as the worst, or close to it. I always had trouble in Kansas City. The first time I ever appeared there was with a six-piece band very early in my career. I played an engagement at Will Wittig's Playmore Ballroom. Curt Massey, later musical director for the Petticoat Junction television series in Hollywood, had the house band at the Playmore then, and it was wonderful. Not only that—it was big! There were about fifteen pieces in the group, and when I first saw that great big orchestra sitting onstage and realized that my pitifully small little band would have to follow it, my heart sank down into my shoes. I almost backed out then and there. I guess I really should have, because the contrast between Curt's big band and our little sextet was just too much and we went down to defeat. I always felt bad about that, and a few years later, when Bill Fredericks arranged a booking for us at the Muehlbach Hotel in Kansas City, I was delighted, hopeful that we could erase the memory of our first failure there. But that whole booking fell through at the last minute, and I never got the chance to try, so when we received a bid to appear at the Tower, I was determined to play a highly successful engagement and "make" it in Kansas City at last!

We played Sioux City, Iowa, just before we left for Kansas City, and while we were there Leo came rushing up to my hotel room in great excitement, "Listen, Lawrence, I've got a friend in the lobby downstairs and he's got the greatest dog act I've ever seen in my life. I think he'd be wonderful for the Tower Theater. Come on down and take a look!" I went downstairs and watched while the trainer put the dog through its paces. He was a great big shaggy-haired spaniel of some kind and he ambled through all his tricks very well. I was such a soft touch where animals were concerned that I hired the act on the spot to go along with us to Kansas City. I had a few other acts with us at that time, too. I believe we had a juggler and I know we had another accordionist. He had a novelty act and he was really very good. He had tricked up his accordion so that when he played a wild version of the William Tell Overture the silver nameplate on the front of it sprang up and smacked him in the face, and when he played a soulful rendition of "Smoke Gets in Your Eyes," smoke poured out of the instrument. Audiences loved it, and although I was a little jealous, I was really happy to have him, because my main concern was to put on a good show.

As soon as we arrived in Kansas City, I went out to check the theater, and when I was still almost a block away I stopped short. There was a big crush of people waiting in a double line clear around the block outside of the theater where my name was prominently displayed on the marquee. I stood watching this lovely and unexpected sight for quite a while, grinning happily. With that many people standing in line so early in the morning to buy tickets, I felt sure we'd be making a good deal of money, so when I saw a men's clothing store nearby with a big "Sale" sign plastered all across the front of it, I decided to celebrate in advance by stocking up on some shirts and underwear I needed. I was so happy about the big crowd that I bought enough underwear to outfit a whole platoon, and then I headed for the theater where I could get a closer look.

A few feet away I stopped dead, almost paralyzed with shock. Just beyond the Tower was another theater, and it was playing a highly popular movie of the day, some sort of sea epic. *That's* what all the people were standing in line for! Nobody was standing in line at the Tower. In fact, there was nobody at all in the lobby of the Tower, except the cashier, who sat in her little glass booth yawning widely and filing her fingernails. She straightened up and smiled hopefully as I entered the lobby, but when I backed off again without buying a ticket, she shrugged her shoulders and went back to filing her nails. She didn't even recognize me.

I carried my new underwear back to the hotel, wondering if I could return it. I was very worried about our forthcoming engagement and as it turned out, I had every reason to be. It was a disaster from start to finish.

Opening day the curtains parted, and I came bounding out onstage beaming and smiling hopefully, determined to play my best for the audience. But there wasn't any audience. Only about twenty-five people sat out there in that gloomy darkness, and they were so widely separated I didn't know which way to look. I don't know of anything more depressing for a performer than trying to play to an almost empty house, and this one was so empty it almost rattled. Added to that, the mood of this audience was very bad, and an audience-mood is highly important. A happy and expectant audience can make any show brighter, but a depressed, resentful one really gets things off to a bad start. Nearly all of those people were disappointed because most of them had been standing in line for hours to see the movie next door, and they had come in to see us only because their feet hurt, or they were chilled to the bone, or both. They sat in little groups almost daring us to entertain them. We tried, but we certainly didn't do very well. After our opening number, which we played with a great flourish, I finished up with my most dazzling run on the accordion and took a deep bow, but only one man, sitting way in the back of the house, bothered to applaud. Somehow the sound of that one lonely defiant handclap seemed worse than no applause at all. A little shaken, I pulled myself together and went ahead and introduced the juggler and the accordionist. Neither of them did much to improve the situation, but when our great new dog act came on, we managed to sink to a new low.

I don't know whether the dog was disgusted at the size of the audience or came down with a sudden attack of stage fright, but he was just plain awful. Everything he did right in Sioux City he did wrong in Kansas City. He got his tricks mixed up or jumped his cues, and finally he just slumped down in the middle of the stage and refused to do anything at all. I never saw such a bad performance and I wasn't the least bit surprised to find the angry manager waiting for me as I came offstage after the first show. He glowered at me for a moment and then shoved his cigar from one side of his mouth to the other. "Get rid of that dog act," he ordered, "and get rid of it now!"

"Oh, please," I said, "I know he was awful, but I think maybe he was just nervous. That act came clear from Sioux City just to be on the show, and it really is a good little act.

Couldn't you give them one more chance, let them try another performance?"

The manager heaved a sigh and looked at me sourly for a moment, but finally he said, "All right. Once more. But that dog better be better, or . . ." he jerked his thumb over his shoulder, "out he goes!"

"Fine," I said hastily. "Thank you very much. I'm sure he'll be better next time." I was absolutely convinced the dog would be better, because I didn't see how he could be any worse. He was though. He really outdid himself. I didn't think I had ever seen a worse performance the first time around, but this dog was teaching me new things all the time. Not only did he sit down stubbornly in the middle of the stage and refuse to do any tricks at all, but he finally yawned widely and lay down, put his big shaggy head on his paws, and went sound asleep. Furious and red-faced, his trainer stopped begging and pleading and began threatening. Suddenly the dog came to life with a bang and began loping in big wide circles all across the stage, barking at the top of his lungs. He skidded underneath the piano, turned and dashed behind the drums, darted in between his trainer's legs, slid past all of us as we reached out frantically trying to grab him, and finally turned tail and ran yelping into the wings, with his trainer right behind him, looking mad enough to kill.

We all stood frozen for a moment listening to the yelps fade away in the distance, and then I broke into a quick accordion number while the audience, for once, broke into gales of laughter. I caught Leo's eye as we played and he shrugged his shoulders as if to say, "Well, how was I to know the dog was so darn dumb?" We went on to finish the show to continual snickers and muffled giggles from the audience.

We never did recover. That whole week had a kind of madness about it, because in spite of our sparse and discouraging crowds, we had one lady who came every day without fail and sat through every show. She sat right in the front row where none of us could possibly miss her, and she rolled her eyes and shook her head from side to side constantly, and kept saying, "Tsk tsk tsk!" over and over, very loudly. It unnerved us all. "If she can't stand the show so much, why does she keep coming every day?" demanded one of the boys. None of us knew, but all during that miserable week she never missed a single performance—and we gave four a day. Toward the end of the run Leo gave up. "Lawrence," he said white-faced, "I don't care what you say. That woman is driving me crazy. I can't stand it another day. I'm going out and getting a bottle."

He came back with a small bottle of brandy and poured himself a stiff drink. By that time I was so upset myself I said, "Here. Give me some, too," and I tossed down a drink, right in front of his astonished eyes. I don't think he ever got over it. Neither did I. That was the toot of my lifetime.

The brandy didn't help either one of us, or the show. We struggled along, and on the last day we discovered that our faithful visitor was a mental patient whose family sent her to the theater every day to keep her entertained and out of harm's way. We didn't know whether to be insulted or flattered by her daily attentions, but we did know that the show, as a whole, was a dismal flop. I had played the engagement on a percentage basis and I lost $2,200 that week, plus a lot of self-confidence. I realized later that the main reason we had failed was because none of our radio broadcasts had reached the Kansas City area and nobody there had ever heard of us. It made me realize again the power of radio, and of course, in later years, the power of television.

In fact, it wasn't until after we had become established with our national television show that I was finally able to play Kansas City successfully. We filled the huge Civic Auditorium to capacity, and I must say that that particular show was a great personal satisfaction to me. I had finally "made" it in Kansas City, even if it had taken me thirty years to do it.

After that disappointing Tower engagement, I returned to

the Trianon minus $2,200 but loaded down with enough underwear to last me for the next thirty years. That's the most expensive underwear I've ever worn in my life.

I began to think that for every step forward, we took two steps backward. That engagement at the Tower was certainly a big step backward; in fact, it was almost a full retreat! But then we played an engagement at the Oriental Theater in Chicago which was a nice step forward. I was very anxious to succeed there, because we had played an engagement at the Chicago Theater a few years earlier which hadn't been quite so successful, and the memory of it still bothered me. At the time we'd gone into the Chicago, we were accustomed to play the "Clarinet Polka" as our closing number, and it always brought down the house. I danced a spirited polka with the Champagne Lady, while Leo and his fellow trombone player, Terry George, not to be outdone, put down their instruments and danced with each other. Our bass player, Holly Swenson, who was six feet seven inches tall, straddled his fiddle like a horse and galloped across the stage while one of the other boys followed along behind him with a broom and shovel. Johnny Reese, our drummer, grabbed another bass fiddle and staggered all over stage balancing it on his chin. All of us did something unusual, and the audience just loved it. We always had to do at least one encore. But the producer at the Chicago didn't like it. "Corny," he said, wrinkling his nose the first time he viewed it. "That has to go. Now I'll buy the 'Clarinet Polka.' That's okay; you're known for that. But the rest of that corn"—he made a face—"forget it! We'll use our line of girls instead."

"But our audiences have always loved this number," I protested. "We always get a lot of requests for it."

He looked at me for a moment and then began speaking very slowly and distinctly, as if he were explaining something very simple to a small, very dumb child. "It . . . is . . . corny," he said. "Chicago . . . is . . . a . . . big city. The people will not like it. Now you just play the number straight and we'll use the line of girls." When I started to speak he held up his hand and said sharply, "I'm the boss here and we'll do it my way."

I was very unhappy about it but, after all, he was the producer and I was in no position to argue with him, so we did as he said. And the number just lay there. Even before the curtains came to a close the audience was out of their seats and halfway up the aisle, and there was just a smattering of applause. For the first time in our history the "Clarinet Polka" just lay there and died. I didn't say anything, but it taught me a lesson. Nobody knows all there is to know about everything. The producer of that theater knew a great deal about some things, but he didn't know what worked best for us. And so by the time we were offered a booking at the Oriental I had sufficient confidence in my own judgment to accept it, provided I could produce the show myself. We worked out a deal whereby I was paid a flat guarantee of $6,500 plus fifty percent of the gross, and I went to work to put together the best show I could.

I hired some extra acts, and my star attraction that time was a young performer named Johnny "Scat" Davis, who played trumpet and was famous for singing a song called "Hooray for Hollywood." I used all the little bits of business and comedy touches that had gone over so well with our audiences for so many years, including the "Clarinet Polka." Corn or not, the audience loved it. We made $12,000 in one week, the highest we had ever made anywhere, and all of us were pleased and delighted. This experience strengthened my conviction that the prime purpose of entertainers is to entertain and give the audience what it wants, always consistent with basic moral standards. To my mind it is not a question of playing up or down to an audience. It is simply a question of honesty. If an audience is promised a certain kind of entertainment, then that is what it should receive, and I have always tried to fulfill that obligation.

There was one time at the Capitol Theater in New York, however, when I was absolutely unable to live up to my principle in this regard. Even today I feel numb all over when I think about it. If our appearance at the Tower in

Chicago

Kansas City was embarrassing and humiliating, then the one at the Capitol was downright agonizing. It all started on such a high and happy note, too. When we were booked to play the Capitol early in 1943, we were all happy. The Capitol and the Paramount were the two theaters in New York which booked only top-name bands in connection with their movies and we felt that this engagement put us right up there with Benny Goodman, Glenn Miller, and the Dorseys. Ralph Edwards was scheduled to appear on the same bill, which made us even happier since he was one of the top attractions of the day, starring in a radio show called "Dr. I. Q." Ralph would stay on stage asking questions while his assistants roamed through the audience looking for contestants; when they found one they would call up to him and say things like, "Here's a man on the aisle who thinks he knows the answer, Doctor," or "Here's a young lady in the front row, Doctor." The show became particularly famous for one line: "I have a lady in the balcony, Doctor!"

At the time I had a sixteen-piece orchestra, and New York was one of the cities which operated under the standby ruling. This was a union regulation which stipulated that whenever a touring orchestra appeared in town, the band leader must hire an equal number of local musicians on the theory that his orchestra was displacing them and keeping them out of work. I decided to hire sixteen extra violinists and have a truly spectacular string section, something I had long wanted to do, but when I told the producer of the show at the Capitol what I had in mind, he shook his head. "Nah, nah, that's a lousy idea," he told me. "What you should do is just double up on the number of instruments you now have. You got three trumpets? Okay, then you'll have six. You got one piano? You'll have two. And so on."

I didn't want to do it that way and argued with him, but of course he had the final say and finally he said it. "You just forget about that string section. It wouldn't work anyway. Leave it to me, Welk, don't worry about a thing. You just wave the baton. I'll hire the musicians myself and fix everything up for you." Well, he was certainly right about that.

When we held our first rehearsal with the sixteen new musicians I was a little surprised to find that the extra drummer was a girl. After everyone else had arrived and we went through our first number together I got more than surprised. I got sick. Half the new so-called musicians couldn't keep in time or play on key, and I was more than a little suspicious that a couple of them had ever played at all before. I couldn't understand where the producer had found this bunch of terrible musicians. Later on I found out where. Right in his own home. Almost all the new players were related to him or his wife or his cousins.

I wouldn't have cared so much if he had picked good musicians, but these were so bad I finally begged them not to play at all. I told them just to sit on the stage and pretend to play while my own band did the work. They refused. I suppose the lure of actually playing at the Capitol Theater in the heart of Broadway in New York City was just too much for them, and they insisted on sawing away on their violins or blowing into flutes and trumpets, and you never heard such discord in your life. Orie Amodeo, who later played in our reed section, happened to be in the audience opening day, and he agrees with my judgment entirely. "Boy, were you awful," he told me years later. "You were so bad my girl and I got up and walked out on you."

I think I would have joined him if I could. I was so ashamed of the way my band sounded it was actually painful for me to come out onstage and smile and pretend to enjoy leading it. I struggled through each performance and I could hardly wait for that terrible week to come to an end. Far from being the wonderful chance we had all expected it to be, the Capitol engagement was so bad it nearly ruined us, and I figured it took almost five years for us to regain our original stature.

All during that endless week Ralph Edwards and I would nod and exchange pleasantries whenever we met, but we never actually talked. I always had the feeling he was secretly wondering how a band as bad as mine had ever made it to Broadway. Many times I felt like explaining the situation to him, but it seemed rather pointless to complain, so I never said anything. I was just grateful that he, at least, was putting on a good show for the audience.

Years later, in 1958 to be exact, both Ralph and I were in Hollywood with our respective television shows. Ralph had an outstanding series called "This Is Your Life," and we had our regular Saturday night show plus our nightly stands at the Aragon Ballroom, and every minute of every day seemed filled with appointments. I was on the run most of the time with never a moment to spare.

One day, however, Jack Minor, a Dodge executive and a good friend of mine, called to tell me that I would have to make some commercials for the Dodge people, who were then sponsoring our show. "Oh, but Jack," I said, dismayed when he told me the scheduled recording date, "I don't think I can do it that day. We're rehearsing all afternoon at the Aragon and then we play that night."

"Oh, this won't take you long," said Jack easily. "All you have to do is change into a good suit and then drive a Dodge into camera range and smile a little. I'll come out to the Aragon and run you into town. It shouldn't take more than two hours, all told."

"Well, all right," I said. "But you don't have to come out and pick me up. I'll drive in myself."

Jack was strangely insistent. "No . . . no. I'll be glad to do it, and besides, you can finish dressing in the car on the way in and that will give you a little extra time."

That sounded sensible to me, so I did as he suggested. The next day, as we drove into town, I buttoned up my shirt and put on my tie and inserted cufflinks and generally got spruced up a little. Instead of going to ABC, however, where we always taped our show, Jack headed out over the Hollywood Freeway toward the NBC studios in Burbank.

"What are you going out here for?" I asked him in surprise. "Why aren't we going to ABC?"

"Well," said Jack in a very reasonable tone, "we're going to NBC because they have the only color camera available right now, and we want to do this commercial in color. Oh, by the way," he added, tossing some white printed cards at me, "here's what you have to say on the commercial. Why don't you look those over a little?"

I looked at the cards and I nearly choked. There must have been eight or ten of them and Jack knew it was difficult for me to get through even one at a time.

"Jack," I blurted out, "I can't do all these. You know I'll make all kinds of mistakes."

"Oh no you won't," said Jack, still in that kindly tone. "You'll be just fine. Let's just stop in this restaurant here for a minute and have a coke and I'll run over the lines with you."

He pulled into a restaurant close by NBC and steered me to a table. I was bewildered by his strange actions. "Jack," I said, "why in the world didn't you send me those cards before? You told me all I had to do was drive the car in front of the cameras. If I'd known I had to do all this I would have studied more. And why are you taking me to this restaurant? I think we should go over to the studio to rehearse." I could feel my stomach muscles beginning to tighten up.

"Now, Lawrence, just calm down," Jack said, as helpful as ever. "We'll go over the lines. I'll help you."

He ordered cold drinks, which didn't do much toward cooling my temper, and I began to read through the cards. Jack helped me whenever I stumbled over a word, which was every other line. He kept glancing out the window all the time, and suddenly he jumped to his feet right in the middle of a line and said, "Well that's fine, very good, no trouble, you're doing great, come on let's go." Jack was a brilliant and able executive, although sometimes unpredictable, but I had never seen him act like this before and I was at a loss to understand his flighty behavior. "All right," I said meekly and followed him out the door.

"You drive," he said as we got into the car. As we neared NBC he began giving me instructions. "See that narrow street right in front of the studio? See where those two big cameras are? Well, you let me out and then drive right up to that marker and park and get out and walk six steps toward the camera and begin reading your lines. I'll give you the cue . . . they've already got the idiot cards set up for you." (I must add that the cue cards most performers use were called idiot cards long before I arrived on the television scene, although I still wince every time I hear the term.)

"All right," I said a little grimly. I really thought Jack was behaving very unfairly, brushing me around like this and not letting me get properly prepared for an important commercial. But I was determined to do the best I could, so I let Jack out of the car and then I drove as directed into the camera range, stopped, parked, got out, and walked six steps and stopped again. Smiling nervously, I said, "Ladies and gentlemen, it is a pleasure to greet you after driving this wonderful Dodge." I continued all the way through the whole eight cards, and for once in my life I didn't make a single fluff. I was beaming with relief and joy when I turned to Jack, but to my surprise he was looking disappointed.

"Well, you did fine, Lawrence," he told me, "but to tell you the truth, when you parked the car you jammed the brakes too hard and they squealed. We'll have to do it again."

"Jack," I said, miffed, "I'm an orchestra leader, not a mechanic! It's hard enough for me just to talk. You know that. I don't know if I can do it again."

"Oh sure you can," said Jack cheerfully. "Okay, fellas," he called to the cameramen, "let's do it once more."

I got in the car, backed up to the starting point, and at a signal from Jack went through the whole thing again. And again I did it without any mistakes. At the end I turned and looked at Jack hopefully.

He was shaking his head sorrowfully. "Nope. Sorry. You know what you did, Lawrence? Well, instead of smiling and looking happy, you had the least little suggestion of a frown on your face. I think we better do it one more time."

"Are you sure I was frowning?" I asked him. "I thought I was smiling the whole time."

"No no, you were frowning all right. I saw it distinctly. I'm sorry, Lawrence, we'll have to do it again."

I got back in the car. I was really getting hot under the collar but I realized how important this commercial was and I willed myself to keep calm. Once more I backed into position and after a moment Jack gave me the signal and again I drove into the line of the cameras. As I parked and got out of the car this time, I suddenly noticed that Ralph Edwards was walking toward me from the other direction. He was holding a microphone and he was walking directly in front of the cameras. After everything else this was just too much and I started to blurt, "Ralph! Don't tell me you're in this commercial, too!" Mercifully Ralph cut me off immediately, and grasping me by the arm he beamed widely and announced, "LAWRENCE WELK—THIS IS YOUR LIFE!"

Before I quite knew what was happening Ralph had propelled me inside the studio, down the long corridor, and out onto a stage in front of a huge audience. Suddenly I understood the reason for Jack's strange behavior. He had been stalling desperately for time until the exact moment when Ralph would appear to begin the show. I stood on stage looking out at the warmly applauding audience and I realized suddenly that we were actually on the air at that very moment. I was just dumbfounded. I could see Jack behind the cameras grinning widely, delighted that all his elaborate deception had paid off so well, and I realized that everyone in Ralph's organization and mine, too, had been conspiring for weeks to keep the whole thing a secret from me. They succeeded beyond their wildest expectations. I was overwhelmed. That show was a truly thrilling experience, one of the real highlights of my life.

For the next half hour Ralph brought out some of the people nearest and dearest to me. I could hardly speak when I saw George T. Kelly come out of the wings, grinning that same warm wonderful smile. And big Tom Archer, always so kind, so helpful. My sister Eva was there all the way from Strasburg, smiling shyly at all the excitement, and so were Fern and the children, pleased that I had been so completely surprised. The Lennon Sisters came out, laughing with delight, and there were others in the profession I hadn't seen in years. Those thirty minutes went by in a blur of sentiment and memories and I was so close to tears the whole time I didn't trust myself to speak. When Ralph presented me with a beautiful scrapbook as a memento, and some specially made cufflinks with a picture of Shirley enclosed in one and Donna and Larry in the other, I very nearly did break down and cry. After the show went off the air and I was still trying brokenly to thank Ralph, Jack rescued the situation by breaking in and saying gruffly, "Lawrence, you did the best commercial you've ever done in your life tonight and it's all a waste. There wasn't a foot of film in that camera."

16

CHAMPAGNE LADIES AND PRIMA DONNAS

BY EARLY 1945 LARRY WAS READY FOR KINDERGARTEN, DONNA was in the third grade, and Shirley was a grown-up freshman in high school. The picture at home was changing rapidly, and so was the picture in the band. Jayne Walton decided to leave. Before she left we held auditions for a new Champagne Lady, and it seemed to me that literally hundreds of aspiring young singers turned up. We finally picked another dark-eyed and pretty brunette named Joan Mowery. She was only seventeen years old at the time, and her mother was not too sure she wanted her daughter to be a band singer, but after she came down and talked to Fern and me, she gave her permission. Jayne stayed on for a week or so, teaching Joan the ropes and giving her some pointers; and then she left to marry and begin a life of her own. But she tells us today that she has never forgotten her days as the Champagne Lady of the Hog Farm, and certainly the Champagne Music Makers have never forgotten her.

Joan picked up where Jayne left off, and was also a big hit with our audiences. Whenever I think of Joan, I recall one of the funniest incidents that ever happened in our career. It wasn't so funny for Joan, however. She fell suddenly ill when we were touring in Galena, Illinois, and the hotel doctor, who was hurriedly summoned, told us she had appendicitis and needed immediate surgery. We were all concerned about her, but after she had been hospitalized and we were assured she would be all right I realized I needed to have another girl singer, and I needed her right away. I put in a frantic call to my agent and good friend for many years, Joe Kayser in Chicago, to rush out another girl singer immediately.

"Well," said Joe dubiously, "I don't know. Most of the competent singers are working now, but I'll see what I can do." A little while later he called back and announced he had found a girl: "Not exactly what you're looking for maybe, but I think she'll do for a couple of weeks, Lawrence. She'll be out on the next train."

The next day, the tallest, skinniest girl I have ever seen in my life walked in the door. I couldn't believe this was the girl Joe had sent, but sure enough it was. She was not only tall and skinny, she was—to put it as kindly as possible—downright plain. In fact, she reminded me rather of a plucked chicken. I could tell at a glance that she was not exactly the type of Champagne Lady our patrons would expect, and after I heard her sing I was more sure than ever. I tried, as diplomatically as possible, to explain that she wasn't quite what we needed at the moment.

She promptly burst into tears. "Oh now, please," I said, "don't do that! Let's go a different route. I . . . it's . . . well . . . I just don't think you're exactly right for this job."

"Oh please, Mr. Welk," she moaned, "please! I've told all my relatives I'm going to be with your band. This is such a big chance for me. *Please* don't turn me down. I'll do anything you say. I'll just do anything! Please!"

I couldn't stand it. "All right," I said unhappily. "How long would it take you to learn a new song?"

Her tears stopped as if by magic. "Oh, I can learn it in two or three minutes! Just give it to me. Where is it?"

I gave her the song, a novelty number called "Doin' What Comes Naturally," summoned Bob Cromer who was to work with her, and explained how we wanted the song presented. As they sang, Bob was to snuggle up close and put his arm around her waist. She was to remove it indignantly. Again he was to put his arm around her, and again she was to remove it. And the third time he did it—as he sang the last lines of the song, which went, "Maw and Paw raised a fam-i-lee, doin' what comes natchurally"—she was to look outraged and turn and slap him firmly on the cheek. Joan and Bob had done the number many times and it was a great audience favorite.

My new vocalist nodded her head constantly as I explained the routine. Yes, she understood. Yes, she'd have no trouble. Bob gave me a look behind her back which indicated clearly he thought I had really slipped my mind when I had hired her, but he went through the rehearsal glumly anyway. "That's the skinniest girl I ever put an arm around," he muttered to me afterward.

"Bob, it's just for a couple of weeks—till Joan gets back. Don't complain," I told him.

We had a full house that night, and after the first few dance numbers I announced that we had a specialty song we'd like to perform, and the audience crowded up close to the bandstand where they could get a good view of the show. Our new young lady was so keyed up and anxious to begin I was afraid she might collapse even before she got started. I smiled at her encouragingly as she and Bob got underway with this great production number.

Bob put his arm around her waist for the first time, and she looked properly insulted and removed his hand firmly. He did it for the second time, and exactly the same thing happened. But when he sidled up for the third time, rolling his eyes at her and warbling, "Doin' what comes nat-chur-leeeee!" her face suddenly got red and she really did look outraged. She turned around and hit him such a crack in the jaw she knocked him right off his feet and flat onto the floor. He was still singing the last note as he went over backward, and he looked absolutely stunned with surprise, while the audience looked on in shock and the orchestra just fell apart! A good many of the boys in the band were jealous of Bob and his curly hair and his success with the ladies anyway, and to see him knocked flat in front of a whole ballroom full of people was just too much for them. The brass section kept trying to play, but they snorted and spluttered so hard they ran out of wind, and finally they just put their instruments down and laughed till the tears rolled down their cheeks. Everything stopped. The audience didn't know whether to laugh or cry, and neither did Bob. My new prima donna stood looking down at him, uncertain as to whether she had been a hit or not, while Bob looked daggers back at her. Finally he got to his feet, dusted off his pants, shouted, "I quit!" and stalked off stage, followed by howls of laughter. That particular piece of business got such a tremendous reaction I decided to try and keep it in, and after I talked Bob into falling down before he got knocked down, he agreed to go along with it. Our new girl stayed with us until Joan came back.

Joan was our Champagne Lady for two years and was followed by Helen Ramsey, who stayed on for another two. In between I had a succession of girl singers, and that's a story in itself. Champagne Ladies and their mothers—oh my! Most of my singers were lovely and contributed greatly to the band, and the Champagne Lady we have today, Norma Zimmer, I consider to be perfect. But some of the others were a bit less than perfect. I remember once asking Freddy Martin why he never used girl singers with his band. Freddy gave me an under-the-eyebrows look and said clearly and decisively, "Girl singers are just too much trouble. I admit they dress up the band and sometimes add a lot to its appeal, but"—he shook his head—"as far as I'm concerned, they're just not worth the trouble."

I knew what he meant.

Our first Champagne Lady, although she did not officially wear that title, was Maxine Grey. When I had been playing the Baker Hotel in Dallas, just after Shirley was born, Fern and I heard her singing on the radio and Fern was impressed with her. "Why don't you hire her?" she suggested. "I think a girl singer would add a lot to the band." I discovered that Maxine was singing from the radio station WFAA in the tower of the Baker, and so, bright and early at five-thirty the next morning when she had her first program of the day, I went up to take a look at her. She looked as good as she sounded, and I invited her to have dinner with Fern and me that night. The upshot was that she returned with us to Yankton and sang with our band for several seasons.

Maxine was a tremendous hit with the Midwestern audiences. She had a New Orleans accent and a smile to match, and was a pretty brunette girl who had all the fellows falling all over their feet as they flocked up to the bandstand to hear her sing. She was friendly and gracious to everyone and danced with the boys, too, which made her even more of an asset to our group. Maxine's mother traveled with us and I used to like to tease her by pretending that Maxine had fallen in love with one of the boys we met as we traveled. "Maxine," I would say, "that fellow who kept asking you to dance last night—he was certainly a good-looking boy. What did you think of him?"

Maxine would go along with me. "Oh I thought he was darling, Lawrence. Did you really like him? I think I might write to him. He asked me to."

"Maxine," her mother would say sternly from the back seat, "now you just stop that nonsense. You're too young to get married. You just concentrate on your career."

Maxine would give me a sidelong wink and we'd keep up our running gag of having her fall in love with every good-looking boy in every small town we came to. It never

Champagne Ladies and Prima Donnas

failed to upset her mother. Maxine had a lovely voice, and she stayed with us until she was offered a job with Hal Kemp's orchestra. It was a big break for her since he had one of the big-name bands of the day, and we weren't quite into that league yet. I was anxious for her to take advantage of the offer even though I knew we would miss her very much. And so Maxine left us in 1936.

I hired girl singers from time to time after that but none of them stayed with us very long until Lois Best, another lovely brunette with big brown eyes, joined our group. By the time Lois came along I had been around the band business long enough to make certain strict rules, and one of them was that none of the fellows in the band was to date the girl singer. This was partly because of the jealousy it stirred up. If the girl singer was pretty, and invariably she was, all the fellows wanted to date her, and if she went out with one of the trumpet players, then the saxophone player would get upset and wonder out loud how she could possibly lower herself to date that trumpeter. Conversely, if she dated the piano player or a violinist, the whole brass section would get upset. It invariably resulted in sensitive feelings and downright fights on occasion, and so I had made this rule, which was strictly enforced.

But I had reckoned without true love. When Lois joined the band, Jules Herman was playing trumpet for us. He was an exceptionally fine man from North Dakota and a top trumpet player. Since he was one of the few single men in the group, I assigned him to watch out for Lois, to make sure that she was not bothered by any of the fellows who always hung around the bandstand after the dance. Jules took his new assignment very seriously and before long it was obvious that he and Lois were extremely fond of each other. I didn't realize how fond until one night when Lois was riding in the back seat of the car as I drove along to our next one-nighter, with Johnny Neil, our pianist, beside me on the front seat. Both of us knew that Lois was wide awake, but we decided to pretend she was sound asleep and began to converse in low whispers, just loud enough to make sure she heard.

"You know," I whispered loudly to Johnny, "I really think it's terrible what Jules is doing to Lois."

There was a stir from the back seat.

"Yes," said John. "And you know, you'd never think Jules was such a no-good guy now would you. He seems to be so nice."

"Yeah. I wonder if Lois suspects anything."

"No, no. She's not that kind of girl. Why, if she knew he was married, she'd never date him."

This time there was a big stir in the back seat.

I got a little carried away. "Married! Why the man has two children. I have half a mind to tell Lois myself. Do you think I should?"

"Yeah," said Johnny thoughtfully. "I think so. Why let the poor girl go on dreaming?"

Suddenly it didn't seem quite so funny. We could hear Lois trying desperately to stifle her sobs in the back seat. Johnny pretended to be astonished. "Lois! Omigawsh, have you been awake? We didn't think you could hear us!"

Lois broke into sobs, and I realized that she believed what we had said and was brokenhearted. "Lois," I said, ashamed of myself, "we were just kidding. Jules isn't married and he doesn't have any children. We were just teasing you. I didn't know you liked him that much."

She couldn't even answer me. She just rolled her handkerchief up tight and dabbed at her eyes, trying to stop crying. I think she finally forgave me only because she was so delighted to discover that we had been kidding about the whole thing. When I realized how very deeply she cared for Jules, I relaxed my rules temporarily—just long enough for them to get married. They now live in St. Paul, Minnesota, where Jules has had the house band at the Prom Ballroom for years, and also plays engagements throughout the Midwest and New York. They have three lovely children, and are dear friends with whom we have kept in close contact through the years.

Lois was followed by Jayne Walton, of course, and then by Joan Mowery and Helen Ramsey, and later on, on the West Coast, by Roberta Linn of the infectious giggle, and

Alice Lon, our first nationwide television Champagne Lady, famous for her smile and her frilly petticoats. All of them lovely, all talented. But I had a few others I'd rather not think about. They invariably had Stage Mother, the kind of mothers you read about. When you describe one, it's very likely you're describing them all. Generally speaking, a stage mother's whole life revolves around her daughter. She comes in to see you armed with a huge scrapbook of clippings and press releases and reviews. As a rule, the bigger the scrapbook, the less the talent. Perhaps the mother herself had wanted a singing career in her own youth, and if she was somehow prevented from attaining it, she tried to regain it through her daughter. In everything, her daughter's career comes first. Husband, other children—everything else is secondary. I have seen more than one marriage break up because the mother of a girl singer is far more intent on furthering her daughter's career than she is in establishing a home for her husband or her other children.

One thing all stage mothers share in common is an overpowering ambition for their daughters, and I spent many an unhappy hour arguing—or rather listening—to an irate mother tell me that her daughter was so talented and so beautiful and so this and so that, that without her my band would collapse. "You're not lighting her right." "Those songs you give her are terrible." "Why don't you put her name above the orchestra. She deserves better billing than that." Such mothers never like the costumes, the salary, the billing, the songs, or anything else, and I got so that I automatically became very busy doing something important whenever Mama hove into view.

One mother wore me down to the point that we had somewhat of a blowup. She had pestered me for weeks about doing more for her daughter, who incidentally, had a lovely voice, although she was a little on the plump side. Things finally got so bad that one night I decided to try a little diplomacy. Maybe if I took the mother and daughter out to dinner where we could have a nice quiet chat, we could work out some basic agreements and life would become a little more pleasant. I deliberately chose an especially nice restaurant and made an early reservation, before the rush hour began. The place was quiet, almost deserted, when we arrived, and after we sat down and ordered I said, "Now I invited you out tonight to see if we couldn't talk things over and come to a better understanding, maybe have a little more harmony in the band!" I laughed at my own little joke and smiled winningly at the mother, but she just glowered back at me while her daughter fiddled nervously with the silverware.

"I can't see that there's anything to understand," she said sharply. "You're not showing my daughter off to her best advantage. Why, she could be singing light opera instead of singing in a dance band. Why don't you show off her voice once in awhile?"

"I can't let her sing operatic arias on the bandstand," I explained patiently. "We can't change tempos like that. We have to play dance rhythms so people can dance. That's what they come for."

"That's what you think." "They come to hear my daughter! Mr. Welk, you really don't have an orchestra at all," she informed me. "My daughter is the only good thing in it. She's the only one with talent. If you didn't have her, you'd all starve to death."

I looked at her in astonishment. "Do you mean what you're saying?"

"I do."

I shook my head. "I think you'd better go see a doctor. And if that's really the way you feel, maybe we'd just better part company."

She jumped to her feet and her daughter got up slowly, too. "That's exactly the way I feel. And if you won't do anything about it, then I'll just have to take my daughter out of your band!"

She sailed out of the restaurant and her daughter trailed unhappily after her just as the waiter brought three orders of food. The evening had been a total loss, except that it ended the constant friction and unhappiness of the past few months because the mother was as good as her word. The daughter didn't show up for the dance that night and I didn't see either of them again until years later, when the boys and I were playing an engagement at Carnegie Hall in New York. I arrived early, as usual, and a lady standing in the crowd near the box office came up to me. I didn't recognize her at first, but as soon as she spoke, I did. It was the Stage Mother, and she was in tears.

"You know I can just never forgive myself for what I did to my baby," she said. "I realize now how unreasonable I was, and I just ruined her career when I took her away from you. Why didn't you stop me?"

I had no reply for that one, but I felt very sad for both of us, and for the girl in particular. Sometimes we hurt most the ones we love, or profess to love, by our own selfish aims. If that mother had truly been thinking of her daughter's happiness, she would never have interfered or caused such constant friction and unhappiness. I have come to recognize that there is a basic human behavior pattern involved here, because I have seen this type of thing happen over and over.

That same situation was repeated in a rather different version with one of the male members of our orchestra. He was a personable young man of very slight build, weighing perhaps 120 pounds. Inevitably, we called him Teeny. Teeny was an average musician who played in our sax section, but he had a real flair for comedy, and he had a special trick: he could roll one of his big brown eyes while he winked with the other one. We dressed him up in baby clothes with a ruffled baby bonnet and had tall Holly Swenson push him onstage in a baby buggy, from which Teeny would pipe one of the popular baby songs of the day—"Won't You Come and Play With Me?" or "Has Anybody Seen My Kitty"—meanwhile rolling one eye, winking furiously with the other, and waving a baby bottle all at the same time.

The audience response was tremendous, and Teeny always had to do an encore. Before long he was taking the whole thing, including himself, very seriously. From a nice, quiet, average musician he changed into a temperamental and demanding fellow who complained constantly. Every day it was something new. The lighting wasn't right, or his costumes didn't fit, or we played too fast or too slow, or I hadn't given him a big enough introduction. The list seemed endless. He threatened to quit regularly, but I always talked him out of it because I felt that basically he was a good man who would eventually straighten out.

Unfortunately his behavior got worse instead of better, and everything came to a climax one time when we were playing some engagements in the hottest weather I can ever remember. I think the temperature stayed up around 106 degrees for several days, and all of us were wilted beyond belief. The worst thing, as far as I was concerned, was that I couldn't sleep at night. By the time we arrived in Des Moines, Iowa, to play Tom Archer's Tromar Ballroom, I was almost in a state of collapse, and when I ran into an old friend of mine from home, Tony Wald, he was shocked at my appearance.

"What in the world is wrong with you, Lawrence?" he asked in alarm. "You look terrible! Are you sick?"

"No, no, Tony," I said, "I'm just so beat. We've been playing all these one-nighters, and then when I do get to bed I can't sleep because it's so hot."

He was a representative for a drug firm. "Oh well, listen," he said, opening up his sample case, "here's a mild sedative. Take one after the dance—in fact, take two, they're very mild—and get yourself a good night's sleep tonight. You really need it."

We played our stand that night and the temperature never wavered—hot, humid, breathless, overpowering. After we finished Tom and I went out for coffee and our usual after-the-dance discussion. It was almost three o'clock in the morning before I got in the car and headed for Carroll, Iowa, our next stop. By the time I got to the hotel it was five o'clock. I got undressed, took both pills, fell into bed, and was sound asleep almost before my head hit the pillow. An hour and a half later, at six-thirty in the morning, the phone rang. Struggling through a haze of sleep I got up and staggered over to the wall phone and took the receiver off the hook.

"Hello?" I croaked.

It was my temperamental singing star. "Lawrence," he began irritably, "I've told you and told you I don't like one-nighters! I've had enough of this and last night was the last straw! You didn't give me enough time to make my exit and the band started playing before I got off. I warned you about that before. So now listen, Lawrence, I am *leaving* the band!"

"Okay," I said sleepily. "Goodbye!" And before he could utter one word of protest I hung up and fell back into bed and was sound asleep again.

After a few weeks had passed he came back and asked for his job again, but by that time I had learned my lesson. I refused. "I'm sorry," I told him, "but I think we'll both be happier if you work with someone else. I'm sure if you're back with me very long you'll find something else to complain about."

I hated to do it, but by that time I had learned one cardinal truth. People who complain constantly rarely get over the habit, and no matter how you try to pacify them, it's never enough. Not only that, but they tend to make other people in the show unhappy, too. And so, in the interest of all concerned, I decided against having him return. Stage mothers and prima donnas—male or female—are two things I can do without. With pleasure!

17

EAST AND WEST

IN SPITE OF THE FACT THAT WE WERE PLAYING REGULARLY AT THE Trianon I was becoming very dissatisfied, and by the end of 1945 I was looking for a new goal. Bill Karzas, Andrew's brother, had taken over the Trianon after Andrew's death. He had had no experience running a ballroom, and we frequently found ourselves at odds over matters of policy. Then, too, we were still earning approximately the same salary as we had the day we started, even though the band was much larger and we were continuing to pull larger and larger crowds. I was restless and disturbed about this, and felt I should be doing much better for the boys.

I was, however, extremely grateful for the fact that we were able to make continuing broadcasts from the Trianon over WGN. Just as in the old WNAX days in Yankton, WGN made our names well-known within a wide radius around Chicago, and whenever we went out on one-night stands we found ballrooms packed with friendly crowds eager to see us in person. Bill Wilson, who handled much of my press relations at the time, agrees with me that our radio exposure was a big factor in our slowly growing reputation.

I first met Bill when the boys and I were playing an engagement at the Chermot Ballroom in Omaha, and he was still a student at Drake University. Tom Archer invited him to come over to the ballroom one night to listen to our music. Bill had an instant reaction to it: he hated it! He said as much to Tom, who immediately told me, and when I met Bill later on in the evening I said, "Well, I'm sorry to hear you don't like our music." Of course he was embarrassed, and stammered and stuttered all over the place, but we got along so well I ended up by inviting him out to the house for a chicken dinner the next day. He came back to the ballroom for another listen that night, and by the time the evening was over he had changed his mind and decided he did like our music. I'm not sure whether it was my accordion or Fern's chicken that did the trick. Anyway, we became very close friends and Bill worked many years with me, traveling thousands of miles with us as we made our one-night stands out of Chicago.

He vividly recalls the time he himself promoted one stand for us in Lansing, Michigan. To his great surprise the evening turned out to be a flop and we lost money. Later he discovered that none of our radio broadcasts had been heard in that particular area. "Lawrence," he said to me earnestly, "it just goes to show that whenever you play a town where they haven't heard you on the air, you won't draw much of a crowd."

"Bill," I said with real feeling, remembering our Tower Theater disaster, "I know that. Believe me, I know."

I kept after MCA to find other bookings for us, or to set up recording dates, or to establish us in long location-jobs, and finally they arranged a six-week stand at the St. Francis Hotel in San Francisco as part of a cross-country tour. I had never played the West Coast before and I really wanted to get established on the East Coast, but of course I was pleased at the new territory which was being opened up for us. I had no way of knowing at the time that that San Francisco engagement would be the beginning of an unalterable shift in our lives, the first step into the television world that lay ahead.

Just before we left for San Francisco that year we played a week's engagement for Eddie Weisfeldt at his Riverside Theater in Milwaukee. My secretary, Dorothy Van, a brilliant and highly efficient young lady, decided to leave at just that time, and she gave me her two weeks' notice. I had depended on her good help for a number of years, and I was in a quandry trying to find someone quickly who could replace her. All my life, however, I have felt that God has had His arms around me, and that one door never closes but that another one opens. And that's exactly what happened when Dorothy left. While I was still fretting about what to do, a young man I knew only slightly came backstage after the show; he had his date with him, a young girl not long out of high school, named Lois Bielefeldt. We chatted for a while over coffee, and I told the two of them about my troublesome search for a secretary who could travel with the band.

"Oh," said the young man lightly, "well, your troubles are over. Lois here is a great secretary."

I took another look at her. "Can you type?" She nodded. "And take shorthand?"

"Uh . . . well a little," she said uncertainly. Her boyfriend added that she had been an "A" student in high school, and Lois volunteered that she was then holding down two jobs in order to help out with the family finances at home. In spite of her youth I was very impressed with her. She seemed so honest and so reliable and so trustworthy—and so available. I needed someone in a hurry.

"Could you start work right away and leave town?" I asked. "We're on our way to San Francisco."

She seemed very excited and said she thought she could, but she would have to ask her parents first. Next afternoon she came down to the theater with her mother. She later told me her father had put his foot down and flatly forbade her to go running off on "any wild goose job like that," but her mother had decided to investigate. After talking with me for a while she gave her permission, and so Lois Lamont (I soon changed her name from Bielefeldt, mainly because I couldn't pronounce it) became my new secretary and returned to Chicago with us.

For her first assignment I handed her a sheaf of papers and some instructions, and sent her off on some errands to my banker and then to my agent, Joe Kayser. Both gentlemen called me up the minute she had left their offices and implored me not to keep her. "Lawrence, that girl doesn't know the first thing about show business," said Joe. "Why in the world did you hire her?"

"Because I was desperate," I said honestly. "I couldn't find anybody else."

There were times in the days that followed, as we traveled westward, when I wondered myself why I had ever hired her. Lois didn't have the foggiest notion of bookings or bands. In addition, Dorothy had long been accustomed to translating my thoughts into business letters, and I had gotten out of the habit of actually dictating a proper letter. Lois nearly collapsed in tears as she listened to my garbled English for the first time and tried to make out what I meant. I would attempt to dictate to her as we drove along in the car from one engagement to another—my car was our office—and Lois would bite her lips and make all kinds of notes in her stenographer's notebook, and then sit up half the night trying to sort them all out and type them into some kind of sensible letter.

We kept on struggling, however, and finally we began to work things out. Lois remembers, with a mixture of horror and amusement, her initiation into "counting the house" at the ballrooms. This was always standard procedure for us. Most ballroom managers were scrupulously honest and never cheated. But there were a few others who tried to hold back an honest accounting of the number of tickets sold, so they could keep a larger share of the percentage of the gross receipts. The only way to get around it was to have some idea of how many people had actually bought and paid for tickets. Lois's job was to stand at the door with a counter and click off the number of people who entered. In this way we had a fairly definite idea of exactly how many tickets had been sold and what our fair share of the proceeds should amount to.

In the very first ballroom we played, after Lois joined us I knew that the manager was not above fixing the count a little. I warned Lois to stay at her post, and she did. The manager tried everything he could think of to lure her away. He brought her cups of coffee and urged her to come over to the bar for a coke or a drink—anything to get her away from the entrance. Lois refused to budge, however, staying at her post from seven in the evening until midnight. Finally the manager gave up. I decided then and there that I had made a good choice, and I have never had reason to change my mind. Lois now heads our large office in Santa Monica and runs it with superb efficiency.

But in those days she was still learning. I gave her as much help as I could, and Orie Amodeo and his wife, Gloria, with whom Lois often shared a room, gave her pointers, too. As we were traveling along one day, I was expounding to Lois on some of the points I had learned from George Kelly and Andrew Karzas—namely, the importance of establishing cordial and friendly relationships with your patrons.

"Oh, I don't think that makes a bit of difference," objected Orie. "All that people really care about is how good the music is—whether it's easy to dance to or not."

"Well, certainly the music has to be good, and we have to play the kind of music they want to hear," I agreed, "but a feeling of personal friendship adds a great deal, too."

We argued pro and con, and the upshot was that Orie and I made a little wager. We were playing a tiny town called Edlestein, Illinois, that night, a village of about 118 people located some nineteen miles from Peoria. The place was so small it didn't even have a ballroom and we played in the local farm implement supply house which was cleared of plows and tractors for the occasion. "I'm going to try an experiment tonight," I told Orie, "and prove a point to you and the boys."

"Okay," he said cheerfully, after I had explained my plan to him. "You're on. Let's see what you can do."

I bought twenty dime-store tablets, the kind school children use, and tacked them all across the front of our bandstand that night, with a pencil attached to each one by a string. "We're on our way to the West Coast," I told the crowd, "for our first big engagement there at the St. Francis Hotel. And if you would like to hear from us, just sign your name and address on one of these tablets and we'll send you our new broadcasting schedule and keep you up to date on what's happening."

All evening people stopped by the bandstand and wrote their names and addresses, and in some cases added an encouraging word of good wishes. Lois collected them all, and as we drove on west she arranged them into a card file, the beginning of a complex cross-reference correspondence file she now has arranged in our Santa Monica office. As soon as we arrived in San Francisco she mailed each one of our Edlestein friends our new radio schedule.

Orie was skeptical. "Well, so far all I can see is that you've spent a lot of money on printing and stamps," he observed, accurately enough. "What do you think you're going to accomplish with all this?"

"You'll see," I told him. I wasn't sure myself, but I had a hunch something beneficial would result.

All of us were impressed with San Francisco. The war years were just ending and the city was bursting at the seams with soldiers and sailors and marines coming home to their wives and sweethearts, who were streaming into town to meet them. In spite of the fact that hotel rooms were impossible to find and planes and trains were always jammed to capacity, there was an overwhelming feeling of joy and happiness in the air. It was exhilarating. I recall going to the Top of the Mark, the penthouse restaurant atop the Mark Hopkins Hotel, one evening at sunset and looking down at the beautiful city spread out on the seven hills all around me. I could see almost every form of transportation in motion at once. The huge bay was crowded with aircraft carriers, troop ships, battleships, destroyers, small tugs, and fishing boats, as well as the white ferry that used to steam regularly from San Francisco to Oakland across the bay. On the dockside were long lines of railroad cars crawling along to meet the ships and ferries, and the streets were choked with cars and taxis and the little cable cars clanging up and down the hills, while airplanes flashed in the darkening sky. It was quite a sight.

The St. Francis Hotel, where we played, was one of the best hotels in the city. It fronted Union Square, a park-like area in the center of town, crowded in those days with servicemen and their girls, sitting on benches in the sun, enjoying the ocean breezes, just happy to be home and alive and enjoying life again.

We drew big crowds right from the beginning, and all of us enjoyed the casual Western informality, so similar in many ways to the Midwestern hospitality at home. Our original six-week booking was extended, and extended again, and then again, until eventually we had played there for six months, and we began to get urgent calls to play the Aragon Ballroom in Los Angeles. Pleased, we accepted the offer, and as we moved down south, Lois mailed off more cards to all our Edlestein friends advising them of the move and promising to send them another schedule. Orie shook his head again. "Well, at least you're helping subsidize the post office with all that mail," he said.

I felt right at home the first time I saw the Aragon. It looked just like a big barn! It was located on Lick Pier in Santa Monica, and in those postwar years it was attracting huge crowds. Charlie Lick, the owner of the pier, had built it originally in 1921, and had seen it burn down in a disastrous fire. He was determined to reopen it again, and using his tremendous talents of organization and executive ability, he brought in workmen from all over the Pacific Coast. Using three shifts around the clock, he rebuilt the entire pier and ballroom and had it open for business in a record three months. The place had a great charm about it, in spite of the fact that it was located in a rundown amusement center in a fading part of town. Shooting galleries and games of chance lined a boardwalk leading to the pier and huge double ferris wheel and carousel lighted up the sky a block or so away. The Aragon was built right out on the pier so you could hear the roar of the waves as they rushed in and slapped at the pilings underneath, and sometimes the whole pier would quiver and shake under their impact.

The ballroom itself was constructed entirely of wood, in narrow tongue and groove design with a high vaulted ceiling, and it had an ornate round chandelier of mirrored glass tiles which revolved slowly while colored lights played on it casting varicolored shadows on the crowds dancing around the bandstand in the center of the floor. Right down the boardwalk was another ballroom, the Casino, which also booked name bands such as the Dorseys or Harry James. The competition was keen between the two ballrooms and kept us on our toes.

Right from the start we did pretty well. Every night big crowds made the long drive down from Los Angeles, or came over from the nearby beach towns of Manhattan and Hermosa and Huntington. Many times they would just press in close to the bandstand where they could get a better look at Joan, and one night I noticed a young curly-haired fellow standing there among the crowd, grinning up at me. I knew I knew him, but at first I didn't recognize him, because he was out of uniform. It was my old friend, Sam Lutz, from Chicago. He had come out to Los Angeles after the war to establish himself in public relations and agency work, and he was finding the going a little rough. He told me about it after the dance, when we went to a nearby hamburger stand for a cup of coffee. "You know what I'd really like, Lawrence? I'd like to handle you as a client. I know what great work you and the boys do, and I think I could do a good job for you."

"I'm sure you could, Sam, but I can't afford to pay you anything. I'm only clearing about $125 a week myself. I have to pay expenses and advertising and that's just not enough to support a family of five and an agent, too."

Sam didn't give up easily. "Yeah, well I don't need very much. Couldn't you pay me just a little?"

I thought for a moment. "The most I could spare would be . . . oh . . . twenty-five dollars a week."

The agent in Sam rose to the surface immediately. "Thirty-five!"

We finally settled on thirty dollars and Sam went to work. He really did a job for me! He was at the Aragon every night without fail, with a newspaper reporter or magazine writer or disc jockey—anyone who could help publicize or promote the band. If I had an early morning engagement with him at, say, seven in the morning, I'd look out of my motel window and there was Sam, waiting patiently, neat, clean, and ready to go. He worked very hard and helped a great deal to make that Aragon engagement an outstanding success. The crowds kept coming, and we began to make a great deal of money for the ballroom, and as the first six-week engagement drew to a close, the manager, Gordon Sadrup (whom we all called Pops), called me in to discuss my replacement.

"Whom would you suggest, Lawrence?" he asked. "I need somebody pretty strong to stand off Tommy Dorsey. He's coming in for the Casino."

"How about Guy Lombardo?"

"No, no, he's booked up years ahead. We can't get him."

"Dick Jurgens? Jan Garber?"

He shook his head. "I think they're booked, too. Lawrence, you've done awfully well for us. Do you think you could stay?"

"Oh," I said, "I just don't know if I could be any real competition to Dorsey, Pops. He's very popular."

"I think you could," said Pops. "Think about it a few days and let me know."

I promised to do so. That afternoon, as I attended to some correspondence, I dropped off one of my regular notes to Edna Stoner, and in it I mentioned the offer. "But the Casino down the street will be bringing in Tommy Dorsey and then some other big-name bands," I wrote, "and I'm just afraid that that kind of competition may knock us out entirely. So I think you'll be seeing us soon, Edna. The boys and I may be coming back to the Midwest right away."

Almost by return mail I got an urgent letter from Edna. "Stay!" she wrote. "Please don't come back yet! Maybe you don't realize something all of us here have always noticed, and I'm sure the same thing that happens here will happen out there. All of the people who are attracted to the Casino to hear one of those big-name bands are really going to be of help to you before the evening is over, because the ones who love to dance will go in and listen to the other band for a while, but then they'll come over to your place before the evening is over so they can dance! And the people who started out the evening with you will just stay on."

Sometimes you are so close to the truth you fail to realize it. I sat in my motel room reading Edna's letter over and over. For a little girl confined to bed for so many years with no real contact with the outside world, she had amazing insight. I had really learned the lesson she pointed out years before at Lake Okaboji, when I spent the summer listening to the seven competing bands and realized that the one with the best dance music was the one which ended up with the crowds. Over the years I had seen the same thing happen again and again in various localities where we had played. Even though we had often been tempted into playing fancy or technically brilliant musical arrangements, we always pulled the biggest, and happiest, crowds when we stuck to what we did best and what they wanted most—playing the most danceable music around. When I realized that I would actually be in competition for the crowds who wanted to dance the most, I decided to follow Edna's advice and stay on.

She was absolutely right. Huge crowds swarmed down to the pier every night and filled the Casino to hear Tommy's artistry on the trombone. But around ten-thirty or eleven the dancers in the crowd walked down a block to our place to dance. With this group added to the crowd we already had, we invariably wound up with a house bulging at the seams by midnight, and we managed to show a very good profit for Mr. Lick every night. Our engagement was extended for month after month. Professionally things looked very bright. But personally that long engagement was a great strain.

Fern said later that this long separation was the lowest point of our married life. "Donna cries herself to sleep every night," she wrote while we were still in San Francisco, "and all the children miss you so much. Don't you think you could see your way clear to coming home to the Trianon?"

I was torn. On one hand, I naturally wanted us to be together and I knew how hard things were for Fern. She was the one who had to put up the storm windows and attend to things around the house, and be both mother and father to the children. I felt badly about that and I wanted to be home with my family.

On the other hand, I knew that these engagements were opening up new fields for us and were important moves professionally. And of course our professional success meant a good deal to our family life, too. I made a flying trip home at Christmas, and Fern made one short two-day visit out to the Coast to see me, but in some ways those short visits only made things more difficult for us.

By the time we had reached Los Angeles to play the Aragon, Fern was even more unhappy. She even called me long distance several times, and that in itself was enough to indicate how desperate she was. But she agreed after a while that it might be a good idea to see how things worked out at the Aragon, and so we went ahead with our original booking.

We were all unhappy about it, though. The children flew out for a short weekend visit one time and we all stayed in a motel in Inglewood. We were so happy to see each other, and we tried to catch up on all the news at once, talking, laughing, walking along the beach together. I realized with a pang how much I had been missing Donna's lively chatter, and she hung onto me as though she would never let me go. Shirley and I had some grown-up teen-aged conversation, and I watched with amazement to see how much Larry had changed in a few short months. I could hardly bear to see them all fly home again. But the engagement at the Aragon was succeeding beyond all expectations; we continued to draw full houses every night, and the weekends were always jammed to capacity. It seemed foolish to leave.

Still, it was so hard on Fern, and finally she wrote again urging me to come home. "If you don't want to go back to the Trianon you can take a job running one of Tom Archer's ballrooms. You know all about that business. It just isn't worth it this way. I don't have a husband. The children don't have a father. Lawrence—we just don't have a home anymore."

I walked down to the pier that night after everyone else had gone home and I stood alone at the railing watching the water rush in, crashing against the pier, foaming and white in the moonlight, looking much like the waters of Lake Michigan back home.

What was the *right* thing to do? I knew that we could play indefinitely at the Aragon and probably return to San Francisco or the Pacific Northwest for other long runs, and I also realized that the television industry, just beginning to emerge then, would probably be headquartered in Hollywood. I felt we might have a future of some kind there, and I hated to miss out on any of those chances after the boys and I had worked so hard and so long.

But I had to face one fact. My wife and my children were not happy. I was not being the kind of husband or father I should be. Earning money for my family was not enough. We should all be together, especially in these young and growing years. After a while I made my decision and the next day I told the boys.

I had decided to go back home.

We played our way back East again, and the closer we got to Edlestein, the more Orie twitted me about it.

"What do you expect to prove?" he asked.

"You'll see," I replied serenely, although I wasn't too sure myself what to expect. We played all our usual one-night stands en route and drew our usual houses, some good, some not so good. I hoped that our Edlestein experiment would result in a bigger crowd than normal. I truly expected to find a pretty good house as a result of our correspondence, but even I wasn't prepared for what happened! Edlestein that night looked like a combination of the county fair, a three-day wedding, and the Mardi Gras all rolled into one. Orie was flabbergasted. "Where did everybody come from?" he wanted to know. I didn't know either, but I was too delighted to care. The crowd was just enormous.

Long before time for the dance to start, the little town began to fill up with people. We found out later they had come from 125 small towns in the surrounding area. By seven o'clock they were jammed into a long line outside the farm implement building, waiting good-naturedly to get in. I was eating a sandwich, watching the growing gathering with awe. By seven-thirty the crowd had become so great that we opened the doors and the dancers streamed in. By the time the boys and I walked onto the bandstand at nine o'clock we were greeted by such a storm of cheers and applause it was like walking into a friendly tornado. The small room was so jammed there was really no room to dance, but no one seemed to care. People took turns all evening long coming up to the bandstand to shake our hands and thank us for the cards. They regarded us as personal friends, and they were eager to hear about marriages and new babies, and they were pleased that their own Midwestern band had been able to play successfully on the West Coast. If ever I saw a powerful demonstration of the value of personal relationships, I saw it that night. Orie conceded.

There was an added magic to it also, quite apart from everything else. The closeness we had established really did strengthen the communication between the audience and us as we played. I have had that feeling all my life for audiences. I come alive most truly when I'm performing. I can be so tired, so exhausted, that the thought of going to bed seems very attractive, but once I'm onstage and the accordion is strapped on and I see the light in the eyes of the people dancing and having fun, it's like a shot of adrenaline. At least I imagine that's what adrenaline is like. I've never needed stimulants of any kind, although the boys used to accuse me of taking something. "Lawrence, don't you ever sleep?" Leo said to me one day in annoyance. "No matter when I get up you're always up!" It's true. I've never needed much sleep and don't to this day. Whenever I do get tired, the music is there to revive me.

From Edlestein we returned to the Trianon. Sam Lutz came right along with me, and he worked constantly to get us good bookings. He set his sights on some engagements in New York City, and he finally landed one that really thrilled me—a booking to replace Guy Lombardo at the Roosevelt Hotel in New York. I felt like a bat boy going in to replace Babe Ruth, because Lombardo had been one of my earliest idols. Being booked to replace him in the spring of 1948, while he went on tour, was a real thrill for me. It wasn't long before I discovered why he took off on tour in the spring though. New York often gets hot and muggy then, and without air conditioning it wasn't always pure pleasure to play in that room.

Still, I was elated to be filling in for the great Lombardo. All dressed up in my white tie and tails I stood on the edge of the platform opening night, beaming at the crowd. I was enjoying the evening immensely until an elegantly dressed couple danced by, with the lady gazing at me through her lorgnette as if she couldn't quite believe her own eyes, or ears. When they got up to me they paused. "What," asked the lady, removing her lorgnette, and speaking in carefully cultured tones, "is the name of this orchestra, may I ask?"

"It's the Champagne Music of Lawrence Welk," I told her.

"It's the—whaaaaaaat?" she said in disbelief.

"The Champagne Music of Lawrence Welk," I repeated.

"Oh," she said, replacing her lorgnette and giving me a look which can only be described as disdainful. "Well, it's *terrible!*" And she waltzed off without a backward glance. A few nights later my self-confidence was shaken even more, when a younger and prettier lady came up and asked me for my autograph. I obliged and she chattered away. "Are you really a Canadian?" she asked with interest.

"No, no. I'm an American," I said.

"Oh really? I thought you were all from Canada."

"Well," I said, "I'm from North Dakota, and that's pretty close to Canada. Maybe that's why you thought I was Canadian." I handed her back the autograph.

She thanked me, but when she looked at it her eyes widened.

"You're not Guy Lombardo," she accused.

"No ma'am, I'm not," I said, a little crestfallen. "My name is Lawrence Welk."

"It's what?"

"Lawrence Welk."

"Oh. Well," she said, shrugging her shoulders, "thanks for the autograph anyway."

Lombardo didn't do much for my ego, and even though my stand there helped our national reputation, it very nearly wiped me out financially. I was so anxious to succeed that I made a practice of appearing on all the disc jockey shows I could, in order to publicize the band. I also invited all kinds of radio entertainers and press people in to hear our orchestra. Of course, I always paid for whatever food or drinks they ordered, and most of them were very fair about the way they shared my hospitality. But the word began to get around that Welk was an easy mark and some of them—one in particular—began to take advantage of me. He often showed up for a few drinks, but he never once mentioned the band on his program. One night he appeared with seven friends. The eight of them sat down and ordered steak dinners with all the trimmings and drinks to match. When the bill got up over eighty dollars, the waiter, who was a friend of mine, came up and whispered, "Lawrence, the bill is eighty dollars now and it looks as though it's going to go a lot higher. That guy doesn't go on the air till midnight and it's only ten o'clock now."

Since this particular man had taken advantage of me so many times before, and also because my bank account was pretty flat by then, I made a decision. "All right," I said, "just go ahead and give him the check. I'm not going to pick it up this time."

The waiter handed the bill to the outraged disc jockey. I heard later from friends that I got plenty of free publicity that night. "All he talked about all night long was you!" said my friends. "Only he didn't call you by name—just referred to you as that cheap son of a gun."

I still had a lot to learn about trusting people and making judgments as to their sincerity and honesty. I had saved up $22,000 before our engagement at the Roosevelt and I spent every bit of it on ill-advised publicity. It took me years to distinguish between honest song pluggers and press people, and those who were just out to use me. But I cannot say I ever lost my faith in people. These experiences simply reinforced the lesson I had learned back in South Dakota when my band walked out on me. Never trust anyone completely but God. Love people, yes; always hope for and expect the best from them. But put your full trust only in God.

We were down to our last penny when we returned to the

Trianon, but after a series of one-night stands we began to earn back some of what we had lost. I never really worried about money and I still don't. The job is, and always has been, the important thing to me. If you put all your strength and faith and vigor into a job and try to do the best you can, the money will come. It will be there almost as a side benefit.

18

THE CHAMPAGNE OF BOTTLED BEER

WHILE WE WERE TOURING OUT OF THE TRIANON I MET AND hired Myron Floren, who is today my right-hand man. I had heard him years before when we toured through his part of the country—he was born in Webster, South Dakota—and he had played for me then. He was good, and had a shy pleasant personality, but I didn't feel that he played quite well enough to join our group. In 1949, however, I heard him again when we were touring through St. Louis. I was astounded. The improvement was almost miraculous.

"What in the world happened to you? How did you improve so much?" I asked him.

Myron said something that endeared him to me at the time, and my regard for him has continued to grow over the years. "I wanted to make something of myself," he said simply. "I practiced four hours before school, part of my lunch hour, and then another four hours after school, when my farm chores for the day were finished." That much practice every day, without fail, had made him a master of the instrument. I consider him to be the finest accordionist in the United States, if not the world, and he can play any type of music—dance, country, or classical.

I hired him on the spot, but when I got back to Chicago and told Mr. Karzas what I had done he was furious. "Welk, you've got to be kidding," he exploded. "One accordion is bad enough . . . but two! Besides, would Dorsey hire another trombonist? Would Benny Goodman hire another clarinet player? Let him go." Karzas was in the audience the first night Myron played with us, however, and toward the close of the first intermission I could see him wending his way through the crowd on the floor toward the bandstand. As he got closer he beckoned to me to bend down so I could hear him. After gazing at me thoughtfully for a moment he said, very softly and very distinctly, "Welk, they tell me that this new accordion player plays better than you do!"

"Mr. Karzas," I confided in the same soft tone, "that's the only kind of musician I hire."

As the forties drew to a close there was no doubt but what many of the big-name bands were fading. Several of them disbanded entirely and the whole profession was undergoing a transition. Nevertheless, we were still attracting big crowds of dancers, and I felt sure there would always be a future in the music business if we gave the people what they wanted. Not only that, I was sure that a radio program featuring a dance band could be a big success, too, and I kept after my good friend Joe Kayser at MCA to see if he couldn't set one up for us.

"Oh come on, Lawrence," said Joe, "Half the bands are not even working steady. You can't get a radio show today."

"Why not?"

"Just what I said! There's no demand for bands. Listen, we've already tried it with Lombardo and the Dorsey brothers, and we couldn't succeed. I like a commission as well as anyone, but it's impossible to get a radio show for a band these days."

I didn't believe him. I still felt deep in my bones that there was a hunger for good dance music and a radio show could be successful. I filed the idea in the back of my mind and decided to work on it myself. My contract with MCA was for booking tours only, and so I was free to do so. Leo unexpectedly put all the necessary wheels in motion one day when we were out driving and passed a giant billboard advertising Miller High Life, the Champagne of Bottled

Beer. "Say, you know, Lawrence," he said, "that could make a heck of a tie-up for you! Champagne Music and the Champagne of Bottled Beer. That would be the perfect sponsor for us, don't you think?"

"Leo," I said, giving my old friend a look of profound thanks, "I think that's one of the best ideas you ever had."

"And I have a friend who knows Roy Bernier, the advertising manager for Miller," Leo went on in excitement. "I'll bet he could get you in to see Mr. Miller himself."

"I'll go see him first chance I get," I said. "I think it's a wonderful idea! Now don't let me forget it, Leo; keep reminding me."

Leo prodded me regularly, and a few days later I drove from Chicago to Milwaukee and met Mr. Bernier. True to Leo's prediction, I was ushered in to see Mr. Miller himself. He was a vigorous, charming man, dark-haired and very handsome with a powerhouse personality. He had built his brewing company into one of the more successful ones at a time when all the major breweries were competing heavily for the public's favor. We took to each other at once. After a few pleasantries I said, "Mr. Miller, I have an idea that could help us both. And it will help you sell a lot more beer."

"Oh?" he said. "Well, I'm always interested in ideas like that. What do you have in mind?"

I explained that since my orchestra was called the Champagne Music of Lawrence Welk, we could do a tremendous selling job for him if he sponsored us on a national radio show: Champagne Music presented by the Champagne of Bottled Beer. "And we could also design music stands and stage decorations with your name on them, so that we could give you constant advertising every time we play. You'd really be getting seven nights of publicity a week for investing in just one night on the air. And another thing— I'm sure we could increase the sale of Miller High Life in every ballroom we play, and we play a great number on our one-night stands."

Mr. Miller sat back in his chair and regarded me for a moment thoughtfully. Finally he said decisively, "I like it. I want you and Roy Bernier to go down to our advertising agency. Tell them I sent you and I like the idea. Maybe we can work something out."

I went down to their agency, Mathisson and Associates, and—naturally—with Mr. Miller's personal blessing, I was very well received. In fact, several of the people in that agency later became very good friends of mine, and the president, C. A. Mathisson, "Matty" as we called him, is a close personal friend to this day. We all set to work immediately making plans for the show. I was in a real fever to keep everything secret. I didn't want anything to leak out until the deal was entirely set, and that wasn't the easiest thing in the world to do because it took three months to set it. All during that time I drove back and forth between Chicago and Milwaukee three times every week. Somehow I managed to keep everything quiet. At one point in the negotiations Mr. Miller asked me which network I preferred. Bill Wilson had gone on to become an account executive for the American Broadcasting Company, so I suggested that network. Mr. Miller was agreeable, so we called Bill and soon the whole thing was wrapped up. We were signed to a twenty-six-week contract calling for one broadcast every week over the nationwide ABC network, with each show to originate from a different city.

I could hardly wait to drive back to Chicago that day and tell MCA and Joe the big news. "Oh say, Joe," I said, as casually as I could, after I got him on the line. "I have a radio show."

"Oh yeah? Who for?"

"Well, it's for . . ." I said, and then had a better idea. "Say, Joe, will you put the other officials there on the phone. I think they might like to hear this good news, too."

"Okay, Lawrence," said Joe, a little mystified. After he got the other men on the extension telephones, I said, "Gentlemen, I have a radio show. It's for twenty-six weeks, nationwide, over the American Broadcasting Company. And oh yes, we have a sponsor, too—The Miller Brewing Company. You know, the Champagne of Bottled Beer."

The Champagne of Bottled Beer

There was absolute silence at the other end of the line and then Joe said sharply, "Repeat that, please!"

I did, enjoying myself hugely, and he demanded again, "Lawrence, is this another one of your jokes?"

"No no. It's really true."

"Well, why didn't you tell us Miller was interested in a radio show?"

"Because," I said truthfully, "I was afraid you'd sell Guy Lombardo instead of me!"

We began broadcasting Wednesday night, June 1, 1949, from New York, and we became known as Miller's Ambassadors. We had all our music stands redesigned to look like silver champagne buckets, complete with plastic ice cubes and a champagne bottle sticking out of the top, its neck wrapped in gold foil. There was a special lighting device inside the buckets which caused the lettering around the top edge to change color from time to time, and it was very effective. Our stage backdrop always carried a huge poster of the Miller "Girl in the Moon" trademark, and decals of the same design appeared on the sides of all the cars we used as we traveled all across the country.

I generally called all the ballroom managers myself, long in advance of our bookings, and I used every George T. Kelly trick I could remember. George would have been proud of me. After I got the manager on the line and dispensed a little Irish charm, all dressed up in a German accent, I'd tell him about our Miller High Life show, how well we had been doing, and what wonderful publicity it would be for their ballroom if we played there. "Just think, you'll have the name of your ballroom announced several times from coast to coast during each show!" I would exclaim. By the time I finished I had them drooling for our appearance. Then I'd say, "By the way, you do have Miller High Life on hand at the refreshment bar, don't you?"

If they did, everything was fine. If they didn't, I'd say, "Oh, well, then I'm afraid I can't appear. It would look pretty funny if the Miller High Life Band played in your ballroom and you didn't have any Miller Beer!" Nine times out of ten they promised to get some, and we always arranged to have Miller Beer in every ballroom we played.

I was very happy about that, and I was also proud of the fact that by intermission time in every one of those ballrooms Miller Beer was always sold out. The next time we returned, the ballroom was always heavily stocked with Miller's product.

Six weeks before our original twenty-six-week contract ended, we had increased our station outlets from 38 to 105; and Mr. Miller had extended our contract for another twenty-six weeks. The program worked out beyond our wildest expectations. Miller became the only major brewer in the country without any surplus stock by November of that first year. In fact, in Lincoln, Nebraska, seventy-two out of his seventy-three retailers complained they couldn't get enough of the product.

I was delighted, both for Mr. Miller and for us. And the show was fun, too. It reminded me in many ways of our old Honolulu Fruit Gum days. In every city where we played we found parades and banners and big welcoming committees, often with the mayor of the town and occasionally with the governor of the state. We managed to open up the Pacific Northwest and Idaho and Utah as brand new sales territory for Mr. Miller. I'm glad to report that he was just as pleased as we were.

We traveled constantly for the next two years under the Miller banner, in between our long stands at the Trianon. Most of the trips were without incident, but one night, when we were driving from Rock Springs, Wyoming, to Salt Lake City, where we were scheduled to play our next broadcast, we ran into such a terrible blizzard that I very nearly gave up the music business in general and one-night stands in particular. It was close to two in the morning when we left and it had been snowing a little all through the evening. As we drove, it continued to fall, gently at first, covering the hills and valleys through which we were driving with soft drifts of white.

Most of us were used to snow and, aside from putting

chains on the tires, didn't pay any particular attention to it at first. But before long the wind began to rise and whistle sharply through the steep canyons, and then the snow fell in such blinding flurries that we had to stop for minutes at a time because we couldn't see the road ahead. It was miserable driving. In some ways it reminded me of the time Johnny Higgins and Art Beal and Howard Kieser and I had driven from Bismarck toward New Orleans and had made our unexpected stop at Yankton. Only then we were twenty-three years younger and we were driving through flat prairie lands which were known to us. Now we were driving treacherous mountain passes on roads which were almost totally unfamiliar.

All of us got very uneasy. We weren't used to these jagged mountain peaks which reared up at one side of the road and dropped into canyons thousands of feet deep on the other. I was in the lead car, concentrating totally on the driving. The windshield wiper froze to the pane regularly and we took turns getting out of the car and working it loose and then scrubbing the windshield so we could see through it. Every time we did, we got chilled to the bone, and before long we were all wet and cold and thoroughly uncomfortable. More than that, we were all scared, although we tried not to show it.

"I think we're having a worse time than Brigham Young did when he first explored this place," I said, trying to joke a little.

"Nah," said Jerry Burke, taking it up. "Don't forget, he had six or seven wives giving him backseat advice. Think about that for a while!"

We thought about that and decided maybe this wasn't so bad, but it was really a terrible night, and it began to seem endless.

We plowed on slowly and as dawn began to cut through the early morning blackness, we came around a curve and saw a small coffee shop, brightly lighted, standing there like a beacon from heaven. With one accord we all drove into the small parking area in front of the place and stamped inside, drinking cup after cup of hot coffee and getting dried off and rested a little. The wind had died down slightly as daylight approached and it seemed to us that the snow was letting up, too, so nobody wanted to stop. We were all anxious to keep our date that night in Salt Lake City, and so we went back and got into our cars again.

We had a new young drummer with us, Nicky Aden from Chicago, and he was fairly new to band traveling. He was the only one who didn't voice an opinion in the restaurant when we decided to continue. He was white-faced and seemed frozen; I realized later on that he was frozen as much from fear as from the biting cold. He never said a word, just sat back in one corner of the car and kept looking out the window constantly as if he could keep us safely on the road by sheer will power.

For the next few miles we drove very slowly. It was now well past daylight, and in some ways that just made everything more frightening. We could see the occasional tip of a bright orange snow marker sticking above the level of the snow at the sides of the road, and we were reassured that we hadn't wandered off the main highway; on the other hand, the daylight made us realize how very deep the snow was. Also, we could now see all too clearly that we were often driving right along the edge of a cliff which plunged thousands of feet into the rocky canyons below. It was not a reassuring sight, and I continued to concentrate totally on my driving.

In spite of the fact that I had been driving for more than thirty years in very similar weather, I cannot ever recall a time when I was more uneasy or an episode of more dangerous driving. The day dragged on and on, and so did we. Inch by slippery inch we skidded and slipped and slithered along. The driving became more hazardous as we continued, in spite of the fact that the snow had stopped, because the temperature had dropped, too, so that everything was coated with a slick and dangerous layer of ice.

We began a long slow steep ascent up the side of one mountain, and I hugged the hill on our right side as closely as possible, trying to keep away from the sheer drop on our left. No one said a word. Our young drummer sat with his hands clenched tight and his eyes fixed constantly on the road ahead. I shifted into low gear as we approached the crest of the hill and we began to inch closer to the top. But just as we were within sight of our goal, the car suddenly began to slide backward as smoothly and quietly and forcefully as though a giant hand were pushing it. I jammed on the brakes but they didn't hold. I threw the car into reverse and yanked the steering wheel to the right as hard as I could so the chains would bite into the road and hold us. Nothing worked. The car continued its silent, relentless slide backward. It was heading right for the cliff. "Jump!" I yelled finally, turning off the car motor and throwing open the door. "Quick!" All of us jumped out and a couple of the other fellows and I ran behind the car and shoved our full weight against it, trying to halt its progress. We couldn't do it. The car, with us clinging desperately to the sides and back, continued its slow descent, and then, with a kind of gentle shudder, it suddenly came to a stop in a slight depression at the side of the road, almost as if it were being cradled in the snow.

Not one of us said a word. In fact, we hardly dared to breathe. We weren't sure just how close to the edge of the cliff we were, and we were afraid to move for fear of dislodging a chunk of snow or ice and sending us all plunging to the bottom. Finally, one by one, we eased ourselves gently away from the car and back up into the center of the road, where we stood together, watching the car settle deeper into its little nest on the side of the road. By that time, the rest of the cars had driven up behind us and all the fellows got out to lend us a hand. We talked the situation over and finally decided to form a kind of human chain and began cautiously exploring all the ground around the car. It was all solid. Finally I got back behind the wheel, and with much shouting and directions from everybody else, managed to drive back into the center of the highway, ready to try again.

I remember the silence more than anything else right then. The mountain beside us loomed so high, and the chasm on the other side was so deep, and all of it was covered with that same deep blanket of snowy silence. We in the car were silent, too, as we began the long slow climb again. We all knew we stood every chance of the same thing happening again, but the second attempt was a little easier than the first because we had already made some tracks through the snow. I drove as carefully as I could and we all leaned forward in the car as though we could push it up the hill that way. After what seemed like ages, we made it all the way to the top, and we all erupted in rather weak cheers. A little further on we came upon the fresh tire tracks of a huge truck that had passed that way earlier, and from then on the going was much easier. But it was still dangerous driving and there was always the danger that the blizzard might start up again.

Our young drummer moaned softly to himself all this time. He was burning with fever, even though the rest of us were miserably chilled, and I was very concerned about him. I began to think some very long thoughts as we bumped and skidded the rest of the way. For the first time in my life I realized that there was such a thing as taking a job too seriously. What good did it do to arrive at a job on time if I had needlessly endangered the lives of my boys? We hadn't expected such a terrible night when we started out, of course, but even so I had to accept full responsibility for the whole trip. I knew I could never again ask the boys to drive under such terrible conditions. I was very unhappy about the whole thing.

We were all exhausted by the time we pulled into Salt Lake City. The boys went to a hotel to grab what little sleep they could and I took our young drummer to the hospital. The attending doctor told me he was running a temperature of 105 degrees and his condition appeared critical. The doctor promised to call me at the ballroom if there was any change, and I drove over soberly to get ready for the evening's broadcast. I went through the preparations mechanically, checking out the program with our announcer, going over last minute arrangements with the ballroom manager, getting washed up and dressed. Just before the boys arrived the phone rang. It was the doctor. "I just thought you'd like to know your boy seems to be making a miraculous recovery," he said. "His temperature is back down to normal and he's hungry and asking for dinner."

I was amazed. "What happened? Did you give him one of those new miracle drugs?"

He laughed. "No, no. Just some tender loving care. I really think the boy was frightened nearly to death. The combination of fear and overreaction to the cold must have sent his temperature sky high. In any event, he seems fine now and he'll be right over."

The news hit me like a shot in the arm. All my depression and fatigue seemed to vanish. I was delighted to hear that our young friend had recovered so quickly, and when the boys came in and heard the good news they were delighted, too. I had been worried beforehand that we were too tired and emotionally wrung out to put on any kind of decent performance that night, but the combination of finally arriving safely and hearing such good news from the hospital affected us all like a tonic, and I think we played one of our best shows. Governor J. Bracken Lee of Utah and Mayor Earl Glade of Salt Lake City both attended the broadcast, and it was really a very festive occasion. I always remember the audience that night as the nicest audience we'd had in years. As a group the Mormons have always impressed me deeply anyway. We have a lovely representative of the Mormon people today on our show in Sandi Jensen Griffiths, the red-headed half of Sandi and Salli. That night the audience was wonderfully polite and well-mannered. After the broadcast the dancers came up to ask for requests, and they were all so pleasant about it, so gentle, that it was a real pleasure to play for them.

We continued to play regular weekly broadcasts for Miller for two years, although we never again had to plow through such a blizzard to keep our engagement. I think we could have worked together indefinitely, but by 1950 I had made a decision which was to affect our lives permanently. But it meant we had to give up our wonderful association with Mr. Miller.

PART FOUR

Television

19

REACHING THE GOAL

I FELT TRAPPED—AND A LITTLE PANICKY. After ten years at the Trianon, we had reached a stalemate, because Bill Karzas still refused to raise our salary. When I asked why, he sent for his account books. "I can't pay you any more," he said. "Look at this." He showed me the returns for Tuesday, Wednesday, and Thursday for each of several weeks, and he was right—they were on the low side. But he quickly flipped past the receipts for Friday, Saturday, and Sunday and I knew they would be much higher, because the ballroom was always jam-packed over the weekends. I said nothing, but I knew the time had come to move on. But where?

Finally I decided to go on tour again. I hated to do it because it meant another long separation from Fern and the children, and that was hard on all of us. And I got no encouragement from other musician friends who thought I was crazy to undertake a tour at a time when so many other big-name bands were either floundering badly or had gone under completely. We were still pulling big crowds to our Miller High Life stands, however, and I felt we had a chance, so Sam worked out a tour for us, concentrating on the West Coast.

One of our first engagements that year, early in 1951, was at the rambling white Claremont Hotel in Berkeley, California, where Russ Morgan held forth for so many years. After that we began to tour through Oregon and Washington. We were booked nightly until the end of April and then we were set to open for four weeks at the Aragon Ballroom in Santa Monica in May. After that Sam had arranged a three weeks' booking at Elitch's Gardens in Denver, followed by another four weeks at the Casa Loma in St. Louis. But that was it. We had no definite plan of any kind for the fall and winter season, and there were times, as we toured through the misty rainy Northwest when I wondered if I had done the right thing in leaving the Trianon. Maybe I had traded in real security for an uncertain future that would leave us all stranded. More than once I worried about what was in store for us, as we moved from one small city to another. But it was during those soft spring days in the Northwest that our real future was being decided. I didn't know it at the time, but our television years had just begun. And suddenly all the pieces began to fit together as smoothly and neatly as the parts in a giant puzzle.

The first piece moved into place in Los Angeles, where Sam was hard at work trying to arrange a television appearance for us in connection with our forthcoming engagement at the Aragon. A local television station, KTLA, had been telecasting all the bands which appeared there, and Sam had naturally assumed they would do the same for us. But just before we were due to arrive, the station had discontinued the broadcasts, due to lack of interest. Sam immediately swung into action, trying to persuade Klaus Landsberg, program director at the studio, to change his mind, at least long enough for us to appear on television. The only trouble was, he could never get through to Landsberg. "I must have placed a couple hundred telephone calls," says Sam today, "but Landsberg's secretary always told me he was in conference or on the air or on a remote or something."

Sam kept at it, however, and one evening about seven o'clock he placed a routine call to the Landsberg home, and to his surprise Landsberg himself answered the phone. Sam talked fast, telling him what a great orchestra we had.

"Welk is sensational, Mr. Landsberg. He has great singers and they do novelty tunes and sketches and his Champagne Lady, Roberta Linn, is a beautiful girl. Big brown eyes, very photogenic, fine singer. Welk himself plays the accordion."

Landsberg cut in curtly. "I'm not interested. None of the bands we've shown have drawn any response. Sorry."

Reaching the Goal

"But Welk is really different! He has a seventeen-piece group and his singers not only do solos and duets, they do choral numbers, too, something like Fred Waring."

For the first time Landsberg seemed the slightest bit interested, and Sam plunged on telling him how good we were. Finally Landsberg said, "Well, I'll tell you what I'll do. We still have our remote control equipment at the ballroom and I'll let you have one shot at it. But you'll have to pay the band expenses yourself. We won't do that. That's the best I can do for you. Take it or leave it."

"I'll call you right back," said Sam hastily. He called me in Portland, Oregon, where we were appearing at the Jantzen Beach Ballroom, and explained the proposition to me. "It will cost close to three hundred dollars," he told me, "but it will give you some local television exposure. Do you want to do it?"

I thought for just a minute. "Yes, I do," I told him. "This may be the break we've been looking for. Go ahead and make the arrangements."

Sam called Landsberg back and the deal was set. We would make our local television debut over KTLA in Los Angeles on Friday, May 2, 1951, the day after we opened at the Aragon.

As soon as we arrived in Los Angeles that time, I went out to Santa Monica to visit Pops Sadrup at the Aragon. I was shocked when I saw the place. The Aragon had never been a thing of beauty, not even in 1946, but by 1951 it was badly run down. Paint was peeling off the outside walls and hung in dejected strips in the ocean air. Most of the windows were cracked or broken. The whole pier looked shabby and deserted. The shooting galleries and games of chance were nearly all boarded up and only a couple of seedy-looking bars were doing any business at all. A few old people, huddled up in sweaters, sat listlessly on the benches along the boardwalk, watching while seagulls picked their way hopelessly among the litter on the ground looking for crumbs of popcorn. It was a depressing sight.

"What in the world happened?" I asked Pops.

He shrugged his shoulders. "Ah well, you know. The ballroom business has just gone to pot. Nobody wants to come way way down here to the pier anymore. It's too far out of town. Why, do you know, the band that closed here last night drew exactly eight couples? Eight!" He shuddered a little and shook his head.

"Well," I said, "we'll do the best we can for you, Pops. We'll really try our best."

"I know you will." He grinned over at me suddenly. "You know why you're here, don't you? Charlie Lick came and asked me who did the best business for us. 'For Pete's sake get somebody in here who can make some money for us!' he told me. 'Well,' I said, 'the one who did the best for us was that accordion player, the one from North Dakota, can't think of his name right now. Anyway, he did the best business for us, back in 1946.' And Lick said, 'Well okay, then get him!' So I did, and I'm sure glad to see you, Lawrence. Only"—his shoulders sagged again—"I'm in so far over my head right now I don't even know if I can meet your regular price."

Pops and the Aragon had been very good to us for seven months in 1946. Maybe we could return the favor now. "Pops," I said, "I think maybe I have an idea that could help us both."

"Yeah? What is it?"

"Well, suppose you just pay us union scale, and then we'll split the profits, if there are any, fifty-fifty. How does that sound?"

His head snapped up and he looked at me almost in disbelief. "I'll tell you how it sounds, it sounds like an answer from heaven!" he said.

Maybe it was . . . for both of us.

Opening night, May 1, at the Aragon, we had a modest crowd but I wasn't too worried. That fit in with the pattern of all our previous experience—start slowly and build solidly. We had a good number of old friends from the Midwest on hand to greet us. Besides, the next night was a Friday,

Reaching the Goal

and that was bound to be better. Early in the evening of that second night, while we were playing our opening numbers at the ballroom, KTLA was broadcasting an hour of Harry Owens' music, live from their studio. Then they began telecasting a famous movie of the day, a picture called "To Have and Have Not," starring Lauren Bacall and Humphrey Bogart. In those rather loose days of television timing we were scheduled to come on whenever the picture finished, and it didn't finish until eleven-twenty that night.

I don't recall our opening broadcast was anything special, but I do recall that Landsberg, a sharply featured man, pushed his way toward me through the crowds around the bandstand, shortly before air time, to discuss the program with me. "How do you want to work this out?" I asked him.

"Just give me a list of the songs you're planning to play," he told me. "We'll take it from there."

I wrote out a list of the numbers we had scheduled, and he and Sam disappeared into the remote control truck parked outside on the Aragon parking lot. And that's how we made our local television debut. Roberta sang, and giggled, and Dick Dale and Jim Roberts also sang. Myron and I played a few numbers, and we called some of the dancers out of the audience to demonstrate a polka or a rhumba. We did the same kind of things we did during our usual ballroom performances, and the cameras roamed across the bandstand and out across the dancers as they whirled around, under the famous revolving chandelier in the ceiling. After the broadcast Klaus came back in and he was smiling, almost in surprise. "Nice show," he told me. "You have great rapport with the audience."

I smiled and nodded. I hoped rapport meant something nice, and from the way he was smiling, I assumed it did.

That show, of course, was on a Friday. The next morning I had a date to play golf at a course out in Pasadena. I was just beginning to pick up my golf game again after years of touring, and I was really looking forward to it. There was a small lunch counter there, and since I hadn't had any breakfast, I sat down for some quick bacon and eggs before I teed off. I hardly got a chance to eat that breakfast, but it didn't matter at all. At least twenty people came up to me as I was sitting there and smiling warmly, they said things like, "Say, aren't you Lawrence Welk? I saw your show last night and really enjoyed it." By the time the tenth or eleventh person had spoken to me, I had really begun to realize what a powerful medium television was. In one evening I apparently had reached more people than I had in weeks of touring. It was WNAX, WGN, and all the other radio broadcasts rolled into one. If a single local television performance could bring this kind of response, what would a national appearance do? I played that round of golf caught up in a haze of dreams for the future. And some of those dreams were pretty high.

Fortunately for my dreams, KTLA also received many telephone calls and letters of approval. The following week they paid *us* to appear. Then they signed us for the third and fourth week of our Aragon booking, and before we left to play our previously scheduled engagements in Denver and St. Louis, they had signed us to a firm six month contract with options. I could feel a small secret inner bubble of happiness, and a conviction that somehow, someway we had stumbled into our real future. I felt an absolutely firm flash of insight that we had finally come home.

Meanwhile business at the ballroom picked up steadily. Every night saw a slight increase in the crowds, and by the end of that first four-week stand we were doing very well indeed and our percentage of the profits was pleasantly healthy. Pops was delighted. "I'm going to get this place painted and fixed up a little," he promised. "By the time you get back here in August, you'll see some big changes."

On August 23 we reopened again at the Aragon. True to his word, Pops Sadrup and Mr. Lick had had the old Aragon spruced up a little. The place had been repainted and the broken windows repaired and the whole pier had taken on a slightly more hopeful air. They had even tuned the piano! We opened on a note of optimism that was to grow and grow during the coming exciting months. We immediately picked up our telecasts again over KTLA, and week after week the crowds at the ballroom increased. We tried to establish a friendly, happy, party-like atmosphere for the folks who came down to the Aragon, and some of this feeling seemed to show through on the television screen. Many a night someone would stop by the bandstand to confide, "You all looked as though you were having such a good time down here, my wife and I decided to come down and find out for ourselves."

Those Aragon crowds were wonderful people; a beer-drinking, shirttail crowd, hard working, respectable folks who enjoyed an evening out and thought that dancing was a good way to have it. They stomped and whirled in polkas, or did the rhumbas and sambas and beguines that were popular in those days, and of course, always, the one-steps and waltzes. Inside that big, vaulted barn-like interior of the Aragon, the mood was just like that of a Strasburg wedding dance magnified a hundred times, a thousand times. I often strolled through the crowd with my accordion, chatting with the folks, finding out what they wanted to hear, playing requests. Roberta was a wonderful addition also, because she was so friendly and gracious with everyone. She was a great favorite, with her pretty voice and infectious giggle, and the fellows used to line up to dance with her, just like they had with Maxine Grey years before in the Midwest.

We began to get so many local sponsors we had a waiting list. I recall that Laura Scudder Potato Chips was an early sponsor, as was Chicken of the Sea. That always seemed very appropriate to me, because I often had the feeling the whole ballroom, pier included, might just break off and float out to sea, particularly during a strenuous polka number. The ratings kept climbing and the Aragon crowds kept getting bigger. KTLA re-signed us to a new and better contract, and the future looked so glowing and so secure that I wrote to Fern to put the River Forest house up for sale and move out immediately.

She wrote right back that she didn't want to come.

Today Fern says laughingly that the only reason she protested against the move to California was because she wasn't convinced that this sudden prosperity would last long, "and I didn't want us to be stranded out there in California with no place to go. I just wanted to be sure it was a wise move before I decided to uproot the children and go so far away."

Fern has often been quoted as saying she didn't want to move because Hollywood was no place to bring up growing children. "I never said any such thing," she says. "I don't think it matters *where* you bring up your children—only how. And besides, by 1951 Shirley was nineteen years old, Donna was almost fifteen, and Larry was twelve. So you can hardly say they were all growing children. No, the real reason I didn't want to move was just because I wasn't fully convinced it was a wise thing to do."

Whatever her reason was, she stalled. I wasn't the least prepared for her reaction, and I began to write her glowing letters about the climate and the fine friendly people and the wonderful future that lay ahead. "No more snowy winters . . . the sun shines all the time . . . there are wide open spaces . . . I know you'll love it out here. We can even live down near the beach if you like." I kept it up, and even threw in a few phone calls which convinced her of the seriousness of my intentions.

Finally I had her and the three children come out for a visit. Meanwhile, I located a house in the Brentwood section of Los Angeles, a roomy, comfortable place somewhat reminiscent in feeling, if not in style, of our place at River Forest. I took them all out to see it soon after they arrived. Fortunately the house was on a street called Tigertail Road and the children just fell in love with that name. They all thought it would be fun to live there, and between their enthusiasm and my continued prodding, Fern began to waver and finally she capitulated. She flew back home with the promise that when that school year was ended, the Welk family would move to Los Angeles and we would establish a West Coast home for ourselves.

One night we had a visitor at the Aragon. His name was Bert Carter, and he was with the Dodge Motor Company of Southern California. Bert's wife Nancy had seen our show on television one night and liked it. "She pestered me for weeks after that," says Bert a little wryly, "to go down and see you in person. 'I think Lawrence Welk has real presence on TV,' she told me, 'and his show is awfully good. You should meet him.'" Finally, at Nancy's urging, Bert decided to go down to the Aragon and see what we had to offer. Our mutual friend, Jack Laven, who used to manage Paul Whiteman before he became head of casting for Disney Pictures, and a man I have long considered my unofficial official adviser because of his valuable common sense advice, arranged for Bert and Nancy and their teen-age daughter Anne to attend one night. Bert remembers a minor crisis at the front door. Since the Aragon served beer, the doorman flatly refused to allow young Miss Carter to enter. Only after Jack assured him that none of the party intended to drink or dance—"We just want to say hello to Mr. Welk"—did he let them come in.

Bert and Nancy watched the show for a while, and then Jack brought me over to their table. After we had been introduced, Bert handed me his card. "Well," I exclaimed, taking a look at it, "you've got a lot of nerve. Don't you know Central Chevrolet is one of my sponsors?" Bert laughed. "Oh, I think we just may get you in a Dodge one of these days," he said lightly.

I liked him immediately and enjoyed our brief conversation, but after he and his party left I returned to the bandstand and thought no more about it. I had no idea at the time of how important that little visit was to be.

It was very important, however, because Dodge at that time was looking for a television show to sponsor on behalf of the Southern California Regional Dodge Dealers Association. Bert was keeping his eye out for the proper show.

Meanwhile, another important piece in the final picture was beginning to move into place with the arrival in Los Angeles of an advertising executive named Jack Minor, who was then associated with the Grant Advertising Agency in Chicago, a firm which was handling radio and television accounts for the Dodge people. Jack had been dispatched to Los Angeles to find the right program for Dodge. "I looked at so much local television in Los Angeles for the first week or so after I arrived," he shudders, "that I could recite the log of every TV station in town upside down and backward."

He also conferred with Bert Carter and, after a couple of weeks of intensive research, narrowed his selection of available shows down to three, which he planned to present at a mass meeting of all the Southern California Dodge dealers when they met to make their final decision as to which show they wanted to sponsor.

I didn't know that all of this was happening, of course, but one day at home, on a Sunday as it happens, I got an urgent call from Klaus Landsberg.

"Can you come right down to the studio and make a record for me?" he asked quickly. "You've got a chance to get a big sponsor for yourself, but you'll have to do this right away."

"But Klaus," I said a little uncertainly, "we've got dinner guests. I can't just walk out like this because . . . "

"It's important," Klaus cut in quickly. "Very important. It won't take you long. Come as soon as you can." He hung up and I went in and apologetically excused myself from my guests.

"But this is Sunday, Lawrence," said poor Fern. "Don't you have any time for yourself at all?"

"I'm sorry, Fern," I said, "but Klaus just insists on this. He says it's very important."

I had no idea what he wanted but I drove down quickly to KTLA and made a recording of a little speech he had written. In it I thanked the Dodge dealers for considering our show and promised to do a good job for them if they sponsored the Music Makers. It was all over and I was driving back home to the dinner guests before the impact of what I had just done hit me. I was up for consideration by the Dodge Motor Company—truly an important sponsor— and I began to get very excited. But why Dodge? Suddenly I

Reaching the Goal

remembered the tall pleasant man who had visited me at the Aragon with Jack Laven a few months previously. He had given me his card that night when he told me he was with the Dodge Motor Company. He must be the one behind all this, I decided, and when I got home I looked all through my wallet for his card. I couldn't find it. I called Jack Laven. "Jack," I said, "what was the name of that man you brought out to the Aragon a month or so ago—the one from Dodge?"

"Bert Carter," said Jack.

"Oh sure," I said. "That's the man. Well, I've just cut an audition record for Dodge, and I wonder if he's the one who recommended me? Do you think so?"

Jack laughed. "I wouldn't be at all surprised," he said chuckling. "I just wouldn't be at all surprised."

At seven-thirty the next morning twenty-seven Dodge dealers met for breakfast to decide on their new television program. Jack Minor, with the quiet and sure assistance of Bert Carter, stood up to begin his presentation. I tell Jack he really ought to go around with a microphone wired to his coat because he comes to life with such a bang whenever he sees a mike. True to form, he began to launch into a fiery pep talk as to what the dealers could expect from a massive and concentrated television program. He then explained the merits of each show under consideration, presenting a detailed account of their individual ratings and sales results, and an appraisal of their potential audience appeal. The three shows he presented for consideration that day were the Connie Haines show, featuring a very pretty and highly popular young singer, Xavier Cugat and his orchestra, and our show.

The dealers listened intently as Jack talked about each one and played excerpts and recordings. (Now, when I think of the stumbling and awkward little speech I had made so quickly for Klaus the night before, I wonder that they ever considered me at all.) Then they had a spirited discussion. Jack made his recommendation, and then asked for their decision, calling off the names of each show. The dealers liked them all and voiced warm approval after each name, but when Jack called out our name almost every man in the room stood up and began to applaud. Before long they were all on their feet applauding, and there were even a few self-conscious cheers.

Jack looked out at all the smiling faces and he grinned a little.

"Well, gentlemen," he said, "you're making my job very easy for me. I don't think I need to take a vote. I think you want the Lawrence Welk show." He was answered by another firm round of applause, and at that moment the most important piece in the final picture moved firmly into place. The Dodge Motor Company undertook to sponsor us on a local basis to the exclusion of all other local sponsors and we began an association that lasted locally and nationally for nine years and is one I still prize highly today.

We were jubilant! We had a local television show with a nationally known sponsor and a nightly appearance at the Aragon which seemed to get more successful all the time. Charlie Lick helped things along with a massive publicity campaign. Lick had access to eight billboards in the surrounding area and he gave us tremendous advertising. With the combined good offices of Charlie Lick and Bert Carter and Jack Minor and Sam Lutz, we were moving into a heady area of success that was highly exciting to all of us. The gate receipts alone at the Aragon were over a million dollars during one of those early years, and Lick was delighted. All of us were.

After a few years Lick offered to sell the ballroom to me. He had proved his point that he could make it into a money-maker, and he had so many conflicting business interests he thought he wanted to sell. He offered me some pretty tempting arrangements; in fact, he finally got down to the point of letting me pay a dollar down and the rest out of the profits. The offer appealed to me in some ways but I finally decided against it. My primary objective was to play the best music and present the best entertainment I could, and if I had to split my interests in two different directions I didn't think I could do a fair job for both sides. I reluctantly turned him down and concentrated on improving our show. Two years later, Lick sold the ballroom for about five hundred thousand dollars, so I don't think that was the wisest decision I ever made!

I began itching for a national television show and I often spoke to Bert Carter about it. He always grinned, his slow, warm, kindly grin. "Just be patient, Lawrence," he'd tell me. "I feel sure it will all work out for you. Maybe soon."

He was right, because suddenly several things happened all at once, all of which had great impact on the final outcome of our television picture. Bert was transferred to the Detroit office of Dodge. Jack Minor went from the Grant Advertising Agency to become head of advertising for Dodge-Chrysler. And a man named Don Fedderson walked into my life.

At the time, Sam and I had established offices in the Cross Roads of the World, a small and rather quaint collection of office buildings not far from the corner of Sunset and Vine, and right next door to the Blessed Sacrament Church in Hollywood, where I often dropped in for a moment of quiet reflection. One day I had a visitor in my office, a tall, ruggedly handsome man named Don Fedderson. He had originally come from Beresford, South Dakota, where, interestingly enough, my little pen pal Edna Stoner also lived, and he had established a brilliant name for himself in Hollywood as a television producer of great ability. He had already catapulted Liberace to national fame via a series of telecasts, and he was also responsible for a show called "The Millionaire." I liked him immediately, both as a man and as a producer. He told me simply that he liked my local television show, and he thought I deserved a break on national television. He said he wanted to act as my television consultant and agent. "I think I can get a national show for you," he said, "and I'd like an option from you to see what I can do."

I agreed, and with that decision the final piece in the puzzle fell neatly into place.

Don immediately began to make arrangements to produce a pilot film for us. He rented a movie theater in Beverly Hills which had been converted into a temporary studio for television and film production, and we made a short film showing off the band and some of the types of music we did. Don also put his public relations man, Les Kaufman, to work arranging a fantastic black and gold leather book; a massive thing with flowing gold script across the front reading "The Man with the Golden Touch." Inside was an impressive array of all the gates and house records we had broken over the years, and an accounting of our local television history. Don included a long story about how the Dodge dealers of the Southern California area had themselves petitioned the head office in Detroit to continue with our show since their sales had improved so much after our show had been on the air. He marshaled all the forces of his background into making an effective presentation on my behalf, and then he and Sam flew to Chicago and took their story to the Grant Advertising Agency.

In those days shows were generally sold to advertising agencies who in turn sold them to the networks, whereas, today the shows are generally sold directly to the networks. Grant listened to Don's story, looked at the film and the big black leather scrapbook, and then called on the Dodge Motor Company headquarters in Detroit to suggest that they sponsor us nationally.

I knew all kinds of activity were going on in my behalf all the time, but I didn't dwell on them too much. I just kept very busy in the office and at the Aragon, and I looked up almost in surprise one day to see Don standing in the door of my office. One look at his smiling Scandinavian face and I felt an almost unbearable mixture of apprehension and hope beginning to rise.

"Well, Lawrence," he said quietly, "you're in. Dodge has bought your show as a summer replacement, and you're going coast to coast. You've got a nationwide show."

I could feel the tears starting to gather, and for a minute I couldn't say anything. I tried somewhat brokenly to thank Don, but he brushed my thanks aside. "It's nothing," he said, "nothing. You had the show they wanted. I'm just happy for you."

I was so delighted, caught by so many different emotions—joy, surprise, deep gratitude—that I hardly knew what to say. But as the sudden shocking glow of surprise wore off, I began to get down to more practical matters. "Well, Don, I just can't tell you how grateful I am. Now I guess the first thing to do is to find a good-looking young announcer who can front the show for us."

Don looked at me impassively. "I don't think I heard you."

I repeated my statement. "Now we need to find a handsome young TV announcer, somebody who can speak good English."

Don sat back in his chair and regarded me speculatively for a while. "Lawrence," he said finally, "Lawrence, they don't want a handsome young TV announcer. They can get those anywhere. They want you. They want *you*, Lawrence."

For the second time that afternoon I was close to tears, but then I went into a slight case of panic. "Oh no, no, Don" I said, "I can never do that. The audience will never understand me. I have to repeat myself all the time as it is. No, we need somebody young and good-looking and a good speaker."

Don just grinned a little. "Uh-uh. You're the one they want. And you're the one they're going to get."

Don later explained to me that everything I had considered a minus was really a plus. "You think your accent is funny and people are laughing at you. They're not laughing *at* you. They're with you. There's a big difference there, you know." I was still convinced my accent was more of a detriment than anything else, and even though I was pretty relaxed in front of a live audience I still froze up stiff in front of the television camera. Despite my doubts, Don finally convinced me to go ahead with it.

Under his tutelage I began to work on short announcements to precede each number. I would talk about the song in my own words and then Don would transpose what I had said into good English, and also into words I could say. I hadn't really improved very much from my Edgewater days and still had trouble with "th" and hard "d" sounds. That's how "wunnerful, wunnerful!" got started. I loved to use the word because it often described exactly how I felt, but somehow the "d" got lost when I said it. And yet when I tried to say the word "that," the "d," far from disappearing, came out something like "dat." The whole thing was a big mystery to me, and I hated the way I dragged out that long "uuh" syllable at the end of some of my words. Again I implored Don to hire an announcer, but he just shook his head. "Nope," he said, "no chance. It's you all the way. You sound fine."

So I kept on rehearsing, but every time I listened to a practice record I was ready to quit all over again. "I'm just not a talker!" I told Don desperately, but he refused to budge, and in fact he wanted to include some of the bloopers I made during a rehearsal for the actual show. One time I said that such and such a song was not my cup of dish. I meant cup of tea, of course. I frequently told Don we were painting ourselves right into a condition, which always broke him up. Those were some of my minor mistakes. I made a few on camera, too, that I would just as soon forget about, and I regularly made mistakes that had everybody giggling. But they all tried to help me, and I tried my best, too.

Roberta Linn had left us in 1954 to take advantage of some of the many night club offers which were coming her way, and almost immediately we found the perfect replacement in Alice Lon, another in our long series of dark-eyed, dark-haired singers. She was an instantaneous hit with both the Aragon and the KTLA audiences, and, along with the band, she began to put in long hard extra hours of practice to get ready for our big nationwide debut.

The great day began coming closer and closer. I planned and re-planned the opening show a dozen times. Alice switched ideas for her costume daily. All of us were eager,

Reaching the Goal

anxious, thrilled at the chance, impatient, literally counting the days till we could begin. And then about six weeks before the show, I found I had one more hurdle to jump.

We had planned an afternoon meeting at the Aragon to go over final details. As usual, I was the first one there and I got busy opening up a stack of folding chairs and setting them into a circle. I was so happy I almost did a polka all by myself. By two o'clock everyone had arrived—Lee Desmond, National Sales Director for Dodge, along with Bert and Jack. Don and Sam came and so did John Gaunt of the Grant Advertising Agency with several of his people. Some officials from ABC were there, too, and just before we sat down Lois came sailing through the front door carrying a stack of papers and a small portable typewriter. All of us greeted each other with smiles and congratulations and pulled chairs into a close circle. "Well," I said with relish, pulling a typewritten sheet from my satchel, "here it is! The opening program all timed and rehearsed."

"May I see that, please?" It was John Gaunt. "Mmmm. Yes. Looks very nice, Lawrence." He handed it back to me. "But, gentlemen," he looked around the group, "I've been reviewing the competition we're facing, and I think we might be very wise to make a few changes in Lawrence's show."

I felt a small warning chill. "Changes? What kind of changes?"

He smiled easily. "Oh, nothing much, Lawrence. Just a few things to spice it up a little. Any of you gentlemen have any suggestions?"

After a moment Bert Carter said slowly, "But John, I was under the impression that Lawrence would do the same kind of show he's done all along. He's certainly done a fine job for us in this area."

"Yes I know, Bert, but you have to remember that a national show is a whole lot different than a local one. Lawrence's music may be all right with the Okies or the folks back home in North Dakota, but it will never hold up with a nationwide audience. Never! What I think we need is—oh, some big production numbers, or maybe a comedian—something to add a little excitement, a little glamor to the show."

"Oh come off it, John," exploded one of the men. "How are you gonna make an accordion player glamorous? That's just not possible." All the fellows burst into laughter and I breathed a little easier until one of them said, "Well, I don't know about a comedian, but what about a line of girls? That would certainly add a little glamor."

"Now *that*" said one of the men instantly, "is a good idea! I'll go for that. Count me in."

"Yeah! You know that really is a good idea." A few happy grins began to appear and several of the men began a spirited discussion of just how much a chorus line would add to the show. After a while the idea of a comedian was introduced again and this time the men were very enthusiastic about it and they got down to specific details: which comics of the day had the biggest following, who their agents were, what the cost would be. Lois's pencil flew over her notebook, writing down all the proposed plans, and there no longer seemed to be any question as to *whether* we should hire a comic and a line of girls—only when—and how many.

I sat where I was and I couldn't believe what was happening. In less than twenty minutes the dream of a lifetime was being destroyed, because I know that nothing in the world could make me put in a line of girls or a comic; not even if I lost the whole show. I just wouldn't do it. And suddenly I found myself on my feet, demanding to be heard over the hubbub of conversation. "Gentlemen," I said loudly, clutching my list of songs. "Gentlemen, just a moment please!" They all turned to look at me in astonishment. I was almost as surprised as they were because I never said much of anything in public, and I certainly never made speeches. Now, however, I did both. "Gentlemen," I said again, waiting for their attention.

Reaching the Goal

"Well yes, Lawrence," said John with a little frown. "Did you want to say something?"

"Yes I do," I said doggedly. "I . . . I . . . I want to do this show more than I can say. . . ." I began to stammer as I stumbled ahead, trying to explain. "I just haven't got the words—the phrases—to tell you how bad I want to do it. But . . . I'll give it up . . . before I'll do it this way!"

"Lawrence," said John impatiently, "you want the show to be a success, don't you? "Well then, you have to do what people want!"

All of a sudden I remembered the theater manager at the Oriental who had stopped me from playing the Clarinet Polka, and the one at the Capitol who had saddled me with all those terrible musicians—and where a minute before I had been groping for the right words, suddenly I knew exactly what to say, and the words just came pouring out. But I spoke very calmly, very quietly.

"Gentlemen," I said again. "May I explain what's in my heart? In television, we're going directly into people's homes—and if we have a comedian who, just *once* says or does anything out of line, then that's a danger point for the children. And that's wrong. But worse than a comic is a line of girls! You hire an orchestra and now you want to put a line of girls in front of it, kicking up their heels! But that's not the real problem, and you fellows know it. Sooner or later some of the men connected with the show, maybe some of you men right here, are going to fall in love with the girls, and you'll be paying more attention to them than your own families, and that's not right either. It makes for an unhealthy atmosphere, and it will show up on the program. The mothers who watch our show are just not going to like it." I took a deep breath and said, "This mother who is watching us—the first time a comedian cracks a joke with a double meaning, or she feels something is not quite right—she will just get up and turn the program right off. You have lost her—and may I say, she's not very apt to go out and buy a Dodge car, either!"

There was a slight pause and then Lee Desmond got to his

feet looking very grim. "Gentlemen" he said finally, "I just don't understand you. You hired Lawrence in the first place because you liked his band and the job he was doing for us. Now you're trying to turn things around and tell him how to run his own business! Well, all I've got to say to you is this: if Lawrence Welk doesn't know what's what in the music business, then we're *all* in a hell of a fix! Now then, you just turn the show over to Lawrence and let him do exactly as he wants!" He glared around the circle. "All right. That settles it. The meeting's adjourned."

He sat down and I did, too, because suddenly my legs wouldn't hold me. After the meeting I wrung Mr. Desmond's hand and thanked him. "That's all right," he told me. "I meant what I said. But tell me something. Would you really have given up this chance to go nationwide if we'd made you hire the girls or a comic?"

"Yes I would," I said. "That meant a lot to me."

He laughed. "Welk," he said, shaking his head, "you're a very determined fellow! You know that, don't you? A very determined fellow."

I guess maybe he was right. And I guess maybe I've known that all my life.

For our national debut, ABC had set aside a rather disreputable studio. It was originally the old Warner Brothers Studio where they had made *Phantom of the Opera*, and had been hastily reconverted into makeshift television headquarters during the forties and early fifties. Today ABC has one of the most modern and highly equipped studios in the world, but then it looked like nothing so much as the Aragon-moved-inland; it was an old barn of a place. All the lights necessary for a TV production hung from newly installed beams which fitted in beneath the catwalks crisscrossing the cavernously high ceilings, several feet below the roof top. The place was so old that there were holes in the roof, and the California sun had a disconcerting way of shining in through all the crevices, and lighting up spots that shouldn't have been lighted up, and on at least

Reaching the Goal

one occasion it rained so hard the stage crew dispatched a dozen men to the roof top to stuff up the cracks with rags. And sometimes the wind whistled through them, too. But I didn't care! Nothing could dim the fact that we were actually going to perform on a big-time network show. It was the first thing I thought about when I woke up in the morning, and the last thing I thought about at night. I went over my planned program again and again. Alice continued to switch ideas for her costume at least once a day and we all teased her about it, but we were just as eager and anxious as she was. We rehearsed constantly, and in some ways the days seemed to drag—but in others they flew—and almost before I knew it, the great day had arrived.

July 2, 1955, I walked into the ABC studios to find an air of barely controlled panic on the rehearsal stage. Everyone was on edge, but determined to do his best, quivering with emotion held tightly under control. It was boiling hot, and since there was no air conditioning, the stagehands had dragged in heavy tubs of ice and set up huge wind fans to blow across them and counteract the tremendous heat from the television lights. Lois seemed to be the cool and calm note in the whole picture. She had made dozens of notes in her neat and legible hand and had everything highly organized. She was right there when somebody asked, panic-stricken: "What's the next number?" "Who took my lead sheet?" "Where's my script?" and she seemed to have the answer for everything.

We were scheduled to go on the air at five-thirty Pacific Daylight Saving Time, and by four o'clock Alice was fully dressed and ready. She must have checked her makeup a hundred times, posing and pirouetting in front of the mirrors. When she was finally satisfied, she stood quietly at one side of the stage so she wouldn't wrinkle her gown. All the boys and I lined up then for our own makeup sessions. In those days we didn't have the fully equipped makeup rooms we do today, complete with makeup artists and hairdressers—we just took turns sitting down at a battered old wooden table topped with a mirror framed with the traditional light bulbs, and waited while the harried makeup men slapped some dark brown pancake powder on us. Then we changed into blue dress shirts—at that stage of the television game, shirts had to be blue in order to photograph white—and after that we walked around very carefully so we wouldn't get mussed up. All of us wore Kleenex tucked in around the collars of our shirts so the makeup wouldn't run and we looked like a bunch of penguins. But nobody laughed. We were too concerned that everything look as good as possible, and the boys took extra pains with their appearance—combing and recombing their hair, peering into mirrors, adjusting their jackets, rechecking the polish on their shoes. They looked the best I'd ever seen them.

At five o'clock the studio audience began to file in and settle down in their seats. I looked out from behind the jungle of cameras and heavy cables wound in tangled heaps on the stage, and my heart contracted when I saw so many dear friends sitting down front—Bert and Nancy Carter, Jack Laven, Jack Minor. Don and Sam sitting in the front row, Sam's hair curlier than ever in the July heat, and Don giving me an encouraging grin and the good luck sign of thumb and forefinger curled together every time he caught my eye. Even Fern broke a long-standing rule and came down with Larry. Shirley was in Washington, D.C., and Donna in Chicago, but I knew from excited phone calls that they were anxiously awaiting the show. All my dear ones were there; in spirit, if not in actuality. I was so grateful. And I thought of all the other friends who had helped so much to make this dream come true: George T. Kelly, Tom Archer, Andrew Karsas, Joe Kayser, Eddie Weisfeldt, Edna Stoner, so many, many more. And I thought of my brothers and sisters back home watching together on one small TV set in Strasburg. And I thought of my mother.

It was time. The studio audience in their light summer clothes were all seated and the doors were closed with the red "no admittance" sign flashing above them. All the boys were in place on the band risers at the back of the stage, Alice sitting in front to one side on a gilt chair, looking as

Reaching the Goal

fresh and pretty as a rose. Ed Sobel, our producer, was in the glass-fronted production booth with his eyes glued to the clock and his hand up, ready to give me the cue the moment the second hand swept around to the top. I stood watching him, clutching my baton tightly, almost frozen with fear, wondering how I had ever gotten into this spot, wondering how I could get out of it, when suddenly Ed's hand came down and he pointed hard at me and I turned and gave the downbeat to the boys. The strains of our theme song filled the air and flowed right through me—and suddenly, my terrible nervousness left me. As always, once the music began, I came fully to life, and I was swept along through the rest of the program on a wonderful emotional crest of feeling that remains one of the high spots of my life. In some ways that hour was a blur, but certain scenes stand out with blazing clarity: Alice, finishing her opening number, "Love Me or Leave Me," and smiling with surprise and delight at the storm of applause from the warm and friendly audience; Myron playing a dazzling version of "Tico Tico," his face so happy, so kind in the spotlight; Rocky Rockwell grinning broadly as he sang "I Love Girls"; our violinist Dick Kesner playing "Silver Moon" with the Heifetz-like quality everyone loved. My dear friend Jerry Burke, his silver hair gleaming in the overhead spots, smiling widely as he played "Unchained Melody"; Aladdin, super-charged with feeling, as he performed "Ciellito Lindo"; Jim Roberts and the entire choral group singing the sentimental Whiffenpoof song, and singing it the best they ever had; the band doing a rousing version of "South Rampart Street Parade" in the Dixieland style I loved so much; Larry Hooper standing tall and straight and summing up all our feelings as he sang "Oh Happy Day" in his deep bass voice. I could hardly believe it when Alice and the group began singing "Good Night, Ladies" and the closing credits began to crawl across the TV screen, and I kept right on leading the band until finally Ed's voice, laughing a little, boomed out of the loudspeaker "Okay! Okay, kids, that's it! Thank you all very much. A very good show."

It was over. Our first coast-to-coast television show was

all over—and suddenly the stage was jammed with friends and guests, hugging each other, shaking hands, pounding each other on the back, kissing, congratulating, beaming, beaming, everyone's face wreathed in smiles, eyes sparkling. The stagehands coming up to shake hands and tell us what a good show we'd done. Alice dizzy with delight, jumping up and down in excitement; Orie almost steaming with joy; Barney Liddell clowning and cracking jokes; all the fellows excited and happy, and I . . . what? Joyful, floating, happy, excited, fulfilled, hopeful—but most of all satisfied—satisfied that we had all done the very best we could. Whatever happened, whatever the reviews or ratings showed, I felt every single one of us in the Music Makers had called out the best talent of which he was capable. I could ask for no more.

The reviews were mixed. One or two of them were good, but most of them asked the question I had been hearing over and over during our years on local television: "How can an orchestra just sitting in front of the camera playing dance music, hope to capture a viewing audience?" Most of the conclusions were not too favorable. But I was not too discouraged. I felt that since we had been able to build up and hold a local audience, we could do the same thing nationally, too, and even though the rest of our company was plunged into despair by our first week's rating—7.2—I didn't feel quite so bad. I had never been interested in a blazingly quick and successful thirteen-week summer run, anyway. I had been aiming carefully for a solid, respectable long-running show—and as the weeks went by and our rating went up slowly and steadily, I began to have hopes that we would eventually achieve it. I watched with deep satisfaction as the rating made its slow climb. From 7.2 it rose to 9.2 the second week, and each week thereafter it climbed by approximately two points, so that by the end of the summer we were in the high twenties, and the Dodge people signed us to appear as their year-round national television show on a permanent basis.

It was one of the happiest moments of my life.

20

THE LENNONS

It's been sixteen years now since that momentous broadcast—years that have brought me such joy and fulfillment that I am constantly filled with a sense of wonder. How could God have been so good to me? Over and over I marvel at the blessings of my life: my wonderful family, my wonderful musical family, my wonderful family of fans and friends. And as I look back over these years that have passed so quickly, two impressions remain firmly with me. Each year has grown better than the last. And each year has made us more determined than ever to improve what we did the year before.

And there are so many wonderful memories! The hundreds and hundreds of telecasts we have done, for instance. I don't know which stand out more strongly, the good ones, or the ones which weren't so good! Maybe it's the latter, because I still cringe whenever I remember our first Christmas show. I'd invited the boys to bring their children down for the broadcast, and they were all determined to make sure the grandparents back home got a good close look at them. You never saw such pushing and shoving in your life! By the time we went on the air, everyone's temper had frayed around the edges and the babies were fussing and crying so much that our timing got off; and when Santa Claus finally arrived on the scene dragging a sleigh full of presents, the show was over! We went off the air to screams and cries of protests from all the outraged little ones demanding their gifts. I thought the whole show was so bad I seriously considered calling up the sponsor and offering to resign, but the next day at Sunday Mass, the parishioners at St. Martin of Tours church in Brentwood came up to me with broad smiles to tell me how much they'd enjoyed the show. "The same thing happens at our house, it was just like home," they said, and I

263

realized, almost with surprise, how much the human touch counts.

Many other shows stand out in my mind as particularly exciting and rewarding, but I believe the one which has meant the most to me was our "Thank You America" broadcast on Thanksgiving in 1970. I meant every word I said on that program, which stressed all the things that are right with this country, and the great gratitude all of us should feel at being Americans. The response was so tremendous, so overwhelming, it indicated a great many other Americans felt the same way, too. That was a happy show for us, one of our best. Right afterward Irving Berlin called to congratulate us, and I told him we were already in the process of preparing a show in tribute to his songs, featuring Kate Smith singing "God Bless America," and that, also, was one of my favorites. But to me each show is so special, it's almost impossible to single one out. We just keep trying to improve.

There are personal memories which come to mind, especially the time President Eisenhower's secretary called from Palm Springs to tell me the General wanted to play golf with me the following day. I remember driving down to the Springs in the moonlight that night, all alone, thinking, "This can't be true! This can't be that I'm on my way to play golf with a President of the United States." But it was true, and even though I arrived at the Eldorado Golf Course very early the next morning, "Ike" was there ahead of me, smiling his warm and friendly smile, putting me at ease immediately.

There have been many honors and awards, too, and I am grateful for all of them, but even so I believe what has meant the most to me is the deep friendship which has grown up between us and our listeners. I first became aware of the depth of this feeling when we played a show in Minneapolis following our initial appearances on national TV. When we landed at the airport that time, there was a huge crowd waiting to greet us, plus the Mayor and other civic dignitaries and a fleet of some twenty Dodge cars, waiting to parade us into town. I was just bowled over. We'd never been treated like that in Minneapolis before! But all during that ride into town I fretted because my managers had insisted on charging five dollars top for a ticket to our show, and since I had only a seventeen-piece band at that time I wasn't sure we could give the audience five dollars worth of entertainment. We did our best, however, and I began to realize, from the continual waves of applause and friendly shouts of encouragement from the audience as the show progressed, that these people really looked on us more as old friends than they did as TV performers. It made us try even harder to entertain them.

I thought we had succeeded, too, except for one bad moment after the show when I was standing out in front signing autographs. One old farmer silently handed over a slip of paper for me to sign, and as I scrawled my name he said sharply, "Mr. Welk, I drove almost five hundred miles to see your show tonight. And I had to pay five dollars to get in!" My heart sank. I was sure he was going to tell me he felt cheated. But then his face creased into a grin, he pumped my hand warmly, and added, "And I just want to say, that's the best five dollars I ever spent in my lifetime!"

I was so relieved, and as we continued to chat I realized again the extraordinary warmth and friendship our audience had for us. I recognized it also by the amount and kind of fan mail we began to receive. Obviously our viewers loved Alice Lon, Jerry Burke, Myron, and Aladdin, and looked on them almost as members of their own families, but I would say that the ones the listeners loved most of all in those early years were the four Lennon girls who became the whole nation's little sisters.

It seems to me only yesterday that my son Larry brought the girls to our house on Tigertail Road. He had met them at school, and for weeks he had been telling me about the great quartet which sang at some of the school dances and church functions. I listened with half an ear—Larry was often subject to moods of great enthusiasm—but I pointed out that a quartet of school girls was probably not professional enough to appear on a national television show.

"But these girls are great, Dad," insisted Larry. And he didn't let it go at that. He worked out a plan which he put into effect one day when I was home sick in bed with a cold. Before I quite knew what was happening he had ushered all the girls into the bedroom, where I was propped up in bed reading. I was charmed at first sight. Janet Lennon was only nine years old at the time; her blonde hair was skinned straight back into a ponytail, and she had a smattering of freckles across her face. The other girls, Dianne, Peggy, and Kathy, were all fresh-faced and glowing, very sweet and very ladylike—the kind of girls I have always liked. After a quick introduction Larry gave the girls a cue and they all broke into song. I was amazed and enchanted! They were young and untrained, but they had a freshness and verve about them that I loved. And they had a quality, a blend, I recognized instantly. If any performer has quality in his voice he can almost always be helped to develop all the other necessary attributes. But quality is the one essential ingredient. I promptly invited them to appear on our Christmas show that year—it was in 1955—and soon those sweet young voices were enchanting the rest of the nation just as they had enchanted me. We were flooded with calls and letters, and after another guest appearance I asked the girls to become a permanent part of our musical family. They accepted, and the Lennon years added a great deal to our musical history.

When they first joined us the girls could not read music, and they sang accompanied only by a piano or a celeste or a guitar. But as they learned more we were able to present them in more complex arrangements until finally they were able to sing with the full orchestra. They were always willing to tackle anything new. I remember the first time Janet danced the polka with me when she was about ten years old. "Oh, but I can't dance the polka, Mr. Welk," she said in alarm when I first asked her. "I don't know how."

"Oh, you can learn it right away," I assured her.
"Do you really think I can?"
"I know you can!"
"Well, if *you* think I can, I'll try."

With her tongue clenched between her teeth in determination, Janet did indeed try, and before the afternoon was over we were whirling around the stage together in a bouncy polka, and I don't know who was having the most fun, Janet or I. Both of us were beaming while Janet's pigtails flew out behind her and the other three girls stood laughing and clapping in time to the music.

Our first six years together were truly wonderful for all of us, and we seemed almost like a family, but by 1961 the girls were beginning to grow up. Dianne left the show to marry her childhood sweetheart, Dick Gass. That was the first real break in an association that had endured so happily for so long. The other three girls continued to perform as a trio but over the next few years each one of them also married. Peggy married Dick Cathcart, a brilliant Dixieland jazz trumpeter; Kathy married Mahlon Fox, also an excellent musician; and Janet, our little baby, married Lee Bernhardi, an ABC staff member who worked on our show. I couldn't really believe that our little freckle-faced girl was old enough to marry, but sure enough she was almost twenty years old and ready to begin a life of her own. It seemed incredible that so many years had passed! Dianne returned to join the group a year or so after her marriage, and the girls performed as a quartette once again.

By the time Janet had married, there were a good many changes in the show. For one thing, it had grown tremendously in size. By 1969, when I celebrated forty-five years in the music business, I also had forty-five people in our musical family. On every level, in every way, the show was moving ahead.

And those years were not only busy and productive for the show—they were extremely productive for the girls, too. All of them began to have children of their own. It got to be almost a standing joke. "We can't stage the number that way," someone would say. "Remember, one of the Lennons is going to have a baby." "Which one?" "Well, I don't know . . . but I'm sure one of them is!" The girls themselves were always very good-natured about the kidding and went cheerfully along with any plans our production staff dreamed up to camouflage their condition. They hid behind a potted palm or a piano or a make-believe telephone switchboard, or else they wore gowns which concealed them from the neck to the floor. "We're wearing our tents again," said Dianne laughingly, as they swirled onstage one night in a cloud of blue chiffon.

I remember once, when I had gone down to Escondido to play some golf, that several people came up to tell me they could hardly wait to see our program every week. "Well, that's wonderful," I said, preening happily. "I'm glad you enjoy it so much." "Well, yes," came the deflating answer, "the reason we can hardly wait is because we're always so anxious to see what you've figured out to hide the Lennons!"

We always arranged things so that whoever was the expectant mamma-of-the-moment didn't have to rehearse, but arrived just in time to get made up and join her sisters onstage for the show. Things worked out very well this way, and with their marriages and new babies the girls began to become wildly popular. They were the darlings of the fan magazines. You couldn't walk past a newsstand anywhere without seeing pictures of them splashed all over front covers.

They began to make more and more guest appearances on other programs. Sam had long been booking them for other shows (something I have always encouraged all the artists on our show to do), and they played the Perry Como and Ed Sullivan programs among others, plus countless fairs and concerts. They were making as much as a quarter of a million dollars a year, and I thought that they were enjoying happy and fruitful lives.

But by 1968 it became increasingly evident that they were becoming restless and dissatisfied. As had happened so many times in the past—for example, when my band walked out on me in Dallas, South Dakota—outside influences came to bear on them. Two agents in particular promised them enormous sums of money and untold benefits if only they would leave. I don't know exactly what the agents told the girls, but over the years the same kind of thing has happened often enough, and I have been told the details often enough, to know that the conversation always follows the same lines. "Why are you wasting your time with this man Welk? Don't you know that without you his whole show would fall apart? Don't you know that without you he would be back on the farm shucking corn, or whatever you do on a farm? Why, you could become the greatest star in the world if you'd only get away from him! That no-talent square is just holding you back." And so on and so on. The agents finally convinced the girls that they should refuse to go on tour with us in the summer, and should perform on our show only as it would fit into a new schedule—perhaps once a month or so.

"But girls," I said in dismay when they told me of their new plans, "I can't go along with that kind of thinking."

"Why not?"

"Because it's not fair to the rest of our musical family." I explained that if I permitted them to play the show on an irregular basis, then all the rest of the performers could do the same thing and the show would just break up. "I want you to stay," I told them. "We all want you to stay. And you can play all the extra engagements you like. But I do need assurance that you'll appear regularly every week, and go on tour with us, too."

The girls promised to think it over, but after a few more weeks it was clear they were making plans to leave. I felt so bad about it. I asked their Uncle Ted, my long-time business manager, to speak with them. "I just haven't been able to get through to them, Ted," I said unhappily. "See what you can do, will you?" Ted tried, pointing out to the girls that they'd be giving up a certain amount of security and protection if they left, including our profit-sharing and other benefits, but he came back to tell me they had definitely made up their minds to leave. I then asked my son Larry to intercede on my behalf. The girls had always considered Larry one of their best friends, almost as another brother, and Larry talked to them, too, but he also came back to say with a rather helpless little shrug, "Well Dad, I'm sorry but they want to go. I think they just want to try their wings."

Of course I would never try to stop anyone from doing that. I was concerned mainly that the girls were not making the right decision. Naturally, I was deeply worried about them.

But the girls had made their decision, and I had—and have—every respect for that. They quietly left the show and began to embark on a series of nightclub appearances. They no sooner had left than we were all engulfed in a flood of wild publicity, hounded by reporters demanding to know the "real" reason for their departure. I didn't talk to anyone for many months in regard to the situation, and the girls were quoted so badly out of context so many times that they finally refused to give any interviews either. But none of the stories which attempted to drive a wedge between us succeeded.

It would be foolish to say that I was not hurt when they left. I was. I was deeply hurt, but hurt by the parting itself, not by the fact they had decided to go. I missed them. They had been a part of our lives for twelve years, and I hated to see those years end.

I suppose none of us should have been very surprised at the storm of publicity which blew up when they left, because much the same thing had happened just a few years earlier with Alice Lon.

Alice was a delight to work with right from the beginning. A pretty and talented girl, she was also so pleasant I was almost suspicious. A few weeks after she had been with us, I took her aside one day during rehearsal at the Aragon and asked, "Alice, are you always this nice?"

She look surprised. "Well, I guess so. If I'm being nice,

this is just the way I always am." She laughed a little but she was right, and everyone in the band enjoyed working with her, until much the same thing happened to her as happened to the Lennons—outside influences began to make her dissatisfied.

In that same old pattern agents began telling her she was being held back, that she wasn't being featured enough. I was aware that she was becoming restive and unhappy, but I didn't realize *how* unhappy until the day I returned from a fishing trip to Vermeyo Park, Colorado, with my old friends Dwight Wilson and Tom Archer. I went immediately to ABC for rehearsal and I was working upstairs in the control booth when one of the fellows suddenly darted out into stage center and held up a newspaper so that I could see it. I peered closer through the glass window and made out a big black headline which read: ALICE LON QUITS IN ROW OVER SHORT SKIRTS. WELK SAYS HER NECKLINES ARE TOO LOW. This was so untrue I burst out laughing and I thought the whole thing was an elaborate gag—that the boys had gotten together and had one of those newspapers which specialize in comic headlines printed up, just for my benefit. "This is no gag," said Ed Sobol. "I know the part about the short skirts is a lot of baloney, but the rest of it is true. Alice has left the show."

I think the thing that hurts most when people leave without any warning at all is that you have invested so much of your time and your trust and yourself in them and their careers. On the other hand, if any of our people want to leave to pursue a career on their own, I will do everything I can to help them, if they will only come and tell me about it. Jo Ann Castle is a case in point. When she first came on the show a great many people liked her, but a great many didn't, and they began to write letters complaining about the way she played her rag-time piano, her personality, and so on. Many of the letters complained that her playing was "sloppy"—that she didn't hit the notes clearly and cleanly and sloughed off the difficult parts without real musicianship. We finally received so many letters that I thought I had better let Jo Ann see for herself what the viewers thought. I took some of the mail down to the Aragon with me one night and left it in her dressing room before I went onstage. When she hadn't appeared after forty minutes I went backstage to find her. Her dressing-room door was closed, but I could hear her sobbing convulsively inside. I tapped lightly. No answer. I tapped again, and finally she blurted, "Who is it?"

"It's me, Jo Ann. May I come in, please?"

Presently the door opened and Jo Ann appeared, her eyes red and swollen, her face mirroring her unhappiness. When she saw me she burst into tears again. "Oh, Mr. Welk," she sobbed, gesturing toward the pile of letters, "how can people be so mean? How can they say such terrible things?" She cried as if her heart would break and I patted her shoulder and finally got her calmed down. Then we sat down to talk the whole thing over.

I told her frankly that some of the complaints about her playing were true. "And here's what I think you should do, Jo Ann," I said. "Get a piano somewhere—buy one, rent one if you have to—and practice an hour every single day. Two or three hours would be better. Otherwise—well, I just don't know if we can keep you on with such strong objections as these."

Jo Ann nodded her head. "All right," she said. "I promise I'll practice an hour a day. And if I can't, I'll tell you."

She was as good as her word. Within three days she had gotten a piano and started to practice at least an hour, and sometimes two, three, or even four hours a day. Her playing improved so greatly and her technique became so refined that the letters began to swing entirely the other way, and she developed a tremendous fan following.

In 1969 she decided to try it alone. She came to me one morning at ABC and we talked it over. "I just want to see what I can do on my own," she told me. "What do you think?"

"Jo Ann," I told her, "we'll miss you on the show. You

know that. But if you want to go, I'll do everything I can to help you." We tried to make the transition as pleasant and easy as possible, and we still keep in touch today. Jo Ann is a classic example of a girl who worked with us, helped us, allowed us to help her, and left only good feelings when she departed. I felt happy about that and I would do the same thing for any of our artists today.

I would have done it for the Lennons, too, if only they had come and told me how they really felt. But I think what really happened in that case was that there was some kind of breakdown in communication between us. I wanted so much to help the girls. I would have been glad to do so if only they had asked, but somehow they were unable to express themselves to me, and so they went ahead and made plans on their own. I suppose that's the thing that really hurt me.

21

GERITOL, SOMINEX, AND A SLEEPLESS NIGHT

IN 1959 THE DODGE PEOPLE AND I PARTED ON THE MOST friendly terms, and the J. B. Williams Company undertook to sponsor us. That also has been a wonderful association. I am delighted about this relationship not only because they are good people to work for, but also because I discovered Geritol and Sominex. If you want to know how I keep my health and strength, I can only tell you that I play golf religiously, swim daily, think good thoughts, take Geritol in the morning, Sominex at night—and sprinkle on a little Aqua Velva in between!

Matty Rosenhaus, the president of the company, is one of the finest men I have ever known, and that's a nice feeling to have about your boss. He has a great sense of humor, too. One time when he was vacationing in Florida I called and told him that one of my best saxophone players was sick and that I just couldn't seem to find a good replacement for him.

"Oh," said Matty, instantly concerned. "I'm sorry to hear that. Is there anything I can do to help?"

I knew that he had played a little sax in his college days so I said, "Well yes, Matty, to tell you the truth that's why I called. Do you think you could fly out here and sit in with the reed section till I can find a replacement?"

"Certainly," he said immediately. "What time is rehearsal?" And then he roared with laughter. After he recovered he said, "Lawrence, I'd do almost anything for you—anything but play in your band."

But you know something? I think if I were really stuck, Matty would get in there and blow a few licks for us.

Working with Matty and his fine associate, Ed Kletter, we continued to try to improve our show in every way we could, and it seemed to me we were doing pretty well, too. But I was still stymied in one direction: I just couldn't seem to get a hit record. From the days when I had paid the Genett Company four hundred dollars back in Yankton to produce our first recording ("Spiked Beer" on one side and "Shanghai Honeymoon" on the other), I hadn't done very well in this phase of the music business. I couldn't understand it, especially after we got on television and our music seemed to be so widely accepted. When my contract with a major recording company drew to a close at the end of 1958, I began looking for the best company to help me find that elusive hit. Finally a man named Bob Thiel introduced me to a young recording executive named Randy Wood from Gallatin, Tennessee, and I went up to his office to find out about his philosophy of music. Randy greeted me at the door, sent out for a cup of tea for me and coffee for himself, and very nearly brought the meeting to an early close when he inadvertently picked up a paper napkin on which I had set my tea cup and dumped the whole thing in my lap. But by the time we got the tea wiped up and had settled down with a fresh cup, we were pretty good friends. We talked for three hours and when I left Randy looked me right in the

Geritol, Sominex, and a Sleepless Night

eye and said with great sincerity, "Lawrence, we will do everything in our power to get you a hit." I went home and thought about it. All my life I have invested in people rather than companies, so the fact that Randy was then associated with one of the smaller organizations didn't bother me. I decided to go along with him. I liked his manner and I sensed his honesty.

He did just what he said, and soon came up with the song we'd all been looking for. The name of it was "Calcutta," and it turned out to be our first gold record. Later we had another million-seller gold record, "Winchester Cathedral," and with Randy's help we have had a series of hits, among them "Galveston," "Moon River," "Candida," and "No, No, Nanette." He has now established his own record company, Ranwood, which produces all our records.

As our television show expanded, so did corresponding areas of our business life. We incorporated all of our various enterprises into one company called Teleklew, and moved into headquarters in the Union Bank Building in Santa Monica, where Julie Jobe is our pretty receptionist. George Thow, our continuity writer, has his offices here, and so does Ted Lennon. Ted first came to work for me as a talent scout, and he was so good that I gradually put him in charge of all our business enterprises, and he has done a magnificent job. It was largely as a result of his efforts that the new sixteen-and-a-half-million-dollar Lawrence Welk plaza at the corner of Wilshire and Ocean Boulevards in Santa Monica was erected. This complex consists of a twenty-one-story office building housing the General Telephone Company, with an adjoining sixteen-story apartment building, each with an ocean view.

Another one of our dream-come-true projects is our mobile home village at Escondido where some two hundred retired families live. The village is equipped with swimming pools and club facilities and an eighteen hole, three par golf course, as well as a large motel and swimming pool for visitors. We also have a restaurant, the Welkome Inn, which gives me a chance to try out some of my ideas—the basic one being that food should be the best you can possibly serve, at prices reasonable enough for the whole family.

Escondido, which is located about forty miles north of San Diego, is an oasis in my life, a chance to get away from the pressures of the show and just unwind for a few days. Bert and Nancy Carter, having retired from Dodge, and Harvard and Irene Noble, formerly of Mitchell, South Dakota, manage Escondido for us, and it was from there that we did our first color show in 1965. By that time my life was truly full to overflowing, both personally and professionally. Fern had long since settled down happily to life in Los Angeles—complete with weekly bridge games—and our daughters had married. Both of them married doctors. Shirley and her Bob now have five children, and Donna and her Jim have three. It didn't surprise me in the least, incidentally, that both girls married doctors, because Fern had always had such great admiration for the medical profession. I was always rather uncomfortably aware that she would much have preferred to see me with a stethoscope in my hands instead of a baton, but I figured there really wasn't much I could do about it. In 1965, however, the North Dakota State University solved the whole problem for me by awarding me an honorary doctor's degree, and the moment I flew home I walked in the front door, handed over the precious roll of parchment to Fern and said, "Here. Now stop complaining! At last you're living with a doctor."

Professionally we were going full steam ahead, too. Norma Zimmer had joined us in 1958 as our first blonde and blue-eyed Champagne Lady and she is a constant inspiration to everyone on the show. Norma just radiates the kind of spiritual serenity which comes from true religious faith, and she is such a fine artist I still wonder how I could ever have been so fortunate as to have her with us. Bobby Burgess and Art Duncan were with us, too, and all our days were jammed full.

But even though I loved every minute of it I began to get the uncomfortable feeling that I was pushing myself to the limits. I was getting old, of course—it *was* some forty

Geritol, Sominex, and a Sleepless Night

years since I had set out from the farm in that horse and buggy, driving down the road toward Strasburg—and now, in spite of the fact that I loved my work more than ever, I began to have nights when I turned and tossed all night long and got up in the morning just as tired as when I went to bed. I had almost continual stomach spasms, too, and finally I felt so wretched, so wrung out, that I went in to see my old friend Dr. John Eagan, whom I had known in the Midwest years before. He took one look at me and clapped me in the hospital for a series of tests. After three days at St. John's Hospital I felt so much better I thought everything was fine and I went right back to work. But a day or so later I got a call from John asking me to come down to his office. I went over, expecting him to prescribe a tonic or perhaps a short vacation. I was totally unprepared for what he had to tell me.

He sat behind his desk, looking more massive than ever with the sunlight coming through the window beside him, touching his white hair. Very solemn and professional in his starched coat, he began going over the results of my tests, explaining that my trouble stemmed almost entirely from tension and overwork. I listened closely and expected him to wind up with a recommendation that I get away for a few days and get a good rest. Instead he said very slowly and with utter seriousness, "Lawrence, as your physician and your friend I must tell you this. If you want to live and enjoy your grandchildren, then you'll have to give up your show."

I can remember every detail about that moment—the look in John's eyes, the sound of the traffic outside the window, the terrible, terrible shock I felt. "Oh no, John," I said, after a moment. "No. You must be kidding!"

"No. I am not kidding. If you don't do it, then I won't be responsible for your life."

"But . . . but why?"

"Because you're killing yourself, that's why! You're on the run from morning till night. You never stop. You're at every recording session, every planning session, every performance. You're involved in so many decisions, so many pressures, that you just can't take it any longer. Nobody could!" John's voice softened. "Lawrence, believe me, I know what this means to you. But you just can't go on this way. You don't have to do the show. You've already taken good care of your family." He stacked all the medical reports in a neat bundle, and then peered at me sharply. "Lawrence, this is your life we're talking about! So think it over. Please."

I nodded and shook his hand almost in a daze. Then I walked out across the cobblestone patio of his office to my car and drove home, almost as if I were in a dream. It couldn't be true! I couldn't give up the show! I loved it, loved everybody in it. John had been right when he said I had taken care of my family, but he meant Fern and the girls and Larry. I had another family who was almost as dear to me as they were, however, and I didn't want to do anything to let them down. I just wouldn't do it. They were depending on me, and somehow, someway, I had to figure out a way to go on with the show. All the way home I tried to think of some kind of satisfactory solution, and I lay awake almost the whole night wrestling with the problem. As always, I felt that God had His arms around me, and so I asked for guidance in making the right decision. Finally, I drifted off into a troubled sleep. I had to find some way to go on with the show. But how?

22

MY MUSICAL FAMILY

EARLY THE NEXT MORNING I AWOKE QUITE SUDDENLY, AND THE answer came to me so clearly and so quickly I almost laughed out loud! I could go on with the show—if I gave it up! Instead of involving myself in every single decision of every single aspect, I would simply turn over many of the tense and nerve-wracking details to my right-hand people, and let them handle things for a while. And I would begin to pay a little more attention to myself.

I knew I had fallen woefully short of doing a good job in that respect for a long time, and I remembered some advice Dr. Eagan's colleague, Dr. Thomas Havel, had given me a few years earlier, after my gall bladder surgery. "Lawrence," he said, "the most important thing for you to do right now is discover which diet works best for you. Keep a list of foods which agree with you, and those that don't, and then stick to the ones that do. And that's something you'll have to do for yourself," he added. "Nobody else can do it for you."

And now, I realized, nobody else could give me the rest and relaxation I needed either. I would have to do that for myself, and I made up my mind to do it. But it was so hard at first! I made myself stay home, read books, take naps, play golf, or go swimming, but all the time I was just aching to go down to the studio and get in all of the excitement myself. In the very beginning the agony of staying home and worrying about how things were going was far harder on me than the actual work would have been. But I stuck to it, and gradually, things calmed down for me. I began to play golf almost every day, mainly with friends, because my handicap was thirty-eight at the time, and nobody but a friend—and a very good one at that—will play golf with some duffer whose handicap is thirty-eight. So Don and Sam and Randy and Jack Minor, Eddie Shipstad, Judge

O'Connor—so many of my good friends—rallied 'round to help me. Eventually I came to love those hours on the golf course so much that I now play every chance I get, and I also play in several tournaments every year, usually the Los Angeles Open, the Bob Hope Desert Classic in Palm Springs, the Phoenix Open (where my good friend Art Coates always whistles along to my accordion accompaniment at post-game parties), and the Tucson Open where Bill Breck is my gracious host.

By the end of four or five years, incidentally, I had whittled my handicap down to eighteen, and in one spectacular month at the Bel Air Country Club I lowered it to thirteen. A notice of this momentous achievement was duly posted on the club bulletin board, and the golf starter, Jack Dover, took me aside and said earnestly, "Mr. Welk, in my thirty years in golf, I've never seen anyone improve as much as you have in a single month!" All this flattering attention just about ruined me. I fell apart completely and my handicap shot right up again. The trouble was, I believed my own publicity.

When I first started on my new regime to regain my health, I also tried to curtail many other activities, but the very next day after my decision, Sam called to say he had another personal appearance arranged. "Sam," I said, "I thought you were going to let me take it easy for a while." "Yeah, well after tomorrow I'll do it, Lawrence," he said, and he has.

(He has?) Over the next few weeks I could see for myself how all the outdoor exercise and enforced rest (plus a little Geritol and Sominex, of course) were doing the trick. When I went in to do my necessary work on the show I was thrilled to see how all my people had come through so brilliantly. In fact, as I felt when Myron had stepped in for me at the Aragon once before, I noticed they were doing such a fine job without me I almost had a relapse. But I didn't, and together we worked out a format wherein none of us had too much pressure. I regained my health completely, and was able to keep on working with this group who meant so much to me.

My Musical Family

I had long been referring to them as my Musical Family because that's really the way I feel about them, and . . . as it turned out . . . one of them *did* become a member of the Welk family in fact, as well as in feeling. In 1968 I hired a little Italian girl named Tanya Falan. When I auditioned her I remember thinking she had the biggest, brownest eyes I'd ever seen since the day I met Fern, and when my son Larry got a look at her, that ended his search for a bride! By the time Larry met Tanya he was twenty-eight years old, and Fern and I had become concerned about him. Like most families of German background, we felt it was very important for him to find a good wife and establish a home of his own, so I used to try and help him find a girl. In fact, I made a point of it. Whenever I met an attractive young lady somewhere I'd make sure to introduce her to Larry, until finally in exasperation one night he said, "Dad, please! I'd rather do it myself!" I took the hint (although I must say he spoiled my fun a little) and Larry did, indeed, do it himself. In fact, I didn't even know that he and Tanya were dating and I was surprised when he told me that they were planning to be married. But I was very happy. Tanya is a delightful addition to the family, and she presented us with Lawrence Welk the Third on February 28, 1970—a wonderful birthday present for Fern and me and, as I immediately began telling all my audiences, proof positive of the wonderful things that can happen when you combine sauerkraut and lasagna!

About the time we hired Tanya we also added several other members to our cast—Sandi and Salli, our sparkling singing duo; Ralna English and Guy Hovis, our first husband-and-wife team; Ken Delo and Clay Hart; Gail Farrell and Mary Lou Metzger; all very talented and hard-working youngsters. Along with Bobby Burgess and Cissy King—to my mind the finest dance team in the country—and our other regulars like Myron Floren, Charlotte Harris, Joe Feeney, Bob Ralston, Arthur Duncan, and Jack Imel (who is our assistant producer as well as our spoon-artiste extraordinaire), we had a very full and highly-talented roster of performers. I was so proud of all of them, and every other member of the band, too. And I felt additionally blessed to have Jim Hobson as our producer-director, and George Cates as musical director. Jim has been with us since we began, and George since our Aragon days. Both are brilliant and I just couldn't do without either one of them. Together with arrangers Curt Ramsey, Joe Rizzo, and S. K. Grundy, costume designer Rose Weiss and set designer Chuck Koon, they helped us put together the best show we could have every week.

We maintained a heavy schedule of weekly broadcasts, recordings, dance dates at the Palladium Ballroom in Hollywood, and our annual cross-country tour, something I insist on doing every year. To my mind nothing can replace that personal contact, that spontaneous reaction from an audience which tells us instantly whether we're doing the right thing or not. And if I live to be ninety (and I'm planning to!) I'll always love performing for a live audience. The communication, the two-way feeling of warmth, is just like the breath of life to me. Lon Varnell, the top tour manager in the country, a real expert, makes all the arrangements for us, and he has everything clocked down to the last minute so that we operate with split-second precision as we fly from one one-night stand to another. And I do mean fly!

Occasionally we have a two- or three-day stand which makes a welcome break for us, and one of our favorites is our week-long appearance at the Corn Palace in Mitchell, South Dakota. This particular palace is decorated on the outside with huge murals made entirely of kernels of corn. There are a few critics who say I should feel right at home there—and they're right, I do! And it's at the Corn Palace, too, that we get to see Edna Stoner, my number one fan. We send an ambulance up to Beresford to get her, if her health permits, and Edna arrives, eyes sparkling, sweet face glowing, so giving, so loving that she inspires us all. Her mother once told me something I keep in my heart to remember on days I sometimes feel a little down. "Whenever people ask me how Edna manages to keep in such good spirits," she said, "I tell them, 'Well, her sister and I do everything in our power to keep her physically comfortable, but it's Lawrence Welk who keeps her happy.'" That makes me feel so good. Edna tells me she still has a feather from one of the pheasants I brought her from a hunting trip one day, but I tell Edna that just knowing her has been a feather in my own cap.

That's another reason we love the tours—because we get to see so many dear friends. In San Antonio we see Jayne Walton. In New Orleans, Pete Fountain. In Bismarck, North Dakota, we are often favored with a visit from our good friends, Governor William Guy and his beautiful wife, Jean, who are always so kind and hospitable to our entire troupe. And in Tahoe we see Bill Harrah who, like all the other friends, is so kind and generous I still can't get used to it. Bill provides Fern and me with a beautiful lake-front "cottage" (to this farmer's son it is a mansion) and a wonderful couple who take such good care of us, Smiley and Julia Rosetta. I would say that Julia is maybe the best cook in the world, but then Fern might get mad at me. And in addition to everything else, there is always a nice selection of Rolls Royces and Cadillacs sitting outside the cottage for us to use whenever we feel like it!

All of us always look forward to Tahoe, and we play there regularly every year. Most of the boys bring their wives and children and it is just like a three-week vacation with pay. And in June of 1970, Tahoe provided us with the springboard for one of the most successful tours we ever had. We were all thrilled and delighted with the reception we received as we toured cross-country, and by the time we returned to Los Angeles in September to begin taping our shows for the new fall season, we were full of renewed enthusiasm. Things looked wonderful for us.

But almost immediately, as the new season got underway, we realized that tremendous changes were in the air. The Federal Communications Commission ordered the three major networks to return one half hour of prime evening time to local stations every night, with the order to take effect the following year. This was done in order to decentralize some of the massive power held by the networks, and allow smaller stations a better chance to develop their own programming, and it signaled a major turning point in television history. I was fully in accord with the idea, since I have long felt that too much power in the hands of a few can be extremely dangerous, but the directive seemed to throw the entire broadcasting industry into something of a panic, and there was much talk of reshuffling or cancellation of shows, because of the cutback in available time.

I was cautiously optimistic about our own chances for renewal, however, because I felt sincerely that our show was better than ever. But as the weeks went by I noticed a few unsettling straws in the wind. In January, 1971, we were moved from the regular eight-thirty time slot we had held for sixteen years, to seven-thirty; and on a few occasions our show was delayed an hour and a half because sports events ran over into our time. Still, we managed to retain a fairly healthy share of the ratings, and my own natural optimism helped me keep a positive attitude.

By March, though, the tension was running very high. We all knew that the final decisions would be made then, and Don and Sam flew to New York for negotiations with ABC. When they returned they were guardedly hopeful. "But things are in a turmoil," admitted Don. "And there will be no decision for another two weeks."

We continued to work. Don and Sam were in frequent contact with New York, and on Monday, March 11, they were assured that no definite decisions had been made and that ABC was extending its deliberations for another week. So I was not too dismayed, although I suffered a momentary heart-stop, when I picked up the trade papers on Tuesday morning to read that our show was "probably" going to be dropped. When Don rechecked with New York, however, he was again told that no decision had been made, and none would be for another week.

I was very much on edge awaiting the outcome of all this, of course, so I tried my usual cure-all—work. I worked hard every day, and at night, too. Tuesday night I wrote articles for a magazine, Wednesday, I blocked out some plans for the show at Tahoe, and Thursday, Fern and I attended the annual banquet of the National Conference of Christians and Jews. On Friday, March 19, very early in the morning, Ted Lennon and I drove down to Escondido, where we were scheduled to play in the Avocado Golf Tournament at nearby Fallbrook. I had developed a miserable head cold by then, and my head was really pounding, and my eyes and nose running like a faucet.

Once we got out on the golf course I felt better. I tried to concentrate on my game, but I kept thinking of the momentous decisions being made, and also, as we walked around the course, I was picking out the best sites to use as background for the "special" we were planning to shoot at Escondido. My mind wasn't completely on my game, and my golf score for that day shows it.

At four o'clock, just as I finished the fourteenth hole—at par—a messenger approached and told me I was wanted on the phone. "Can't it wait till I'm finished?" I asked. "I only have four more holes to play."

"Well . . . " he seemed a little hesitant. "It's long distance and they say it's very important. Harvard Noble is waiting to drive you back to the clubhouse."

The moment I heard those words I felt that this was the call that would tell the tale, and when I got in the car I looked at Harvard questioningly. He shook his head. "I don't know what it is," he said quietly. "Only that it's very important. They're calling you from New York again in five minutes. You'll just about make it."

He drove quickly to the motel office and I jumped out of the car and ran inside where Irene Noble took me to the small, quiet room behind the lobby. It seemed rather dim in the fading light of the afternoon, and she switched on a lamp as she left, closing the door softly behind her. I sat down alone at the desk to wait, gazing fixedly at the shiny black telephone. Suddenly it shrilled and I picked it up instantly, but I waited a split second before I held it to my ear. Finally I said, "Hello?"

"Mr. Welk?"

"Yes, speaking."

"This is Rick Du Brow of UPI." He paused. "Mr. Welk, ABC has just released its official list of shows for the new fall season. Your show is not on the list." Another pause. "How do you feel about that?"

"Mr. Welk? Sir?" He was waiting. I had to say something, and so I said exactly what was on my mind and in my heart. "Naturally," I said slowly, "I am very, very disappointed, both for my Musical Family and for our television audience, too. I believe there is a place . . . maybe even a need . . . for a program such as ours. No," I added, in answer to his question, "as for myself it's not so important. But I am very concerned for my Musical Family. I hope I can arrange something for them."

Then things blurred. Harvard and Irene came in, and Ted Lennon and Bert Carter. It somehow seemed very fitting that Bert, who had helped start it all, should be there with me then. We talked, made small jokes, and I remember saying, "Well, it's bad enough to get fired, but to be pulled off the golf course to be told, that's just too much!" The telephone began to ring and it didn't stop. Don called; he had been notified by ABC at just about the same time the reporter had called me and he'd called every ten minutes thereafter trying to get through to me. Sam called . . . all my good friends. Wires and calls continued to come in all that night and for the next several days. I had scheduled a dinner party that evening at the Welkome Inn and it seemed pointless to cancel it, so we went ahead even though I was feeling dizzy and sick, partly from my cold and partly from shock and disappointment. I was almost glad my eyes were watering from the cold. It made tears a little easier to hide.

At the restaurant, diners came up constantly to express their surprise and anger at the news, or offer encouragement and good wishes. And then, midway through dinner, I received another long distance call, this one from Florida, and I left the dining room to take it. When I came back I went directly to Bert and Nancy Carter and put an arm around each of them. Then I looked at each one of those dear and familiar faces gathered round the table. "Friends," I said, my voice hoarse from emotion (and my pesky cold!), "that was Matty Rosenhaus calling. And he said . . . he said, 'Lawrence, we just heard the news about your show and I want to tell you this. Whatever you and the orchestra decide to do, we would like to go along with you. We're with you all the way.' " I stopped, and even as I said the words, I knew beyond a shadow of a doubt what I was going to do. I was going to go on with the show. I wasn't sure just how, but I knew we would go on. And in a matter of days, the way was pointed out very plainly for me.

We were inundated with mail, and we received so many requests from television stations across the nation to go on with our program that we decided to go into syndication, and in less than a week we were booked solidly from coast to coast. The newspapers began to refer to the new "Welk Network," and confirmed that we would stay on TV, without a break, as usual. We were off on a new adventure, the biggest one yet, and I felt sure that everyone in our Musical Family would go along with us and work harder than ever to achieve mutual success. I had no real proof that they would, of course, just my own deep feelings of love and faith in them. And my faith was justified a hundred times, a million times over, when we opened at Tahoe a few months later.

I was sixty-eight years old. I had been performing with my orchestra for a long, long time. We had just been through a stunning upset together. But that wonderful engagement in Tahoe was to prove that our future together was brighter than ever.

23

TOMORROW

FROM THE MOMENT OUR BOYS AND GIRLS APPEARED ONSTAGE singing and dancing, until the finale when the entire cast gathered to sing the closing number, the show moved with a sparkle and glow beyond anything we had ever done before. We all noticed it. Never had I heard my band play better. Night after night I stood in the wings listening, as Myron led the boys through their paces. And night after night I could feel the chills go up and down my spine, they played so well. I could have rested between numbers in an offstage dressing room, but I never did. I stood in the wings during the whole show, watching and listening. "You're still stage-struck, Mr. Welk," whispered Sandi one evening. I nodded. I guess I always will be.

I could hardly wait to get down to the theater every night. Fern and I generally had an early dinner with our guests, but by seven at the latest I was off on the ten-minute drive into Tahoe village. At Harrah's I parked near the stage door and then walked into the dim, quiet interior. I love backstage anywhere. There is always a feeling of excitement in the air, a feeling of wonderful things about to happen, and you sense it whether you're in a luxuriously equipped theater like Harrah's, or in some broken down firetrap of an old fair building, out in the middle of a prairie somewhere. I'm not sure what it is. Sometimes I think it's because the walls have sort of soaked up all the hopes and fears and excitement of all the other people who have played there over the years. Then again, maybe it's not in the walls at all, but in you; maybe it's something just peculiar to performers, and it's your own anticipation which always seems heightened in the quiet that precedes any performance. Whatever it is, I love it, and I always arrived early.

But no matter when I arrived, Myron was always there ahead of me. I could hear the soft sounds of his accordion as soon as I began walking down the long sloping ramp backstage, and when I peeped around the back drape I could see him sitting far across the stage in the dim work lights, on a black stool, running over and over the scales on his accordion with the bellows almost closed, polishing up his already considerable skills. (And one time I came in unexpectedly in the afternoon to pick up some music from my dressing room and found Johnny Zell hard at work, rehearsing a tricky figure from one of his trumpet solos. And I knew that Bob Ralston often stayed on after the last show at night, all by himself, playing the grand piano till two, three, four o'clock in the morning. Perfectionists, every one of them. And I'm a lucky man to have them.)

My dressing room was always lighted and ready for me when I arrived, stocked with fresh hot coffee and tea and a wide assortment of other refreshments. I went over the mail and greeted the kids as they came in one by one. When Lois arrived we checked out any business at hand and conferred with Cliff Kehl, the maître d', who handles the reservations so capably. Sometimes a party would arrive unexpectedly, or a "relative" would show up. Sometimes he was a relative and sometimes he wasn't, but we tried to accommodate them all.

The tension began to mount as show time neared. By eight o'clock I was always fully dressed for our opening number, and at five minutes after eight I picked up my baton and climbed the wide, red-carpeted stairs to the stage above. All the boys and girls were waiting in the wings for their first entrance, milling around nervously—girls in yellow full-skirted chiffon dresses, boys in yellow jackets and white flannel pants. There were hurried jokes, little spurts of muffled laughter, girls fluffing their hair, boys straightening ties and jackets, everybody keyed up, everybody happy. Then at exactly eight-fifteen, the house lights dim, the stage lights come up, and it starts. It begins. The moment that still makes my heart pound with excitement after forty-six years in the business. And for the next hour and a half we are all caught up in the happy task of entertaining the audience the best way we know how.

All during that run I was aware of an extra feeling of cooperation, of "giving," of . . . well, happiness was the only word I could think of. I couldn't quite put my finger on it, but I was certainly aware of it. Those three weeks just flew by. During the day I played golf with some of the boys in the band or friends who came by to visit us, and I enjoyed that so much, but it was the music, the show, I really looked forward to.

We had fine crowds every night for both performances, but on the closing night we were really swamped! When I drove into the parking lot a little after seven I could see unusually large crowds of people waiting outside, and when I had my usual pre-show conference with Cliff, he sounded slightly harassed, and for an unflappable man like Cliff that is really something. He managed to cram in as many folks as possible for the dinner show, but he was so snowed under with requests for the midnight show that he finally put some tiny round tables, which could accommodate four people, in the aisles and tucked into the corners. He managed to crowd in just as many as the law allowed. There wasn't one square inch of extra space, and that room, twinkling with lights and jampacked with smiling, friendly faces, was one of the most wonderful sights I've ever seen. We all responded to it, and played a longer show than usual, with extra solos and encores. I don't think any of us really wanted to stop. Finally, of course, we did, bowing repeatedly to the warm and generous storms of applause from our enthusiastic audience. Then, as those big gold curtains pulled to a close for the last time that season, I turned around to face my orchestra—my boys—and to my great surprise, they were all standing and applauding, too, the violin section, who never show any emotion, rapping their bows on the music stands, all the rest of the fellows applauding. The singers crowded around me closely, clapping too, holding their hands out toward me, some of them with tears in their eyes. It was almost more than I could take. After a while I waved them all into silence and tried to make a closing speech. But it was no use, so finally I just said, "Boys and girls—I don't have any criticisms to make tonight!"

There was a chorus of disbelief at the announcement. "What! Not one! Oh come on, Lawrence, you're kidding! We must have done *something* wrong!"

"No," I said, looking at these people who were so very dear to me. "No, I don't think you did. You just did a wonderful job tonight. The whole three weeks. And I thank you from deep within my heart."

The men came up to shake hands then, and the girls crowded around for a quick hug and kiss, and then they clattered downstairs, talking and laughing with excitement. Watching the younger girls in the cast giggling their way downstairs, Russ Klein, my saxophonist, shrugged comically and said, "Teenyboppers! That's what they are, teenyboppers!" We all laughed and I walked on slowly down the stairs, lost in my own thoughts. There's a strange feeling at the end of any successful run—joy that it's successful, sadness that it's over.

Back in my dressing room I packed the brown satchel that goes everywhere I go. (Our fan club president, Mary Lee Schaefer, gave it to me, and I am never without it.) It carries my notes and books and papers and an extra pair of golf socks and the little souvenirs I keep on hand to give out to my friends, as well as a package of cookies or other goodies. I could hear the shouts and jokes winging up and down in the corridor outside as the cast got packed up and ready to leave. I finished my own packing and then went in to say goodnight to Lois, who was busy gathering up her papers and notes. Then I walked up the ramp toward the exit. I paused for a moment and looked out at the vast stage, empty now, deserted, the band risers standing with props stacked neatly beside them, the big black back drape swaying gently in the breeze which always seems to be blowing backstage. I looked for a long, long moment at that empty stage, still hearing the applause and the music, and then I turned and went on slowly up the ramp.

At the stage door the doorman came out to bid me goodbye. "I hate to see you go, Mr. Welk," he said, wringing my hand. "It's a real pleasure to have your show up here. We look forward to it all year long."

"Thank you so very much. It's nice of you to say that," I told him.

"It's the truth. I don't know why, but your cast always seems so . . . well, so happy."

The words struck me. "Thank you. Thank you very much. It makes *me* feel happy to hear you say that."

"Well, it's the truth. You've got a real nice bunch of people there."

We shook hands again and I went on down the steps and got into the Rolls. It was a spectacularly beautiful night, with the moon shining in a clear, deep blue sky, and as I drove through the gaudy lights of the village and on out into the quiet of the surrounding countryside, something of the peace and beauty of that moment began to touch me, and a feeling of great contentment came over me.

I was tired, exhausted really, but it was a wonderful kind of tiredness, the kind that comes from doing the thing you love best, the very best you know how. How lucky I was! I had just seen my "kids" . . . my family . . . come through in a way that surpassed anything we had ever done before. Somehow we had achieved a deep sense of commitment that had communicated itself to everyone in the company, and expressed itself in work done beautifully with a happy heart.

It seemed to me now that we had reached this fine state of affairs because of three things. First, and most important, we had truly exceptional people in our organization, people with strong characters. Second, they were all willing to work to their topmost potential. And third, they were allowed to share in the success of the show as a whole. If the show succeeded, so did they. If our company made more profit through our combined enterprise, they did, too. We had long ago established a profit-sharing and incentive plan for everyone in our Teleklew family, and even though I had expected it to work well, I had not fully realized until just this very moment how very well it had worked. Our system had given us material advantages and extra benefits certainly, but more than that, it had given us those intangibles of good will and mutual helpfulness which help achieve the kind of life for which most of us strive—a life of love and care and genuine concern for the other person's welfare. That was what I had felt so strongly up there on the stage! That was what had moved me so deeply—that feeling of love, the feeling that we truly cared for each other. It mattered very much to each one of us what happened to the other fellow. In a way, our system was an extension of the Christian philosophy of love-in-action, and it had come to full flower only because we were all lucky enough to live in this wonderful country where we have the chance to live out our dreams. How truly blessed all of us were.

I turned off the main highway and began the drive down the gently curving hill to our lakeside home, where I parked and then just sat for a while, listening to the sounds of the wind blowing softly through the trees and the slap of the waves rolling in on the shore, letting the tension drain off, still savoring the warmth and love of that last performance. After a while I picked up my satchel and walked on up the stone and redwood path to the big double doors. Fern had left the porch light on and I let myself in quietly. The house was absolutely silent—one lamp shining softly in the living room, another out in the kitchen where Julia always left an after-the-show snack for me. I tiptoed out to the refrigerator to see what surprises there were. Ah! She had left a beautiful strawberry pie and a bowl of her famous tapioca pudding. The pie looked delicious, but I know my limitations.

I fixed a big bowl of tapioca and then sat down at the small kitchen table to eat, my mind going back over the years and going ahead a little bit, too.

After a while, I finished the last bite, rinsed out the dish, and then took a glass of milk and some homemade cookies, and walked into the living room. It was quiet and peaceful there, and the light from the lamp bounced back from the sliding glass doors which opened out onto the balcony above the shining waters of the lake. It reminded me of the time more than a half a century before, when I had gone out into the barn at Strasburg very early in the morning with my brand-new accordion, and played as the sun came up. I had felt then as if the whole world were opening up for me, and now I felt somewhat the same way again.

I stood and looked out at all that beauty for a long, long time. How marvelous! What a wonderful life God had granted me. I could never thank anyone enough for all the blessings I had been given. But I could spend the rest of my life trying.

DATE DUE

NOV 20			
NOV 27			
DEC 4			
DEC 11			
SEP 26			

92
WEL   WELK   72 5

Stankevich Wunnerful,
XXXXXXXXXXXXXX wunnerful!
Two green bars

DATE DUE	BORROWER'S NAME	ROOM NUMBER
NOV 20	F. Duleba	19
NOV 27	F. Duleba	19
DEC 4	F. Duleba	19
DEC 11	F. Duleba	

92   72 5
WEL

Christ the Good Shepherd School
1590 RIVERBANK
LINCOLN PARK, MICH. 48146